A YEAR OF CHAMPIONS

The 1996 Green Bay Packers

Remembered by

Gilbert Brown

Written by **Chris Havel**

Library of Congress Cataloging-in-Publication Data

Brown, Gilbert, 1971-
Havel, Chris, 1962-

A Year of Champions: The 1996 Green Bay Packers /
Remembered by Gilbert Brown and written by Chris Havel
p.cm.

This book is available in quantity at a discounted rate.
For further information, write to:

Petasek Promotions, LLC
499 Tyrolian Dr.
Green Bay, WI 54302

email: gbubake@tds.net

Manufactured in United States of America
ISBN-13: 978-0-9791198-0-4
ISBN-10: 0-9791198-0-4

Design by Elizabeth Krogwold
Design production by Elizabeth Krogwold & Jayne Fuehrer
Front and back cover designed by Mark A. Wallenfang and Chris Havel

All photos courtesy of Mark A. Wallenfang unless otherwise indicated. Photo on back cover courtesy of Cas Salas.

November, 2006
First Edition

In Memory of

LeRoy Brown, Jr.

March 31, 1944 – February 20, 1992

LeRoy Brown Jr. preceded in death Ann, his devoted wife; LeRoy III, Gilbert and Carlos, his proud sons; and Carla and Joann, his loving daughters.

"He was a tough guy, a man's man and a great dad. He always did the best he could by mama and us kids, and I love him for that. I just wish he could have seen me play for the Green Bay Packers at Lambeau Field. He would have been so proud."

"I love you Dad!"

Your son,
Gilbert "Jesse" Brown

Table of Contents

Foreword

BY BOB HARLAN

Packers chairman and chief executive officer

The thing that gave me such great pleasure was while we were struggling through the 1970s and 1980s fans kept saying, "We're never going to get to that point again. That (Lombardi) era was the last great era, the last great teams, we're ever going to have."

Once Ron Wolf got here and put his team together it gave me great satisfaction to see the Packers back among the NFL's elite, and we did it during the salary cap era when everyone said the Packers were going to suffer because nobody's going to go there.

Ron never used the words "Super Bowl" leading into the 1996 season, but he kept saying, "We're going to be damn good this year." He had great confidence in that club. I look back at what we had at defensive line, and I look at the defensive lines around the NFL today, and I think what a great front four we put out there every single Sunday. They were dynamite.

Ron was someone I knew before I hired him. I knew if I was going to get him to come in as the Green Bay Packers' general manager he had to have total authority or he wasn't going to leave his job with the New York Jets. I offered him total authority and I hired him during the season because I wanted him to live with that team rather than watch it on video in January and February.

Ron had such definite ideas and he was in such a hurry about what needed to be done and how we needed to do it. He just took charge and ran with it. The atmosphere in that building changed overnight once he walked through the door.

When he came to me with something a little drastic, I would say, "Hey, I promised total authority. It's your team to run." We caught some heck for a few things, and we caught a lot of heck from fans about the Brett Favre trade. Ron wasn't fazed.

I loved his daring. He was willing to take chances to make the club better. He wouldn't stand for mediocrity. He wasn't going to stop until we got successful.

I felt we were going to get better when Ron Wolf and Mike Holmgren got there, but I never dreamed we would get that good that soon.

Mike was a teacher and an authority figure. He was the one guy that could take this young quarterback and corral him. The thing about Mike is that it's still in his makeup. I saw him in March at the league meetings and he said, "Hey, is your guy going to come back this year?" I told him I thought so. Mike told me all Brett needed was for someone to reel him in. He said the Packers would have won a lot of games if somebody could have done that. When we were finished visiting, I came away thinking, "Mike would have reeled him in."

Mike cast such a great presence, and the temper was there, too. I know players had tremendous respect for him, but they also had a bit of fear, too.

I am amazed that it has been 10 years since we won Super Bowl XXXI. I look back at how lucky we were to have Ron Wolf and Mike Holmgren. When you talk about a foundation, you have to go with Ron Wolf, Mike Holmgren, Reggie White and Brett Favre. Those were the four guys that took this franchise and put it back on top, and they did it at a time when nobody said it could be done in Green Bay in the salary cap era.

Respectfully,
Bob Harlan

BUTLER
36
21
Riddell
THE FAN
SIX

A Perspective

Lombardi to Holmgren

BY BUD LEA

When I joined the Milwaukee Sentinel in 1953, the year the Boston Braves moved into spanking-new County Stadium, I was the low man in the sports department on the morning paper. I didn't have a beat until the next year when the sports editor assigned me to cover the Green Bay Packers because he got tired of driving up to Green Bay after covering a Big 10 football game on Saturday.

The team was so bad that the Sentinel didn't staff the Packers on the road. Nobody on the expanded staff wanted the Packer beat. The Milwaukee Braves were the hottest thing in town. The University of Wisconsin football team was coming off a Rose Bowl year. Marquette University had a darn good football program.

Hell, there was more interest in the Milwaukee Hawks of the National Basketball Association than pro football. The Packers were losers - Sunday leftovers.

It didn't matter to me.

Having been born and raised in Green Bay, I couldn't have been happier than to get a chance to write about the team I grew up with. My dad used to take me to all of the Packers' games at City Stadium, and I remember the awe I felt watching Don Hutson, Clarke Hinkle, Arnie Herber, Tony Canadeo.

I listened to their games on radio. I was among the hundreds of jubilant fans at the train station to welcome the team back from triumphant championship games and those annual treks to Chicago after beating the hated Monsters of the Midway.

During the 50s, however, things had turned dreadful. In 1958, Green Bay found itself with one of the poorest teams on the planet and getting worse. I was assigned to cover a game in Baltimore and I had a hard time explaining to my readers how Scooter McLean's team could lose, 56-0, against the Colts.

While I was thinking of a lead on my story, a Green Bay sportswriter turned to me in the Memorial Stadium press box and said, "Gee whiz, the Packers can't be that bad and the Colts that good." I told him, "Yes they can."

The arrival of Vince Lombardi the next year changed everything. Suddenly the worst sports beat on the newspaper became the best as Lombardi built a dynasty at Green Bay and I was on the ground floor to report on it.

What a ride! I covered five NFL championships and victories in Super Bowl I and Super Bowl II. The media could catch a ride on the Packers' buses to the stadium in those days and traveling with Lombardi and his juggernaut team was like riding with Gen. Patton and the Fifth Armored Division into battle.

I was in the Orange Bowl on Jan. 14, 1968, when Lombardi coached his last game with the Packers. After beating the Oakland Raiders, 33-14, in Super Bowl II the mood in the Green Bay locker room was more relief than jubilation. Normally, Lombardi would have been very, very excited about winning and saying, "We'll do it again, boys."

"From a humbling start, covering the Packers was the best beat."
- Bud Lea

There was no talk like that. He was very reserved.

Lombardi made no mention about his future plans.

Two weeks later, at age 56, he announced his long-awaited decision in Green Bay. He told a packed press corps gathered at the Oneida Golf & Riding Club that he would remain as general manager of the Packers and then he introduced his handpicked successor, Phil Bengtson. Now, Bengston was a fine defensive coordinator but he was way over his head stepping into Lombardi's shoes.

Through the years the Packers' failed coaches passed in a steady parade: Bengtson, Dan Devine, Bart Starr, Forrest Gregg, Lindy Infante. The great Green Bay teams were a thing of the past. The Super Bowl trophies were gathering dust.

This was an organization that kept cranking out coaches to see if they could light a fire under the players, but it always fizzled. This was a team that drafted busts like Tony Mandarich and Rich Campbell and gave a fistful of high draft picks for an over-the-hill quarterback named John Hadl. This was a team that drove tough-guy Forrest Gregg up the wall.

The Packers had not won a playoff game in ages. Kids born in the year of the Packers' last Super Bowl appearance were 24 years old. Bart Starr was a grandpa.

The Roman Empire of the National Football League had crumbled. This was a franchise that desperately needed direction.

On Nov. 27, 1991, Bob Harlan hired Ron Wolf, a 51-year-old director of player personnel for the New York Jets, and gave him total authority over every phase of the football operations at Green Bay, including the power to hire and fire the coach.

I questioned the move, pointing out in a column that Harlan really stuck his neck out this time and if Wolf couldn't turn this franchise around in five years, Harlan would be the next one out. I ended up with egg all over my face.

Wolf was a genius. He knew talent. He could find players. He was light years ahead of his competition when it came to putting together a winning organization.

Wolf fired Infante, who had three years remaining on his contract, and hired Mike Holmgren, then a 43-year-old offensive coordinator from the San Francisco 49ers.

The Packers fans' jaws could not have dropped lower if Mike Ditka had campaigned for the job. The Packers had fallen into the hands of a man who had never been a head coach at any level of football.

As it turned out, the Wolf-Holmgren union was a marriage made in football heaven. Holmgren arrived with the intention of lighting a torch under the Packers. When Wolf got Brett Favre and Reggie White, Holmgren got what he needed – the heart of football success – a quarterback, and the soul of a leader who rejoiced playing in Green Bay after years in Philadelphia.

Things were happening fast. The whole mood of the franchise changed.

The Packers, coming off a 4-12 season, finished 9-7 in 1992. Four seasons later, they finished 13-3 – the NFC's best record – and returned to the Super Bowl after 29 years of broken promises and unfixable teams.

Super Bowl XXXI was played inside the Louisiana Superdome, and the Packers were favored to win it against the New England Patriots. And no matter where you went around Wisconsin the week of the game, you could find a happy fan tell you what the big team from the little city in the upper Midwest was about to do to those pompous guys from Boston. Naturally, they were right.

After 42 years, I had retired from the paper in 1995 when the Milwaukee Sentinel and Milwaukee Journal merged, but I continued to write columns for Packer Plus, a separate football magazine the paper publishes 40 times a year. When they told me to pack my bags for New Orleans, I was rarin' to go.

I didn't know the 1996 Packers so well as I knew their ancestors. The much younger members of the media had rightfully taken over. I was a has-been who was hanging on, but I sure did enjoy following this team.

Brett Favre was a sportswriter's delight. He was as available for interviews as a guy running for sheriff. He was the great opposite to Sterling Sharpe. I never saw a man who seemed to get more fun out of playing a game than Favre.

Throughout my career I had covered major events – the Olympics, World Series, NBA Finals, Muhammad Ali heavyweight fights, the Indy 500, college bowl games, NCAA Final Fours, major golf tournaments.

This trip to New Orleans rejuvenated me.

The game was only three-and-a-half minutes old when Favre, sensing a blitz, called an audible and threw a pass to Andre Rison, who was wide open and running a post-pattern. Rison made the catch in full stride and a few yards from the end zone he began celebrating the 54-yard touchdown play with an exaggerated duck walk.

Favre went slightly crazy. He raced to the sideline with his helmet in his hand and that wonderful grin on his face. I'll never forget that scene.

From the upper deck of the press box, I got more worked up than I ever thought I would be. I didn't jump up and down, but inside my emotions were running wild. Inside, I was rooting for the Packers to dismantle the Patriots, which they did.

Green Bay, Wisconsin, the city that skeptics once said didn't belong in the National Football League, owned the best team in all of professional football.

IT WAS THE RIDE OF A LIFETIME.

A View From The Press Box

BY CHRIS HAVEL

When I think of the 1996 Green Bay Packers, winners of Super Bowl XXXI, I think that is the way a championship team prepares, practices and plays.

That is how a winner looks, talks and acts.

That is the way a general manager builds, a coach teaches and a team responds. That is how a veteran leads, a playmaker delivers and a role player steps up. That is the way a fan base unites, a community supports and a country is swept away.

I think that is just about as good as it gets.

There is nothing chance or haphazard about being the best team in pro football.

It is sensational, but it isn't overnight.

The Packers prevailed in Super Bowl XXXI by defeating the New England Patriots 35-21 on Sunday, Jan. 26, at the Louisiana Superdome. They were world champions, Green Bay's first in 29 years, and they were adored and admired.

Today, they are beloved.

Packers' fans enjoy celebrating the 10th anniversary of Super Bowl XXXI because they earned the right. They did more than follow that team from July through January. They followed it on a first name, first down basis. They measured the Packers' success, and their own happiness, in 10-yard increments. They gauged it by the first downs the Packers converted, and the third-down attempts their defense thwarted.

For the better part of seven months, Packers fans woke up each day feeling like they were facing first-and-goal to go. They were in a good place and it was only going to get better. The debate wasn't whether the Packers would win. It was by how much. Third-and-long? That was somebody else's nightmare.

The Packers' rise to long-forgotten heights became the feel-good sports story of the year. When the Packers became an irresistible force for the first time in forever, their fans were mesmerized by the moment.

They felt the rush and it was a beautiful thing.

They first felt it in the 1995 NFC Divisional Playoffs at San Francisco. On the 49ers' first play from scrimmage, fullback Adam Walker caught a seemingly harmless pass in the flat and promptly was flattened by Wayne Simmons. The Packers' linebacker separated Walker from the football while he drove him into the turf.

Craig Newsome, the Packers' left cornerback, alertly picked up the loose football and sprinted 31 yards for a touchdown. It gave Green Bay an early 7-0 lead, and it gave fans a reason to believe the Packers truly were the better team.

That singular play – a turnover that resulted in a touchdown – foreshadowed the 1996 season. That's when Green Bay's defense led the NFL with 39 takeaways, and the 39 takeaways led to 132 points.

The dye was cast. The story was just beginning.

The Packers defeated the 49ers 27-17 at 3Com Park that day to advance to the 1995 NFC Championship Game the following week at Dallas. The Packers lost to the Cowboys, 38-27, at Texas Stadium, bringing the 1995 season to a close.

The Packers left Texas Stadium feeling disappointed, to be sure, but they also left feeling more determined than ever to advance to Super Bowl XXXI the following year. The loss at Dallas was embarrassing, but the mindset it forged was invaluable.

It created a theme that was irresistible, unfailing and consistent in 1996. Whenever anything bad happened, it wasn't long before something good came of it.

For instance:

** In May of 1996, Brett Favre revealed a serious off-the-field problem. He entered rehabilitation at the Menninger Clinic in Topeka, Kansas, where he received treatment for an addiction to painkiller medication. When he completed the 45-day rehabilitation program, he looked the picture of health and he sounded hell-bent on proving his critics wrong. He intended to conquer the NFL.

"You know, I'm going to beat this thing," he told reporters during a news conference at Packers headquarters. "I'm going to win a Super Bowl. And all I can tell people if they don't believe me is, 'Just bet against me.' "

Favre delivered the football with aplomb, and he delivered on his dare with a vengeance. He had 20 touchdown passes through six games. It put him on pace to throw 53 touchdown passes, which would have been a league record. Ultimately, he didn't break Dan Marino's single-season record of 48, but he did OK just the same.

Favre threw 39 touchdown passes, the offense rolled up a league-high 456 points and he was voted the NFL's Most Valuable Player for a second straight season. Just six months after completing rehab and challenging the world to bet against him, Favre stood tall inside the Louisiana Superdome and soaked in the victory in Super Bowl XXXI.

** Reggie White, the Minister of Defense, played like he was 35 going on 25 throughout the 1996 season. He started every game and routinely dominated during it.

It was an amazing display considering his dire situation in December of 1995. That is when he was diagnosed with a torn left hamstring, an injury doctors determined would require surgery and could end his career.

Just when it looked bleak, White said he was lying on a table in the training room when a white-hot light seared through the damaged hamstring and healed it.

White first felt renewed while playing in the hallway with his children, Jeremy and Jecolia, at home that evening. He called Kent Johnston, the team's strength and conditioning coach, to request a late-night workout at The Don Hutson Center. After his hamstring checked out OK, he drove to his head coach's house to spread the news.

Mike Holmgren was reaching down to switch off the lights on the family Christmas tree when he heard a tap at the front door. First startled, then curious, he wondered if Santa Claus might be paying a late-night visit.

It was Reggie White, in all his glory, bearing the best present of all: Good health.

"I can play," he declared.

White practiced the following day and continued to play at a high level for the balance of the 1995 season as well as the 1996, 1997 and 1998 seasons.

He punctuated the Packers' victory over the Patriots in Super Bowl XXXI with three sacks to set the single-game record, and his left hamstring never felt better.

** By early November, the Packers' receiving corps was seriously depleted due to Robert Brooks' season-ending knee injury and Antonio Freeman's four-game absence with a broken left forearm. Don Beebe played masterfully and Terry Mickens, Desmond Howard and Derrick Mayes contributed at times, but the passing attack wasn't the same.

The offense needed a spark. That was obvious. The problem was finding it. The trade deadline had passed and the pool of so-called "street" free agents offered nothing nearly as good as the receivers on their 53-man roster and practice squad.

The Packers' offense was in trouble.

Defenses were beginning to attack with eight men at the line of scrimmage. While the cornerbacks jammed the Packers' receivers, the defensive linemen, linebackers and safeties kept a vigilant eye on the backs and tight ends.

The strategy worked.

The Packers lost at Kansas City, 27-20, on Sunday, Nov. 10, and again at Dallas, 21-6, on Monday, Nov. 18.

Several hours before the Packers-Cowboys kickoff on Monday Night Football, general manager Ron Wolf spied Andre Rison's name on the waiver wire. The Jacksonville Jaguars had released Rison, the much-maligned receiver, and the Packers promptly put in a waiver claim.

"Their season featured a soap opera's twists, a drama's intensity, a sitcom's lighter side and a fairy tale's ending."
- Chris Havel

Twenty-four hours later, Rison arrived and the Packers didn't lose again.

Their locker room was too strong to be fractured by Rison's potentially disruptive presence, although the controversial receiver proved to be a good teammate and a perfect short-term solution. In his debut at St. Louis, he caught a team-high five passes for 44 yards and the Packers defeated the Rams, 24-9, to end a two-game losing streak.

Rison contributed mightily in his short but sweet stint with the Packers. He caught 13 passes for 135 yards and a touchdown in five regular-season games, and seven passes for 143 yards and two touchdowns in three playoff games.

When Freeman returned to catch 10 passes for 156 yards in a 28-17 victory over Chicago on Dec. 1, Freeman and Rison became a formidable pass-catching duo.

Even the Packers' Super Bowl XXXI victory parade was a resounding success despite the fact that it possessed all the elements to be a disaster. The route was hastily chosen, the weather was brutally cold and the parade's pace was insufferably slow.

Nobody complained. Not much, anyway.

The Green Bay Press-Gazette published a photo of fans standing along the parade route in downtown Green Bay. It circled a man wearing an overcoat and a fedora, and it playfully begged the question: Could it be the Packers' legendary coach, Vince Lombardi, joining in the celebration?

I smiled and thought, "Not a chance. Lombardi would neither promote nor attend such a poorly planned team function."

It didn't matter because the parade – like the season – was a huge success.

Once again, something bad ultimately turned into a good thing.

For that reason, fans love to relive the 1996 season. But it isn't the only reason. Fans savor the memories because a decade's passing provides the benefit of perspective.

Everybody knows the '96 Packers were obscenely popular.

Their team flags waved a good-natured Packers hello from every other automobile on the road. Their previous game and upcoming game were bridged by a running commentary throughout the community. Their every action was superimposed upon fans' subconscious.

The Packers' success was too new to get old, too inescapable to ignore and too compelling to want to try. Their season featured a soap opera's twists, a drama's intensity, a sitcom's lighter side and a fairy tale's ending.

For all that, something important was lost in the euphoria.

While fans in Dallas and Green Bay quibbled about which franchise truly was "America's Team" and Packers fans basked in a return to "The Glory Years," the fact that the '96 Packers were among the NFL's all-time great teams was glossed over.

Their exploits were so fantastic that their place in history got lost in the shuffle.

The '96 Packers were more than an answer to the prayers of long-suffering fans. They were a team for the ages. They could stand up to any Super Bowl champion, past or present, without fear of embarrassment. They may not win, but they wouldn't be routed.

They could hang with everyone from Chuck Noll's Pittsburgh Steelers and Tom Landry's Dallas Cowboys to Bill Walsh's San Francisco 49ers and Bill Belichick's New England Patriots.

The '96 Packers went 13-3 while becoming the NFL's first team since the undefeated 1972 Miami Dolphins to lead the league in points scored with 456 and points allowed with 210. Green Bay yielded 19 opponent touchdowns to establish the 16-game, single-season record. The 1985 Chicago Bears had previously held the record, and that '85 Bears' defense is widely accepted as one of the league's all-time greatest.

The 1996 Packers' defense isn't even in the conversation.

It ought to be.

In retrospect, Mike Holmgren is among the

NFL's finest head coaches of all time. He has taken teams to three of the past 10 Super Bowls.

A secret to success as a NFL coach is the ability to make OK players good and good players great, while wasting minimal time on players who don't belong there. Another trick is to define and design a specific role for each player, and then to encourage, challenge and enable them to perfect it.

Holmgren did both.

Antonio Freeman, Robert Brooks, Mark Chmura, Edgar Bennett, Frank Winters and others were really good players that maximized their talent under Holmgren.

Dorsey Levens, Desmond Howard, Don Beebe, Bruce Wilkerson, Mike Prior, Travis Jervey, Bernardo Harris and others were role players that routinely made significant contributions to the team's success.

Meantime, Holmgren helped Favre develop into one of the greatest quarterbacks the NFL has ever seen.

Holmgren's game planning, play calling and preparation were so consistently strong that it came to be expected. When he was out-coached, which rarely happened, it drew far more attention than the many times he simply said, "Check mate."

Holmgren isn't the only one.

LeRoy Butler merits strong consideration for induction into The Pro Football Hall of Fame. The strong safety made 953 tackles in 12 seasons. He registered 20 1/2 sacks. He intercepted 38 passes. He invented the Lambeau Leap, with an assist from White, and he forced opposing offenses to game plan around him.

Thanks to defensive coordinator Fritz Shurmur's clever schemes, many of which were designed with the strong safety in mind, Butler changed the way the game is played.

Furthermore, Butler was as good a teammate as he was a player. He stepped aside when veteran free safety Eugene Robinson was acquired on the eve of training camp. Butler could have been envious of Robinson's acumen as a defensive leader.

Instead, he promoted it.

Robinson, 33, was the perfect alter ego.

Robinson directed the defense and Butler executed it.

Six safeties have a bust in The Pro Football Hall of Fame in Canton, Ohio. If Butler isn't elected to take his rightful place among them, the 1996 Packers' defense has one less voice to sing its praises, and one less advocate to advance its story.

The '96 Packers' defense already has lost Fritz Shurmur, Reggie White and Wayne Simmons. Butler's election into the Hall of Fame would honor their memory.

White's posthumous induction into The Pro Football Hall of Fame in the summer of 2006 was a foregone conclusion. It cemented his place among the all-time greats, but it stopped short of recognizing him as the most dominant defensive end in NFL history.

White, who died at 43 on Dec. 26, 2004, just might be the greatest defensive player of all time. He was unparalleled as a pass rusher, and he was so strong against the run that few offenses were foolish enough to test him. He made big plays, created turnovers and flashed a combination of power, speed and agility that was frightening.

If they lined up the greatest defensive players of all time, and they polled every general manager that ever presided over a draft, the majority would use the first pick to select Reggie White.

He was that great.

When I think of the 1996 Green Bay Packers, winners of Super Bowl XXXI, I think of Wolf and Holmgren ... White and Favre ... Butler and the rest.

I think how fortunate I am to have written about them. They weren't merely one of the greatest teams in Packers history, although that is something special.

THEY WERE ONE OF THE GREATEST TEAMS IN NFL HISTORY. IT JUST TOOK THE PASSAGE OF TIME TO REALIZE IT.

36

A View From The Sideline

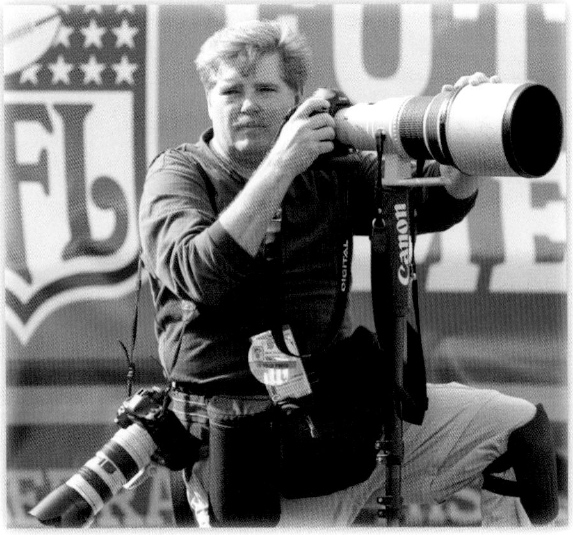

Photo by Patrick Ferron

BY MARK A. WALLENFANG

When I started editing photographs for this book, I realized how these photos held such great memories of stadiums, games and players. I was reminded of how cold it was that Sunday in Kansas City, for example. I had forgotten how I tried to keep my equipment dry and my lenses from fogging up in the January playoff game against the 49ers. I was reminded of how my fingers were so cold and stiff in the championship game against the Panthers, it was hard to change the film in my camera.

I forgot about some of the small moments until I started looking at it game by game, photo by photo. Like when William Henderson got that touchdown against the Chargers and then did the Lambeau Leap. Or when Brett Favre pulled pranks on guys at training camp. Or the memories of things I could see and hear on the sidelines.

One moment that stands out was when Reggie White and Wayne Simmons were having one of their usual friendly arguments. Reggie said, "Hey Fritz, come here." Fritz Shurmur walked over and listened to their argument, then Fritz exclaimed "Reggie is right." Then Reggie said, "See Wayne!" and they both laughed it off and went about their business. Why that small moment came back to me is that I see the photos of those three guys now and I know they're gone.

It was quite a season and I was at every game. Super Bowl week was one of the best weeks of my life. There were so many Packers fans on Bourbon Street that by Friday night it seemed that the Packers fans outnumbered Patriots fans by ten-to-one. Some Packers fans didn't have tickets for the game but just wanted to be there.

I had never seen so many photographers gathered for one game as I did at that Super Bowl. Some were assigned to designated zones along the sidelines and they had to stay there throughout the game. I was lucky enough to have a full roaming field pass that allowed me to go anywhere, on either sideline or along the end zones. It was tough sometimes to get a good shooting position. We were stacked two, three or four deep in some areas. I hoped to God that nobody ran off the field. There was no way I could get up and move if a running back came out of bounds.

I knew the Packers were going to win when Craig Newsome intercepted Drew Bledsoe halfway through the fourth quarter. He was one of the many unsung heroes that day. I knew the game was sealed at that point. You could feel the electricity in the air. The fans felt it. The players knew it.

It occurred to me that I had been very young the last time the Packers won a Super Bowl and what a dream it was to be part of the excitement first hand. I've got the photos to prove it.

Gilbert Brown Introduction

THE GRAVEDIGGER
IS DELIGHTED TO DIG UP THIS PAST

BY GILBERT BROWN

One evening Gabe Wilkins and I decided to get out of our room at the team hotel, a fancy place called The Fairmont, and check out The French Quarter.

We needed to stretch our legs and we needed to take a break from the tension and the routine of Super Bowl week. The game was still a couple of days away, but already I was starting to climb the walls, and Gabe was feeling about the same.

We were messing around and walking along like a couple of tourists who had nowhere to be and no place to go when a man with a booming voice called out my name.

"Hey, Gilbert!" he barked. "Good to see you."

It was Ray Nitschke.

I had to blink because I couldn't believe my eyes.

We talked about New Orleans and the playoffs and how our defense was going to whip the Patriots' butts. It was short and sweet. We shook hands and said our good-byes, and as I started to move on, Ray grabbed me by the arm. He looked me in the eye and said, "Son, you're a player."

I damn near fell over.

I thought, "I'm nobody. I'm just a young pup trying to make a name for myself, and Ray Nitschke came up to me to say that?"

I'll never forget it as long as I live.

Mr. Ray Nitschke, the greatest middle linebacker in NFL history, stopped to shake my hand and wish me luck. Man, it doesn't get any better than that. I was ready to kick New England's butt right then and there.

About a year later, give or take, I heard on ESPN that Ray had died.

It made me sad because Ray was a great man, and he was too young to pass. It made me think of my daddy – LeRoy Brown, Jr., the original Bad Bad LeRoy Brown – who also died of heart disease at an early age.

It's been 10 years but I promise you this: Not a day goes by but I don't think of my daddy, and not a Super Bowl goes by that I don't think of Ray.

It is a big reason why I wanted to write this book.

As a son I wanted to honor my father's memory.

Without my daddy and my mama and my brothers and sisters I seriously doubt I would be here today. Without the two people that mean the world to me – Bob Dozier, my football coach at Detroit's MacKenzie High School, and Fred Roll, my friend and workout guru at the University of Kansas and beyond – I would be in a world of hurt.

As a member of the 1996 Super Bowl XXXI champion Green Bay Packers, I wanted to honor the great players that came before me, like Ray Nitschke. I also wanted to honor the great players I had the privilege of calling "teammate." Men like Brett Favre and Reggie White and LeRoy Butler and Santana Dotson and Sean Jones and all the rest.

Ray and Reggie and Fritz Shurmur, our great defensive coordinator, and Wayne Simmons, are tough-as-nails linebacker, are all gone. I don't want them to be forgotten. I don't want that great 1996 Packers defense to be forgotten, either.

It's a shame we don't get respect like some of the other great defenses. The 1972 Miami Dolphins' defense is praised because that team went undefeated. The 1985 Chicago Bears' defense is praised because they had a bunch of big names.

What about the guys that grabbed their lunch pails, rolled up their sleeves and went to work every day? What about the guys that hung together and trusted each other and counted on each other? What about the guys that were more interested in what was best for the team instead of the individual? What about being a record-setting defense?

Why do we have to fight for respect when we were the world champions in '96? Why? How many quarterbacks come down the bench just to tell the defensive linemen that they thoroughly appreciate "the way ya'all are kicking butt" out there today?

When we came off the field, nine times out of 10 we weren't sitting on the bench. We wanted to watch Brett and those boys go to work. We knew they would go out there and get the job done, just like they knew we had their back if they didn't. We were a team in every sense of the word, and that meant Desmond Howard and the special teams, too.

We dominated but it's really never been about the defense. It was always the offense. We knew our role so we're not fussing about that, but from my perspective I want to talk about the defense. I want people to remember the guys. I want people to remember how hard it was to get to that point.

We had the best defensive lineman in the game. We had the premier safety. We had another defensive end, Sean Jones, who finished with 113 ½ career sacks. We set the NFL's 16 game single-season record for fewest opponent touchdowns allowed with 19.

It's been 10 years and we've had three guys go. Ten years ago, we were the champions of the world. The world! That's something to be remembered.

Ron Wolf, our general manager, and Mike Holmgren, our head coach, made stars out of guys other teams threw away. Guys like me. Our assistant coaches knew how to put their players in the right position, but they also were smart enough to listen to us. Some coaches don't pay attention to their players. They pay attention to their schemes. Those coaches paid attention to everything.

The first thing out of Fritz's mouth every day was, "Pay attention to the details."

That went for the coaches as well as the players.

When you look at the '96 Packers you've got so many players that put it on the line every day, every practice, every game. There are so many players that should be in the Pro Football Hall of Fame. Reggie is there. Brett is going to be there.

But LeRoy Butler belongs there, too. So do Sean Jones and Keith Jackson. If they don't make it they damn sure deserve some serious consideration. That's why I wanted to write this book. That's why it's important to me.

Everybody asks about my Super Bowl XXXI ring but I seldom wear it. That ring means too much to me to wear it every day. I wore it to my son Jesse's Christening, and I wear it if it's requested at a function where it's going to be distinguished. That's it.

It's something I'm very protective of because I worked my whole life to get it. I suppose that's why I'm also very protective of my teammates. I know they worked their whole life to get that ring, too.

It means too much to be forgotten.

93

The Team

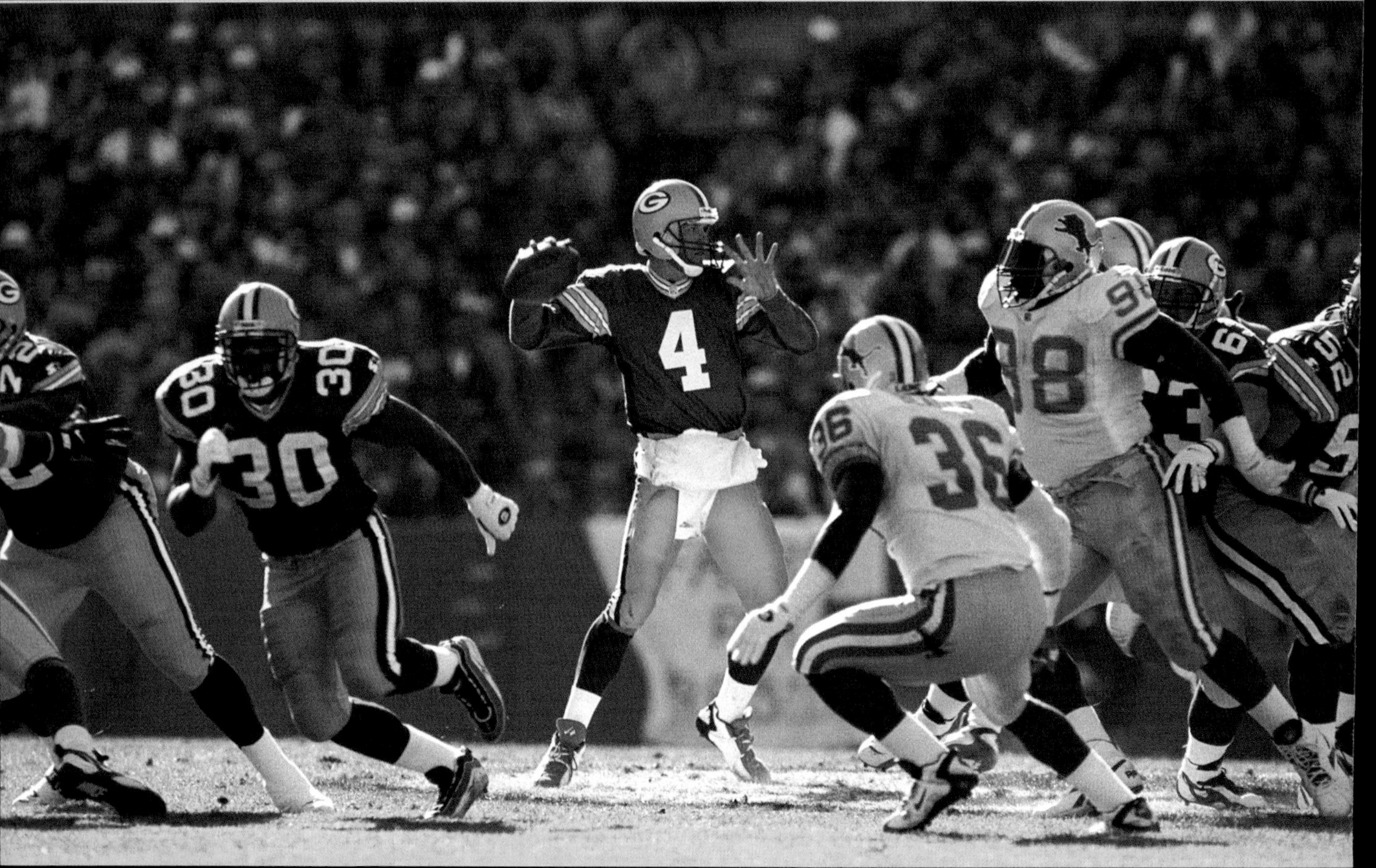

Offense

Brett Favre 4
Edgar Bennett 34
William Henderson 30
Robert Brooks 87
Antonio Freeman 86
Mark Chmura 89
Bruce Wilkerson 64
Earl Dotson 72
Adam Timmerman 63
Aaron Taylor 73
Frank Winters 52
Dorsey Levens 25
Travis Jervey 32
Don Beebe 82
Andre Rison 84
Keith Jackson 88
Gary Brown 68
Lindsay Knapp 65
Ken Ruettgers 75
John Michels 77
Doug Pederson 18
Jeff Thomason 83
Derrick Mayes 80
Terry Mickens 85

BRETT FAVRE
4

Position: Quarterback
Vitals: 6'-2", 225 lbs.
Age: 27
NFL Experience: 6th season
Acquired in February 10, 1992 trade with Atlanta (for 1993 first-round pick)
College: Southern Mississippi

Noteworthy: Favre threw 39 touchdown passes to set the NFC and Packers records for the most touchdown passes in a season. At the time it was the third-highest total in NFL history behind Dan Marino's 48 in 1984 and 44 in 1986. He was named the NFL's Most Valuable Player for a second straight year. He threw just 13 interceptions in the regular season, and improved his win-loss record to 50-27 (.649) as a starter. He was even better in the post-season, where he completed 44 of 71 passes for 617 yards and five touchdowns to just one interception for a passer rating of 107.5.

"If he can stay healthy, Brett will be the cornerstone of our football team for many years to come." – Mike Holmgren, head coach

"What can you say? He's the two-time MVP and I'm sure he'll make a strong run at it again. The remarkable thing is that he has stayed healthy and hasn't missed a game in five years. He's a great leader, a great competitor. He loves to play in the big games. Cold weather doesn't seem to bother him. The players really love him and rally around him. And I just think he's going to get better and better. He's the guy – we go as far as he goes." – Sherman Lewis, offensive coordinator

"The greatest. The best. The most unselfish, the most competitive player, plus he's a guy that you just know, "He's got your back." You know he's going to show up. You know he's never going to leave you hanging. You know he's going to be there for you when you need him the most. That's why he's going to be a first-ballot (Pro Football) Hall of Famer." – Gilbert Brown, teammate

4

34
34
Riddell

EDGAR BENNETT

34

Position: Running back
Vitals: 6'-0", 215 lbs.
Age: 27
NFL Experience: 5th season
Drafted 1992 fourth round (103rd overall)
College: Florida State

Noteworthy: Bennett was unselfish, committed and productive, a model running back and tremendous leader. He led the team in rushing for the third straight season with 899 yards in 222 carries and a career-high 4.0 yards-per-carry. He also caught 31 passes for 176 yards and one touchdown. He saw his streak of 60 games with at least one catch come to an end Dec. 1 against Chicago. It was the longest streak by a running back in team history. In three post-season games, he led the team in rushing with 219 yards and three touchdowns on 59 carries. In his first five seasons with the Packers, Bennett handled the ball 1,178 times and lost only three fumbles.

"The one thing I love about him is that he never drops the ball. I hate to use the word 'never,' but I mean he fumbles very, very seldom. He's a steady guy, he's always there, and he can play hurt. But he's been very productive for us. He's an excellent receiver coming out of the backfield, he's excellent inside the red zone, and he's just a tough, hardnosed runner." – Sherman Lewis, offensive coordinator

"Edgar Bennett is the only running back that I've ever put on my wall and that's no lie. I love Eric Dickerson. I love Eric Dickerson to death. But Edgar Bennett is the only running back whose poster I've ever put on my wall. I had a game room in my house in Green Bay and Edgar Bennett's poster was THE ONLY ONE.

When I first got to Green Bay we hung out. We were homeboys. After I saw how Edgar plays and how he carries himself and how he did his thing, I thought, "That's my boy. That's my running back. I'm going to put him on my wall." I admired his toughness and his ability to never get rattled. I remember that time when he left (via free agency) for Chicago and his first game against the Packers, Santana (Dotson) and I were talking trash to him. We were telling him, "Edgar, we're going to bust you up. We're going to tear you apart." He got that ball and busted a run for like 60 yards and we looked at each other and said, "Wow. We should've known that Edgar was going to try to bust us up." – Gilbert Brown, teammate

34

William Henderson

30

Position: Fullback
Vitals: 6'-1", 249 lbs.
Age: 25
NFL Experience: 2nd season
Drafted 1995 third round (66th overall)
College: North Carolina

Noteworthy: Henderson was a powerful lead blocker whose impact was felt in 1996, his first year as a full-time starter, when the Packers rushed for an average of 114.9 yards per game, up from 89.3 yards per game in 1995. He rushed 39 times for 130 yards and caught 27 passes for 203 yards and a touchdown.

"He gave us a better inside running game. He was a great lead blocker on those linebackers inside the tackles. He did an excellent job. When we drafted him we were looking for a guy who could be a big, physical blocker and that's what he is. But he can also catch the ball pretty well coming out of the backfield. In looking back, he caught the ball well and he gets the ball up field after he catches it. And he's a good pass protector, too." – Sherman Lewis, offensive coordinator

"Big Will. That's my guy. You might as well say that we grew up together. I have never met a guy that is a consummate pro like William. I'd see him bust his butt on offense, on special teams, whatever, and he never complained. He just went out and did his job. It amazed me that with all the stuff he's been through, and all the things that he had to do in his career without much recognition, to finally get to the Pro Bowl in his 10th season is amazing. When you talk about a pro's pro, you're talking about William Henderson. Big Will was the heart of those special teams units and he was a doggone good fullback, too." – Gilbert Brown, teammate

30

30
Reebok

Riddell
87
87
87

ROBERT BROOKS

87

Position: Wide receiver
Vitals: 6'-0", 180 lbs.
Age: 26
NFL Experience: 5th season
Drafted 1992 third round (62nd overall)
College: South Carolina

Noteworthy: When called upon to replace Sterling Sharpe in 1995 he responded by eclipsing Sharpe's club records for receiving yards (1,497) and 100-yard receiving games (nine) in a single season. In 1996 he caught 23 passes for 344 yards and four touchdowns in seven starts before suffering a season-ending knee injury versus San Francisco on Oct. 14. He was a team leader whose courage in the wake of such a serious injury, coupled with his diligence in rehab to come back, solidified a special place among his teammates and in Packers history.

"Robert was our go-to guy when he went down with that injury against San Francisco. He's really one of our leaders. He's such a great example – his work ethic is as good as anybody's I've ever been around. He's dedicated, he works hard, and he's a great, great competitor."
– Sherman Lewis, offensive coordinator

"Robert Brooks was a tough character. He was cut up to be so small. He would get lumps on his body and I wondered what caused it. He was so chiseled and lean that those lumps were the only way he could have body fat. That was amazing. Me, I'm sitting here looking huge, and he was so fit. It hurt for me to see him sitting on the sideline during the Super Bowl and not playing. I could see the pain in his eyes because he wanted to be out there so bad. That's horrible. You start out the season playing really good and doing your thing and then you've got to sit there during the Super Bowl and watch. It makes you feel like you're not contributing. I'm sure he felt like he wasn't contributing, but he meant a lot to that team and that season. That's something I always wanted to tell him but you know how that goes. He was a big part of that team when he was healthy, and a big part of it when he was hurting. He was a heckuva guy." – Gilbert Brown, teammate

87

ANTONIO FREEMAN

86

Position: Wide receiver
Vitals: 6'-1", 194 lbs.
Age: 24
NFL Experience: 2nd season
Drafted 1995 third round (90th overall)
College: Virginia Tech

Noteworthy: He caught a team-high 56 passes for 933 yards and nine touchdowns in the regular season. He also made at least one big play in each of the team's playoff games. That included an 81-yard touchdown catch along the right sideline when he beat the Patriots' Lawyer Milloy in bump-and-run coverage, and then outran Willie Clay to the end zone. Freeman's touchdown catch was the longest in Super Bowl history. His toughness is unquestioned. He missed four games during the regular season after fracturing the ulna in his left forearm but returned with a cast and a vengeance. He caught 25 passes for 452 yards and four touchdowns during the team's 4-0 December run.

"He's an outstanding receiver. He's probably picked this offense up quicker than anybody that I've ever been around. He's a big-play guy. I think he's really excellent in the red zone. When we get down inside the 20-yard line he's going to make some plays for you. I think another thing he does, he gives you that guy that has the ability to run after the catch. And he's a good target – he's good-sized. So he brings a lot to the table for us." – Sherman Lewis, offensive coordinator

"Free was the toughest receiver I have ever met. He played with a broken jaw, a broken forearm, all the bumps and bruises, and it didn't slow him down a bit. He had the best double-move in the business. He was a body catcher, and we could hear that ball 'thump' into his chest, but I can't ever remember him dropping anything. He was money in the clutch, and he was a big-time playmaker, which is what you need out of your top receiver. I loved Free because he got the most out of his talent, he was always on the same page with Brett and he never bitched. He was a winner." – Gilbert Brown, teammate

Reunion, September 10, 2006

Reunion, September 10, 2006

MARK CHMURA

89

Position: Tight end
Vitals: 6'-5", 253 lbs.
Age: 27
NFL Experience: 5th season
Drafted 1992 sixth round (157th overall)
College: Boston College

Noteworthy: Pro Bowl tight end that doubled as a reliable pass receiver and formidable run blocker. He proved to be a consummate pro by not griping about sharing tight end duties with fellow Pro Bowl player Keith Jackson. He caught 28 passes for 370 yards in the regular season, and two catches for 13 yards plus a two-point conversion in Super Bowl XXXI. He was a versatile player that served as the long snapper on punts when healthy.

"He can make the tough catch. He's an excellent receiver down the field. He's an above-average blocker and getting better every year. He's a big target, and he and Brett (Favre) have a nice feel for each other, and Brett likes to go to him in clutch situations." – Sherman Lewis, offensive coordinator

"When I first met Mark Chmura I thought he was just a big pretty boy. He was put together and all that but so what. Then I saw him get on that field and I saw how hard he worked and how he blocked his butt off, sometimes people don't get their just due and I think he was one of them. He was a key part of that offense because he created major match-up problems for every defense we faced that year." – Gilbert Brown, teammate

89

BRUCE WILKERSON

64

Position: Left tackle
Vitals: 6'-5", 310 lbs.
Age: 32
NFL Experience: 10th season
Free agent signed April 19, 1996
College: Tennessee

Noteworthy: Replaced rookie John Michels as the starting left tackle in the regular-season finale versus Minnesota (Dec. 22). He held the job throughout the playoffs and Super Bowl XXXI. He did not allow a sack in his first two post-season games.

"Bruce has played in some big games in his career, and knows how to handle the pressure. When he steps up, you know you're going to get a professional game out of him. He may have lost some speed, but he knows how to get in front of a guy and get the job done. He's effective."
– Tom Lovat, offensive line coach

"He was older and undersized, especially for a left tackle, but he protected Brett's backside like it was his home, his family and his children. He got the job done. It's funny how when a guy's back is against the wall, and he knows everybody in the world is watching him, and you've got to protect one of the best quarterbacks in the league, the question is this: What are you going to do? Everybody thinks you're not good enough and you're mediocre and you're just OK at best. He proved everybody wrong. He got out there and I don't think Brett was ever worried because he knew Bruce was going to die before he let anyone get a hand on Brett." – Gilbert Brown, teammate

64

Riddell
64

Reunion, September 10, 2006

EARL DOTSON

72

Position: Right tackle
Vitals: 6'-4", 315 lbs.
Age: 26
NFL Experience: 4th season
Drafted 1993 third round (81st overall)
College: Texas A&I

Noteworthy: Anchored the right side of the offensive line while paving the way for running backs Edgar Bennett and Dorsey Levens. His long arms, quick feet and quiet determination made him an effective pass blocker. He possessed a nasty streak that was unknown to most fans and media but was totally appreciated by his teammates.

"Earl was probably our most highly graded offensive lineman – and most consistent – last year. He just goes along, and you never hear much about him, but he very seldom gets beat by the pass rush. He's an excellent run blocker – very strong. He can knock people off the line of scrimmage. He's also an excellent pass protector – he's got good feet. I think Brett (Favre) feels real good with him on that right side. We think he's a Pro Bowl-type tackle eventually." – Sherman Lewis, offensive coordinator

"Big Earl. Man. He was a guy that was the thug of the line. He was the meanest cat that you can get. He may not be out there showing it where you could see it, but he would be whipping your butt and talking trash at the same time. Earl had that mean streak that if you ticked him off, he'd really come out and show you how he could play. Earl had injuries and people trying to take his position but he always came out ready to play. He had those long arms, and he was a pretty darn good pass blocker. Teams need to have a certain number of Earl Dotsons if they want to be any good."
– Gilbert Brown, teammate

72

ADAM TIMMERMAN

63

Position: Right guard
Vitals: 6'-4", 295 lbs.
Age: 25
NFL Experience: 2nd season
Drafted 1995 seventh round (230th overall)
College: South Dakota State

Noteworthy: Became the starting right guard in only his second NFL season. He is a fierce and intense competitor whose versatility enables him to play both guard positions at a high level. His selfless attitude and work ethic is reflected in the fact that he started at right guard and played on special teams.

"Adam is a very much-improved football player. He is a hard worker. Adam is doing everything we ask him to do." – Tom Lovat, offensive line coach

"He was a late-round pick out of some school not many people ever heard of and he had that buzz cut, crew cut, but the dude could play. After we played San Francisco in the playoffs – I know (49ers defensive tackle) Dana Stubblefield – and Timmerman was banging with him and pounding on him, our defensive line gave him a name. He was 'The Brawler.' He was out there going against guys that we thought, 'Oh, man, they're going to kill Timmerman.' But he went out there and fought everybody he faced and he got the better of most of the guys he went against. At the end of the day, we all felt like Adam Timmerman was maybe our best offensive lineman." – Gilbert Brown, teammate

63
NFL
Riddell

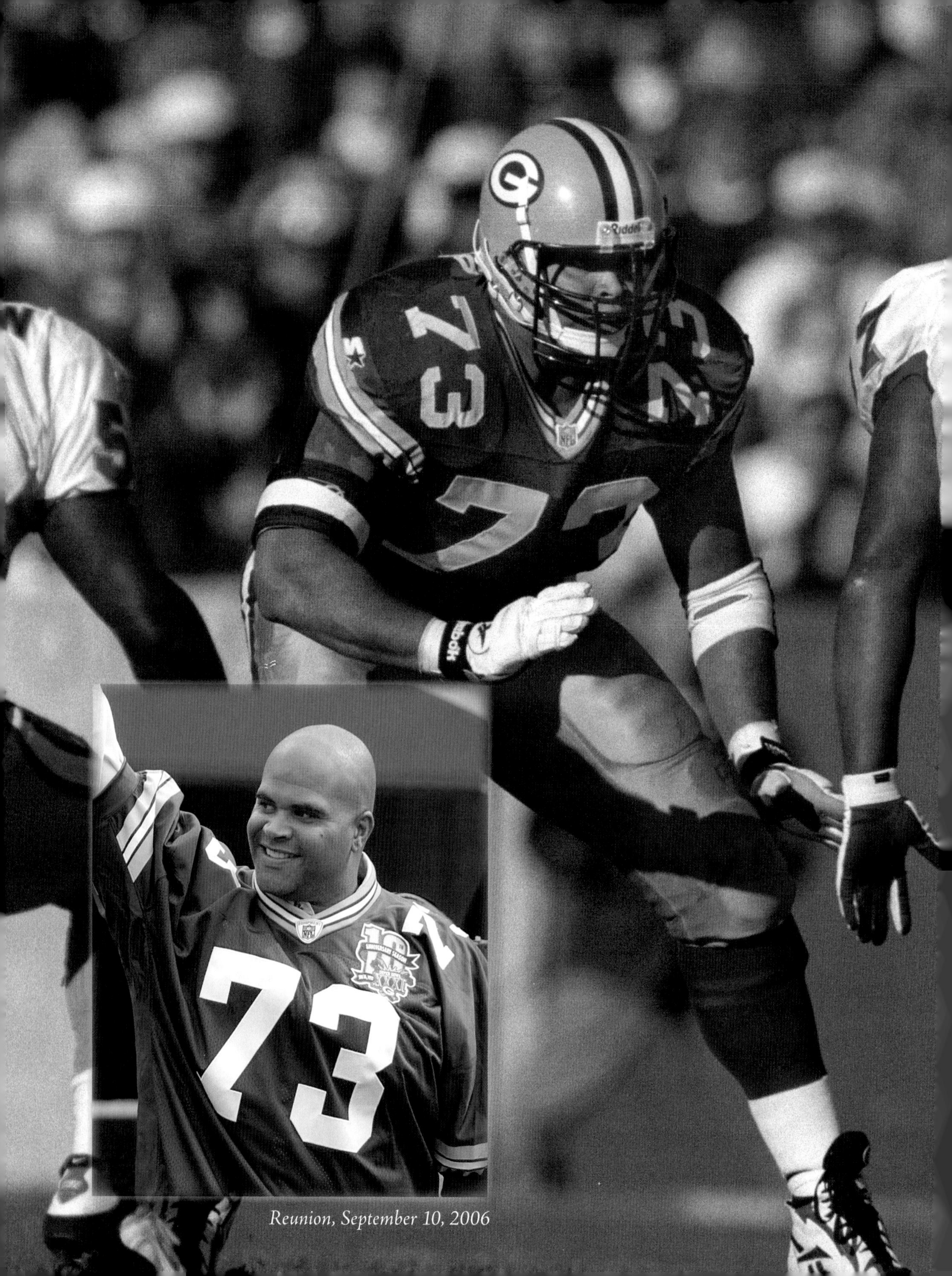

Reunion, September 10, 2006

AARON TAYLOR

73

Position: Left guard
Vitals: 6'-4", 305 lbs.
Age: 24
NFL Experience: 3rd season
Drafted 1994 first round (16th overall)
College: Notre Dame

Noteworthy: Tore the patellar tendon in both knees each of his first two seasons. He reclaimed the starting left guard job upon his return during the final week of the 1996 training camp. Smart, mobile lineman that possesses the strength to battle defensive tackles and the agility to lead on sweeps and screens.

"A.T. is a good football player. We've seen a progression with him since he's come in here. He's a good athlete. He's got a great work ethic and he's got a lot of pride in his work. He wants to be the best – he works hard, studies hard, he's a real professional." – *Tom Lovat, offensive line coach*

"Aaron Taylor was a guy that wasn't powerful, but he was crafty. He was technique sound. Some guys that got over him tried to overpower and muscle him but he had a knack to find that way to slow you down, or get his body in front of you, so the running back could get off and do his thing. He was an intense guy. He was out of that mold of Notre Dame offensive linemen. We were always competing over a lot of things on and off the field. He'd get the better of me. I'd get the better of him. The thing about it is we're both man enough now to sit back and say, 'That was fun.' He had that serious knee injury the first day of practice in one-on-one blocking drills against Don Davey and I don't think he ever became the great player that he could have been. But he still was smart enough and tough enough to have a pretty good NFL career." – *Gilbert Brown, teammate*

73

FRANK WINTERS

52

Position: Center
Vitals: 6'-3", 300 lbs.
Age: 33
NFL Experience: 10th season
Plan B free agent signed March 17, 1992
College: Western Illinois

Noteworthy: A model of consistency that rarely missed a snap. Played in 80 consecutive games with the Packers from 1992 through 1996 to tie Edgar Bennett for longest streak during that period. Finally got his due by being selected to represent the NFC in the 1996 Pro Bowl.

"Frank is a dependable player who I think is underrated as a football player and as an athlete. He has good leadership skills. The players respect his knowledge of the game and the fact that he lines up on every down. He kind of sets the tone." – Tom Lovat, offensive line coach

"At first, I didn't like Frankie. I looked at Frankie and I thought, 'He's a smart aleck.' He had a chip on his shoulder, and the way he talked and walked it seemed like he was arrogant. You've got to grow to learn to like a guy like that. When we got out there on the practice field, we battled. Man, did we battle. After a while you start to really like a guy like that. He really grew on me. If you were whipping his ass, or whatever, he'd get right back up and go to the huddle and do it all over again. He'd get me sometimes. I'd get him sometimes. He may do some dirty stuff. I'd try not to because he was older than me and I didn't want Mike (Holmgren) fussing at me because that was one of his boys. It was great competition that made everyone better. He was a tough cookie. I know they used to call him Frankie Bag 'O Donuts or whatever but he would come out every day – and I mean every day – and try to beat your ass. He wasn't the best body guy in the world, but he took care of his body. Frankie knew what he was doing on and off the field. Frankie was always on top of his game. What he did was the same thing that centers after him had to know. If we had a Thursday practice and it was good on good, and I'd stumble, some centers would just hold the snap. Not Frankie. He'd snap it and shout, "Offsides, 5 yards." And Brett knew enough to always have his hands under center for that reason. And the way Frankie would bitch at Brett was unbelievable. Here he was, an offensive lineman, and he would tell it to Brett just the way it was. He wanted to win. That was what mattered most. I'm pretty sure Brett didn't like to hear it. I wouldn't have had the balls to talk to Brett that way, but Frankie did what he had to do to help us win and he didn't care what anybody thought about it." – Gilbert Brown, teammate

52

Riddell
52
52
52

Reunion, September 10, 2006

DORSEY LEVENS

25

Position: Running back
Vitals: 6'-1", 230 lbs.
Age: 26
NFL Experience: 3rd season
Drafted 1994 fifth round (149th overall)
College: Georgia Tech

Noteworthy: Levens served as the primary running back in single-back sets and rushed for a career-high 566 yards on 121 carries for 4.7 yards-per-carry. He was unstoppable in the Packers' victory over Carolina in the NFC Championship Game, rushing for 88 yards on 10 carries and catching five passes for 117 yards and one touchdown. His 29-yard touchdown catch remains the stuff of legends. That performance earned him NFC's Player of the Week honors. He edged out William Henderson for the starting fullback job in 1995, a testament to his versatility and unselfishness, but moved to running back at the start of the 1996 season.

"He's got a rare combination of size and speed. He can run really fast for a guy his size. He's more elusive than some of our other backs – he can make people miss. He's got quickness and he can change direction. Plus, he's got enough speed that he can out-run angles. And he catches the ball well, too – he made some big catches for us (in 1996) coming out of the backfield." – Sherman Lewis, offensive coordinator

"Unbelievable. To sit there and watch that catch he made (in the NFC Conference Championship Game) against Carolina was unbelievable. From the field you can only see a certain angle, but then when you looked up at the Jumbotron it was an amazing catch. The way he made the catch, and made sure he corralled it in, and made sure his feet were in for a touchdown – it was something else. I wouldn't say Dorsey was a perfectionist, but he was a guy that took pains to hone his craft. He was behind Edgar Bennett battling him for the halfback spot, or William Henderson at fullback, and it helped make him a better player. Dorsey was really, really good." – Gilbert Brown, teammate

25

TRAVIS JERVEY

32

Position: Running back
Vitals: 6'-0", 222 lbs.
Age: 24
NFL Experience: 2nd season
Drafted 1995 fifth round (170th overall)
College: The Citadel

Noteworthy: Jervey was a key special teams contributor on the kick coverage and kick return units. He played in all 16 regular-season games and each of the three post-season games. He ranked sixth in special teams tackles with nine during the regular season, and tied Bernardo Harris for the team lead with six in post-season play.

"Travis has outstanding speed. He is the fastest of all the backs. He worked very hard after the (1996) season to improve his handling of the ball." – Sherman Lewis, offensive coordinator

"He was a surfer dude. Travis was one of those guys you look back on and say, 'Man, he had that look like he couldn't play.' But then when you get out there and you see him run and doing his thing, he wasn't always the smartest guy on the field, but you know if you tell him what to do he'd get it done. He'd bust his butt to get it done, and his speed on special teams really made a huge impact on that team. Like I said, he wasn't necessarily always the smartest guy on the field, but he knew his role and he fulfilled it to a T." – Gilbert Brown, teammate

32

Reunion, September 10, 2006

Reunion, September 10, 2006

DON BEEBE

82

Position: Wide receiver
Vitals: 5'-11", 183 lbs.
Age: 32
NFL Experience: 9th season
Free agent signed April 1, 1996
College: Chadron State

Noteworthy: Beebe turned the 40-yard dash in 4.25 seconds at a private workout to convince GM Ron Wolf to sign a 32-year-old receiver. The transaction paid huge dividends when Beebe hauled in 39 passes for 699 yards and four touchdowns. He also returned 15 kickoffs for 403 yards, including a 90-yard touchdown against the Bears. His Super Bowl experience (three trips with Buffalo), savvy and high character proved invaluable to the Packers' cause.

"He's a guy who still has great speed for being in the league as long as he has. You now, most guys start losing it after six or seven years, but Don is still as fast as ever – probably one of the fastest guys on our team. He's a guy who's been in the trenches, performs well under pressure and is probably the favorite receiver down the field of Brett (Favre) for his deep throws." – Sherman Lewis, offensive coordinator

"Don Beebe and I got along great especially for a receiver and a defensive lineman. I respected him for a lot of reasons but especially because of all the heartaches he endured in Buffalo. They'd get to the Big Dance every year, or at least it seemed like it, and then for one reason or another they would lose. He was such a professional the way he came in and proved he could still run and still play. He wasn't young anymore, but he laid it on the line for that team. He put it down for the younger guys, and he did what he had to do to help us get to the Super Bowl that year. He had high morals, everyone knew that, but he didn't make it like he was better than you were and he didn't force it upon you. He was a true leader in every sense of the word." – Gilbert Brown, teammate

82

ANDRE RISON

84

Position: Wide receiver
Vitals: 6'-1", 188 lbs.
Age: 29
NFL Experience: 8th season
Claimed on waivers November 19, 1996
College: Michigan State

Noteworthy: Rison, nicknamed "Bad Moon" Rison by ESPN anchor Chris Berman, wore out his welcome in Jacksonville when Jaguars coach Tom Coughlin decided to release him. The Packers, in need of a play-making receiver due to Robert Brooks' season-ending knee injury, decided to give him a chance. He responded by catching 13 passes for 135 yards and a touchdown in the final five regular-season games. He topped that in post-season play by catching seven passes for 143 yards and two touchdowns, including a 54-yard touchdown grab on the Packers' second play from scrimmage in Super Bowl XXXI.

"I wanted to show people they were wrong, who put this on me, that I was undisciplined and ran bad routes and was a distraction to a team. Over the past several days, I've read every negative comment that someone could write about me. That hurts for me to see my children read things about me that aren't true. Tonight was a special night for me to play on national TV and for my kids to watch and for me to perform well. It was important for me to prove to people that I am one of the best receivers in the game." – Andre Rison, receiver, after his Nov. 24 Packers debut at St. Louis

"He was a spark for us. The season kind of rolls along and goes the way it goes, and then all of a sudden you get a guy that comes in and sparks the team. That made an impact on us. When you get a new guy that comes in late in the season, it makes other guys go harder because this new guy that came in is getting all the attention. Everyone was talking about Andre Rison. What? Did they forget about us? We better hurry up and get it done. That addition helped our team be even better." – Gilbert Brown, teammate

84

Reunion, September 10, 2006

Reunion, September 10, 2006

KEITH JACKSON

88

Position: Tight end
Vitals: 6'-2", 258 lbs.
Age: 31
NFL Experience: 9th season
Free agent signed July 11, 1996
College: Oklahoma

Noteworthy: Originally acquired in a March 29, 1995 trade with Miami that sent the Dolphins a second-round pick in return for a Jackson and the fourth-round pick the Packers previously surrendered for receiver Mark Ingram. He reported after the Packers' 4-2 win-loss record at outset of 1995. He retired after the 1995 season, then re-signed with the Packers. He caught 40 passes for 505 yards and 10 touchdowns during the regular season.

"He dresses us up offensively. Suddenly, we're explosive as the dickens." – *Ron Wolf, general manager*

"I love Keith Jackson. There are certain people that you know are genuine and Keith Jackson is one of them. I do stuff for guys that deserve to have stuff done for them. It was that way for Keith and Reggie (White) and Brett Favre. I'd do whatever they asked me because I respected them so much as teammates and friends. I'd go to Reggie's camp in Chattanooga, Tennessee. Now who wants to go to Chattanooga, Tennessee? But I went because Reggie wanted me to be there, and I have those same feelings for Keith. I grew up watching Keith Jackson when he was at Oklahoma. Of course, I went to Kansas so whenever they played we'd have to bet on it. The first year I just knew they were going to crush us, but Keith was running off at the mouth so I had to bet him anyway. My boys beat them. I had a pink T-shirt made that was cut real high like a midriff and he had to wear it for a couple of days. I still laugh when I think about that. Those are the fun things you remember. On the field, we had Keith Jackson and Mark Chmura. What a tandem at tight end. It was like a world wrestling championship tag team. When we put both of them on the field, defenses didn't know what we were going to throw at them or how we were going to attack them. Shoot. It was funny because he would appear wide open in the secondary and you'd think, 'How can a defense lose a guy who is that big with hands that soft?' His hands were as soft as pillows. What a great player and an even better person." – *Gilbert Brown, teammate*

GARY BROWN

68

Position: Tackle-Guard
Vitals: 6'-4", 320 lbs.
Age: 25
NFL Experience: 3rd season
Claimed on waivers August 29, 1994
College: Georgia Tech

Noteworthy: He played in eight regular-season games, including five early season starts at left tackle.

"We moved him around quite a bit. We like Gary's size and we think he's more of a natural guard than tackle." – Sherman Lewis, offensive coordinator

"Gary's nickname was Bertha. He was a really nice guy and very pleasant to be around. He had lots of talent, too. For whatever reason it didn't quite come together for him, but when he was right the man could play." – Gilbert Brown, teammate

68

LINDSAY KNAPP

65

Position: Guard
Vitals: 6'-6", 300 lbs.
Age: 26
NFL Experience: 4th season
Acquired in August 27, 1995 trade with Kansas City
(for 1996 fifth-round pick)
College: Notre Dame

Noteworthy: A reserve offensive guard whose primary action came on special teams. He played in nine regular-season games and all three post-season games.

"Lindsay is a dependable guy who knows our offense. He's a good kid with a great work ethic. He's a very reliable backup." – Tom Lovat, offensive line coach

"Lindsay was a hard worker. He showed up. He did his job. He gave everyone a sense of security regarding our depth on the offensive line." – Gilbert Brown, teammate

65

KEN RUETTGERS

75

Position: Left tackle
Vitals: 6'-6", 295 lbs.
Age: 34
NFL Experience: 12th season
Drafted 1985 first round (seventh overall)
College: USC

Noteworthy: Ruettgers played in 153 games, including 139 starts, going into the 1996 season but chronic knee problems forced him to retire Nov. 20. After 12 seasons of top-notch play at left tackle, Ruettgers' body gave out just as the Packers were making their playoff push and eventual run to Super Bowl XXXI.

"There's nobody in this organization that doesn't appreciate Ken Ruettgers as a left tackle."
– Tom Lovat, offensive line coach

"Rut wanted to be on the field in the worst way but his knees just wouldn't allow it. He played a lot of years for the (Packers') organization, and he was a true pro. It wasn't until later that I knew how much it hurt him to retire." – Gilbert Brown, teammate

Reunion, September 10, 2006

75

JOHN MICHELS

77

Position: Left tackle
Vitals: 6'-7", 304 lbs.
Age: 23
NFL Experience: Rookie season
Drafted 1996 first round (27th overall)
College: USC

Noteworthy: Michels started nine games at left tackle in the regular season and saw action in all three post-season games.

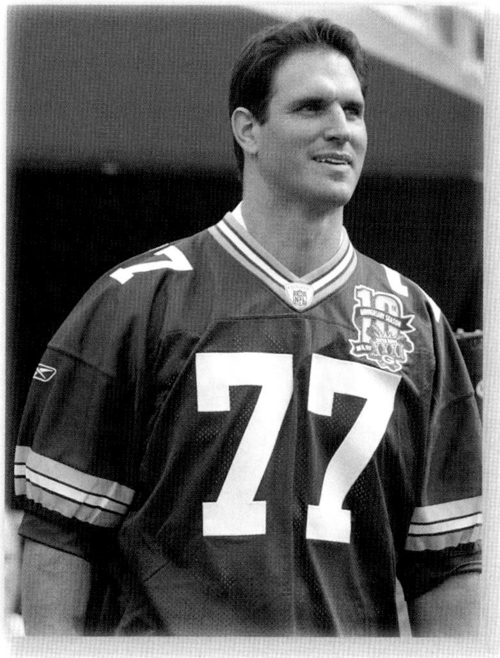

Reunion, September 10, 2006

"When he came in we were hoping that we could hold him a year, let him sit back of (Ken) Ruettgers and learn, and then let him step in (the 1997 season). Unfortunately, Ken got hurt and we had to play John a little before he was ready."
– Sherman Lewis, offensive coordinator

"I saw him at our 10th anniversary reunion the weekend of the Packers' opener against the Bears. I didn't recognize him at first. He has changed physically, and he's doing really well for himself. As a first-round draft pick, some people thought he was disappointing. As a person, he is tremendously successful." – Gilbert Brown, teammate

DOUG PEDERSON

18

Position: Quarterback
Vitals: 6'-3", 216 lbs.
Age: 28
NFL Experience: 4th season
Free agent signed Nov. 21, 1995
College: Northeast Louisiana

Noteworthy: Pederson, a veteran quarterback, may have felt like the Maytag repairman backing up Brett Favre. But before he was signed by Green Bay, he proved in Miami to be a capable NFL quarterback. He came off the bench to rally the Dolphins to a 19-14 victory at Philadelphia to give coach Don Shula his 325th win.

"Doug showed he has outstanding leadership qualities. He showed the staff he can move the team and win. He's got a nice presence about him in the huddle. In addition, he has a good strong arm with the ability to throw on the run."
– Sherman Lewis, offensive coordinator

"A pro's pro. Doug understood the game as well as anybody, and he used that knowledge to help Brett and the offense in every possible way. He didn't get much attention, but he didn't need any. He was great in the locker room." – Gilbert Brown, teammate

18

Reunion, September 10, 2006

JEFF THOMASON

83

Position: Tight end
Vitals: 6'-5", 250 lbs.
Age: 27
NFL Experience: 4th season
Free agent signed January 12, 1995
College: Oregon

Noteworthy: Served as the No. 3 tight end and core player on special teams units. He finished fifth on the team with 11 special teams tackles, and contributed three catches for 45 yards during the regular season. Made a resounding tackle of the Patriots' Dave Meggett on the kickoff return following Desmond Howard's kickoff return for a touchdown in Super Bowl XXXI.

"Jeff has shown steady improvement over the years. He has shown excellent improvement on his run blocking. He always has been an excellent receiver." – Sherman Lewis, offensive coordinator

"Dependable. He was really good on special teams, and when he had to fill in for Mark Chmura or Keith Jackson things kept rolling along." – Gilbert Brown, teammate

83

DERRICK MAYES

80

Position: Wide receiver
Vitals: 6'-½", 200 lbs.
Age: 22
NFL Experience: Rookie season
Drafted 1996 second round (56th overall)
College: Notre Dame

Noteworthy: Mayes caught six passes for 46 yards and two touchdowns in the regular season. He was slowed by a shoulder injury his rookie season and never reached his full potential.

"He has soft, sure hands and he can run after he catches the ball. He's got good body control and he's very aggressive."
– Sherman Lewis, offensive coordinator

"D-Mayes. He had great hands. He made catches in practice that would make us go, 'Are you kidding?' We had such a great receiving corps he never really got a chance to shine."
– Gilbert Brown, teammate

80

Terry Mickens

85

Position: Wide receiver
Vitals: 6-0, 201
Age: 25
NFL Experience: 3rd season
Drafted 1994 fifth round (153rd overall)
College: Florida A&M

Noteworthy: Mickens battled a nagging ankle injury early in the season, but when called upon he responded wonderfully. With starters Robert Brooks and Antonio Freeman sidelined by injuries, Mickens caught seven passes for 52 yards and two touchdowns in his first NFL start to help the Packers defeat the Lions. He started the following week against Kansas City but left late in the game with a concussion. He started again versus Dallas and caught five passes for 38 yards. He finished the season with a career-high 18 catches for 161 yards and two touchdowns. Mickens also played in each of the Packers' post-season games.

"I think Terry's strong suit – the thing that makes him so valuable to us – is that he's so versatile. He can play anywhere when we've got four receivers in the game, and those are four pretty distinct assignments. If somebody goes down we can put him in and he'll go in and he knows what he's doing. He won't make a mistake." – Sherman Lewis, offensive coordinator

"T-Mick was stronger than he looked and he didn't mind sticking his nose in there on special teams. The man also always did his homework. He knew every route on every play for all three receiver positions, the X, Y and Z. When we had receivers getting hurt left and right, Mickens stepped in and helped us beat the Detroit Lions in a big game at home. He knew his role and he played it well." – Gilbert Brown, teammate

85

Defense

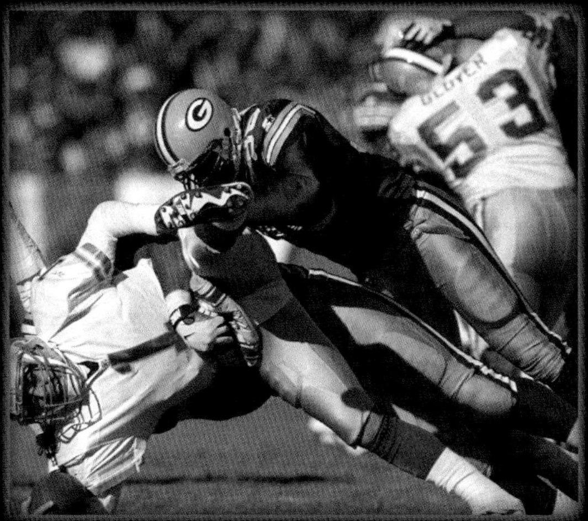

Reggie White 92
Santana Dotson 71
Gilbert Brown 93
Sean Jones 96
Wayne Simmons 59
George Koonce 53
Brian Williams 51
Craig Newsome 21
Doug Evans 33
LeRoy Butler 36
Eugene Robinson 41
Ron Cox 54
Mike Prior 39
Gabe Wilkins 98
Shannon Clavelle 91
Bob Kuberski 94
Keith McKenzie 95
Darius Holland 90
Bernardo Harris 55
Lamont Hollinquest 56
Tyrone Williams 37
Roderick Mullen 28

REGGIE WHITE

92

Position: Defensive end
Vitals: 6'-5", 304 lbs.
Age: 35
NFL Experience: 12th season
Free agent signed April 8, 1993
College: Tennessee

Noteworthy: The cornerstone of the Packers' defense, White led by word and deed to create a winning atmosphere and a sense of pride. He registered 8 ½ sacks, 36 tackles, an interception and three forced fumbles during the regular season. However, it was his dominance in Super Bowl XXXI that stands out. He tallied a Super Bowl-record three sacks of New England quarterback Drew Bledsoe.

"He is the cornerstone and foundation of this football team. Actually, when we look around at our team and what's happened with our team, the most important – the pivotal move – was to bring Reggie White here. When he came here, he came here with the idea that he was going to help this team get to a Super Bowl, and did about everything he could as an individual to try to get there. He is a rare football player and a rare individual." – Fritz Shurmur, defensive coordinator

"Oh, man. Big Dog was amazing. I love him. That's all I've got to say. I'm not uncomfortable saying that. I know that without him I wouldn't be the guy that I am today, period. There's no way, shape or form. I learned so much from him. The funny thing about it was he didn't have to tell me. I watched him and I wanted to be exactly like him on and off the field. You can't be Reggie White, but you can try, and believe me I tried. Do we win a Super Bowl without him? No way. We wouldn't even be talking about a 10 year Super Bowl anniversary. There wouldn't be any. He was the Big Dog and the Lead Dog and he meant everything to that defense and that team." – Gilbert Brown, teammate

92

Reunion, September 10, 2006, represented by his family

Reunion, September 10, 2006

SANTANA DOTSON

71

Position: Defensive tackle
Vitals: 6'-5", 285 lbs.
Age: 27
NFL Experience: 5th season
Free agent signed March 7, 1996
College: Baylor

Noteworthy: Dotson provided a consistent inside pass rush while being strong against the run. He was third on the team with 5 ½ sacks and his 45 tackles ranked second among the team's defensive linemen. In Super Bowl XXXI, he contributed a fourth-quarter sack to help the Packers seal their victory over New England.

"Santana made a big difference on our defense, especially in the inside pass rush. Santana gives us speed and movement as well as tremendous height for an inside player. He has exceptional quickness for a big guy and is an excellent run player as well as a pass rusher." – Fritz Shurmur, defensive coordinator

"That's my road dog, my homey and my guy. I love that clown to death. There isn't anything I wouldn't do for that guy. He was a year longer in the league with me, but we were like two brothers. One time during the '96 year we were playing San Diego and they were getting pretty rough with us. I looked up and I had three guys around me and they were trying to take me out. They had me surrounded even though the play was going away from us. I thought, 'Uh oh.' And then all of a sudden I see this big soup bone come flying out of nowhere and he cleared out two of them. It was Santana Dotson, Big old No. 71 to the rescue, and he wouldn't take anything from anyone, and he wouldn't let anybody mess with his boys. He had your back at all times. I was Batman and he was Robin, although he'd say it was the other way around. That's OK. We were as close as could be, and we still are to this day."
– Gilbert Brown, teammate

GILBERT BROWN

93

Position: Defensive tackle
Vitals: 6'-2", 345 lbs.
Age: 25
NFL Experience: 4th season
Claimed off waivers August 31, 1993 from Minnesota
College: Kansas

Noteworthy: Brown's unselfish approach and mammoth size enabled him to take on and occasionally defeat double teams. He anchored the interior defensive line on a unit that allowed an NFC-best 88.5 yards rushing per game. He led the Packers' defensive linemen with 56 tackles, 30 more than his previous career-best, plus a sack and a forced fumble.

"Gilbert Brown has a unique ability to control the middle of the offense. And it usually takes more than one guy to block him. Gilbert and Santana Dotson complement each other extremely well. Gilbert is the big guy who pushes the pile and Santana is the quick guy who makes the move on 'em. Gilbert, in terms of football strength, is the strongest player on the team." – Fritz Shurmur, defensive coordinator

"A team player first and foremost. If they asked me to jump off the Tower Drive Bridge, if that's what they needed me to do for us to win, then I'd do it. I just loved my teammates, and they didn't have to do anything for me. I loved my teammates and the rewards that we would get as a team, and that was always more than enough." – Gilbert Brown on himself

93

Reunion, September 10, 2006

96

SEAN JONES

96

Position: Defensive end
Vitals: 6'-7", 283 lbs.
Age: 34
NFL Experience: 13th season
Free agent signed April 18, 1994
College: Northeastern

Noteworthy: Jones, a savvy veteran, teamed with Reggie White to become formidable bookends. He played in more than 200 NFL games and registered 10 or more sacks in five seasons. He was a steadying influence and unquestioned leader on the field and in the locker room. He had 37 tackles, five sacks and two forced fumbles during the regular season.

"On the field, (Sean Jones) has always been a leader and just really stepped up his game when we needed to have it. He's the ultimate student of the game. I mean, he works very hard at trying to find an edge." – Fritz Shurmur, defensive coordinator

"Sean Jones was one of the smartest guys on that team. On our defense you had the Big Dog, and then you had Sean Jones, who was second in command and everyone knew that. Maybe back in Sean Jones' younger days he would work his tail off, but when he got to Green Bay he paced himself. But I'll tell you he'd put it down on game day. He'd put it on the line when he had to do it. He had his own routine. Do as I say, not as I do. He used to kill me. He'd always have a huge pad on one side of his arm. I wondered why he would do that. Then you'd see it in the game. He'd take that arm and he'd slam it into guys, and he'd be taking on blocks, and he knew how to protect himself. Without Reggie White and Sean Jones we wouldn't have been there." – Gilbert Brown, teammate

96

WAYNE SIMMONS

59

Position: Left outside linebacker
Vitals: 6'2", 250 lbs.
Age: 27
NFL Experience: 4th season
Drafted 1993 first round (15th overall)
College: Clemson

Noteworthy: Simmons was a fierce, intense competitor that provided the defense with much of its rugged, take-no-prisoners attitude. He was one of the NFL's best at mauling opposing tight ends into submission. He dominated San Francisco's Brent Jones, a top-flight tight end, like few linebackers could. He had 76 tackles, 2 ½ sacks, an interception and 2 forced fumbles in the regular season. He tied for fourth on the team with 13 tackles, including one sack, in the post-season.

"Wayne is very physical and has the capacity to play over the tight end as well as anybody in the league, from both a pass and run coverage perspective. He has the ability to be able to defeat the tight end and get the ball carrier on the ground. What he does can be very disruptive to our opponent. He brings a dimension to our defense that no one else does in terms of just the physical aspect. He's also a very bright guy who has a great feel for what we're trying to do defensively." – Fritz Shurmur, defensive coordinator

"He's a guy that a lot of people didn't understand, and a lot of people didn't like. But as a teammate and a friend, he was one of the best guys you could have around. People didn't see what we saw, and people didn't hear what we heard. If he was in a bad mood and that was the first time meeting him, that's what people would think of him, and there's no doubt he was a rough, tough man. I thought he always got a bad rap. He was the bad guy. He was the bad guy on our defense. He was just straight up raw and that was his personality. He was never a fake or a fraud, and that's more than you can say for a lot of people. He'd never bite his tongue or hold back what he thought. He was the bad guy on our defense, and we needed him to be the bad guy and he did that role to perfection. If you had a beep machine to censure what he said, he'd have broken it the first day. I'm not saying that was bad or good, but it was just the way it was with him." – Gilbert Brown, teammate

59

Riddell
53
53
53
Franklin

GEORGE KOONCE

53

Position: Middle linebacker
Vitals: 6'-1", 243 lbs.
Age: 28
NFL Experience: 5th season
Free agent signed June 1, 1992
College: East Carolina

Noteworthy: Koonce entrenched himself as a top player on the NFL's best defense after a lengthy, humbling journey. He was cut by Atlanta in 1991, and then played for the worst team in the World League before signing a free agent contract with Green Bay. An extremely versatile player, Koonce has played each of the three linebacker positions in his first five seasons with the Packers. He registered 100 or more tackles in three of the past four seasons, including 117 stops, plus three interceptions, in 1996. A season-ending knee injury in the Packers' NFC Divisional playoff game versus San Francisco forced him to miss the NFC Championship and Super Bowl XXXI.

"He's a fine linebacker who has an excellent nose for the ball. He works very hard at his job and because of that he can lead by example. We moved him inside because he had played there and played effectively, and we needed to find a spot for Brian Williams to play because he had been so outstanding. George understood our defense as well or better than anybody that we could move to the middle."
– Fritz Shurmur, defensive coordinator

"George is a guy that knew his position and knew what was going on. He was one of the funniest guys in the world. If we were going on a trip, and there's nobody that could shut LeRoy (Butler) up when we got to playing cards, the only guy that could was George Koonce. It hurt me to see him on the sideline because I knew he put everything he had into that year. Just like Robert Brooks put his all into it. But George Koonce was one of our guys. He was one of our defensive leaders. When we saw him go down, and we had to visualize that, it was tough to take. Like Robert, I could see the hurt in his eyes when we went to the Super Bowl. He was so happy for us because that was the kind of guy that he was, but it also tore him up not to be on the field. He wanted to get out there and help." – Gilbert Brown, teammate

53

BRIAN WILLIAMS

51

Position: Right outside linebacker
Vitals: 6'-1", 240 lbs.
Age: 24
NFL Experience: 2nd season
Drafted 1995 third round (73rd overall)
College: USC

Noteworthy: Williams was among the most pleasant surprises in 1996, when he stepped into the starting lineup after a nondescript rookie season. He racked up 95 tackles and three fumble recoveries in the regular season, and then tied LeRoy Butler for the team lead with 15 tackles in the post-season. He also added an interception, a forced fumble and a fumble recovery in the playoffs.

"Brian had a marvelous 1996 season, his first year as a starter, and he brings exceptional speed to the position. He has the capacity to be an All-Pro performer." – Fritz Shurmur, defensive coordinator

"Good old B.W. He was the craziest cat around. I don't know why but we would butt heads in a playful way. I used to tell myself when I'd get up every morning, 'Screw B.W.' I told him that and we would laugh about it. But he was a really good player. He could run from the weak-side and make a lot of tackles." – Gilbert Brown, teammate

51

Reunion, September 10, 2006

Riddell
21
21
NFL
Reebok
Reebok

CRAIG NEWSOME

21

Position: Left cornerback
Vitals: 6'-0", 190 lbs.
Age: 25
NFL Experience: 2nd season
Drafted 1995 first round (32nd overall)
College: Arizona State

Noteworthy: Newsome was one of the NFL's most tenacious cornerbacks that played the run as well as the pass. He didn't incur a pass defense or illegal contact penalty through the first 18 games (including the playoffs) in 1996. He had 71 tackles and two interceptions as well as a team-high 23 passes defended while starting every game for the second straight season.

"Craig doesn't back off anybody – never would – and knows how to be aggressive. He never misses an opportunity to get better. Every play in practice, whether it's in pads, without pads or whatever, he is a 100 miles an hour guy. He's going full speed, he's trying to make plays, he is trying to get better every time he goes out there." – Fritz Shurmur, defensive coordinator

"C. New was a very physical player. You wouldn't think it by looking at him, but if C. New got a shot on you he'd take it, and he'd be glad to do it. He was fast. He was quick. He was one of those guys that didn't say too much. He would do his talking on the field, and that was fine with us."
– Gilbert Brown, teammate

21

DOUG EVANS

33

Position: Right cornerback
Vitals: 6'-1", 190 lbs.
Age: 26
NFL Experience: 4th season
Drafted 1993 sixth round (141st overall)
College: Louisiana Tech

Noteworthy: Evans blossomed in his fourth year as a starter by intercepting five passes, making 68 tackles and registering three sacks. He even pitched in with six solo tackles on the special teams' coverage units. A quiet, self-assured and durable player, Evans started 47 games and participated in all 64 during his first four NFL seasons.

"Doug Evans, I think, has positioned himself as one of the top corners in the league. He had three magnificent interceptions that turned games around (in 1996). One was on the first play of the Philadelphia game. The second one was the second play of the second half of the Rams game, where he intercepted and went in for a touchdown. And the third one was the big interception he had in front of our bench in the Super Bowl. We like everything he represents as a football player." – Fritz Shurmur, defensive coordinator

"The Greyhound. He looked like a raggedy old greyhound. Man, he could run. He was another joker, too. One of those guys when you get up in the morning and you don't feel like joking, well sure enough, Doug Evans would be smiling and joking and talking away. He and Craig Newsome were the perfect complement to each other. One was quiet. One was a talker. Let me tell you, brother, they both could play. They were out there by themselves and playing the game against all types of receivers. Short. Tall. Fast. Slow. And they would handle them. They were like, 'Let's tango and dance.' They were like Tango & Cash. Guys don't like to brag and boast, but when you'd come back to the sideline, you'd know Doug Evans would have a smile on his face and be joking and having a good time. Every team needs guys like that." – Gilbert Brown, teammate

33

Riddell
33
EVANS

Reunion, September 10, 2006

LEROY BUTLER

36

Position: Strong safety
Vitals: 6'-0", 200 lbs.
Age: 28
NFL Experience: 7th season
Drafted 1990 second round (48th overall)
College: Florida State

Noteworthy: The Pro Bowl safety was a playmaker of the highest magnitude. A cornerback in his first two NFL seasons, Butler moved to safety and never looked back. He had 92 tackles, 6 ½ sacks and five interceptions in an outstanding '96 season. The originator of the "Lambeau Leap," Butler's freewheeling style and ability to thwart offenses by lining up at every conceivable position endeared him to the fans.

"LeRoy is as instinctive a player as there is at the safety position in the National Football League. He is good deep, as a cover guy, but especially effective as a dogger and blitzer and playing up close to the line of scrimmage. He has amazing instincts and a feel for where the ball is going." – Fritz Shurmur, defensive coordinator

"The Butler. He amazed me. When Fritz (Shurmur) started putting those defenses in for LeRoy, the first time I saw it I was like, 'Those dudes at running back are going to run over, around, and through LeRoy.' I was thinking it wasn't going to be pretty because LeRoy doesn't look that strong at all. The only part of LeRoy's body that's cut, is if you took a knife and cut it. And all the while he's telling everyone what a bad dude HE is, and what HE's going to do to them. That's what amazed me so much. Look at me. Look at Sean Jones. Look at Santana Dotson. And then there's LeRoy. Well, it turned out he was a lot stronger than he looked. I mean he's filling holes and knocking people out and pounding on quarterbacks. One of the things that made him so great was that you knew he was going to do whatever it took to win a game. He was one of those guys that when you're picking sides on a playground, you'd want him to be on your team because you just knew he was going to be a winner. He knew football. He was never scared. He didn't have time to be scared. He was too busy making plays and making sure we got it done out there. He loves to laugh and have fun, and that smile of his is the best. But when it came time to be serious and get after it, LeRoy Butler was the man. When everything was on the line he didn't have any time for foolishness. We were locker mates all the way through and I learned so much stuff from him. It's not like he taught me how to play my position, but he did teach me how to be a pro's pro. That's why he was such a great, great pro." – Gilbert Brown, teammate

EUGENE ROBINSON

41

Position: Free safety
Vitals: 6'-0", 197 lbs.
Age: 33
NFL Experience: 12th season
Acquired in a June 27, 1996 trade with Seattle (for Matt LaBounty)
College: Colgate

Noteworthy: Robinson was a smart, vocal leader in the defensive secondary whose six interceptions in 1996 swelled his career total to 48. The veteran was a last-minute addition by GM Ron Wolf that paid off in a big way. He finished fourth on the team with 87 tackles and also defended 12 passes. He was the glue of the secondary, and the reason LeRoy Butler could roam and use his unique talents to the fullest.

"He has great range, great tackling ability and exceptional mental capacity to run the defense and make all the adjustments. Eugene is a playmaker, a bright guy and an exceptional leader." – Fritz Shurmur, defensive coordinator

"Eugene was like a quarterback. I've never seen anyone do the things he could do. He was always telling people where they needed to be at all times during a game. Every time we came off the field he was telling us what (the offense) was doing, why they were doing it and what we had to do to stop it. He would tell us what would be coming and sure enough, almost every time, it would happen just like he said. When he would tell us that a certain play was coming, we didn't even ask who, what, where or why. We just listened to what he said because we knew that he knew. To hear him say, 'They're going to run this or that,' and then to see it happen, it was a thing of beauty. All that film study he put in and all those hours of figuring out a team's tendencies and habits and what they would do based on personnel and formation and situation, and then to take that knowledge and make an educated guess depending on all those factors, and to be right almost all the time, it was a thing of beauty."
– Gilbert Brown, teammate

41

54

RON COX

54

Position: Middle linebacker
Vitals: 6'-2', 235 lbs.
Age: 28
NFL Experience: 7th season
Free agent signed March 29, 1996
College: Fresno State

Noteworthy: Cox was the backup middle linebacker throughout the regular season and the first playoff game before replacing the injured George Koonce. Cox started in the NFC Championship game and Super Bowl XXXI, registering a total of four tackles.

"He's all football player and he's got the great instincts. He works hard at the game and loves to play football – and it shows when you watch him play. He plays it with enthusiasm, he plays it physically and he's got some athletic ability to go with that." – Fritz Shurmur, defensive coordinator

"Nobody could take George Koonce's place, and we all knew that, but Ron Cox stepped in and did what he had to do to help us get to the Super Bowl. I always thought of him as a throwback. I remember looking at a picture of us playing against San Francisco and he was muddy, dirt all over the place, and he was just sitting there like a warrior. I want to thank him for helping us get to where we had to go." – Gilbert Brown, teammate

54

MIKE PRIOR

39

Position: Safety
Vitals: 6'-0", 208 lbs.
Age: 33
NFL Experience: 11th season
Free agent signed April 16, 1993
College: Illinois State

Noteworthy: Prior was a sure tackler, heady defender and versatile athlete that relished, rather than languished, in his role. He was steady on the special teams' coverage units, served as the punter's personal protector and occasionally returned punts, too. Defensive coordinator Fritz Shurmur put Prior in position in the "nickel" and "dime" defenses to utilize his talents, highlight his skills and diminish any weaknesses.

"Mike is a veteran who whenever called upon plays extremely well. Mike has been a very valuable piece of the puzzle." – Fritz Shurmur, defensive coordinator

"He would get his lunch pail and go to work. Just like a bricklayer. Somebody you could rely on. He was an unsung hero. All the work and hours he put in, this guy's not fast, he's not this or that, but he was savvy enough to be where he was supposed to be to make plays. It takes men like Mike Prior to win a Super Bowl." – Gilbert Brown, teammate

39

Reunion, September 10, 2006

Gabe Wilkins

98

Position: Defensive end
Vitals: 6'-5", 295 lbs.
Age: 25
NFL Experience: 3rd season
Drafted 1994 fourth round (126th overall)
College: Gardner-Webb

Noteworthy: Wilkins played in all 16 regular-season games and posted 18 tackles and three sacks. He was the primary backup to Reggie White and Sean Jones, and when Jones retired after the 1996 season, he stepped into the starting job at right end.

"Gabe has improved every year he's been here. Gabe can play inside and outside, though he is probably better equipped as a defensive end. He has been productive every time he has played."
– Fritz Shurmur, defensive coordinator

"That's my roommate. Gabriel and I were tight, best friends, and I always wanted the best for him. He came from a small school and he was kind of shy at first, but he broke out of that in a hurry. He had a ton of talent, and he made some big plays during his time in Green Bay."
– Gilbert Brown, teammate

98

SHANNON CLAVELLE

91

Position: Defensive end-tackle
Vitals: 6'-2", 287 lbs.
Age: 24
NFL Experience: 2nd season
Free agent signed October 25, 1995
College: Colorado

Noteworthy: A role player on the Packers' 1996 team, Clavelle saw action in eight regular-season games on special teams and as a backup.

"He has excellent hands and he plays and practices hard." – Fritz Shurmur, defensive coordinator

"Shannon had excellent quickness and he gave our offensive linemen a really good look in practice." – Gilbert Brown, teammate

91

BOB KUBERSKI

94

Position: Defensive tackle
Vitals: 6′ 4″, 295 lbs.
Age: 25
NFL Experience: 2nd season
Drafted 1993 seventh round (183rd overall)
College: Navy

Noteworthy: Kuberski was inactive for 14 regular-season games and the post-season.

"Bob is a tough, determined player. He is a very dedicated player who gets the utmost out of his ability." – Fritz Shurmur, defensive coordinator

"Bobby Kuberski, that's my man right there. He was one of the ringleaders on that defensive line. He was one of those guys that you looked forward to seeing in the locker room each day. He was just a great guy." – Gilbert Brown, teammate

94

Reunion, September 10, 2006

KEITH McKENZIE

95

Position: Linebacker-defensive end
Vitals: 6'-3", 255 lbs.
Age: 23
NFL Experience: Rookie season
Drafted 1996 seventh round (252nd overall)
College: Ball State

Noteworthy: McKenzie caught the coaching staff's eye when he led the NFL with 5 ½ sacks in the preseason. He went on to become a situational pass rusher and special teams player as a rookie. He played in 10 regular-season games and the three post-season games.

Reunion, September 10, 2006

"He's an excellent pass rusher. He's got a great feel for working off the corners of the blocker, which is what pass rush is all about. And he's relentless in his effort."
– Fritz Shurmur, defensive coordinator

"Keith had a great outside pass rush. He could bring it. He's a Detroit guy, just like me. On one side of Seven Mile Road people like Aretha Franklin live. Guys like Keith and me lived on the other side. He was from Highland Park. I was from Griggs and Schoolcraft. When we'd go home to visit we'd put the word out so we had permission to go through each other's 'hood. He's one of my boys." – Gilbert Brown, teammate

95

DARIUS HOLLAND

90

Position: Defensive tackle
Vitals: 6'-5", 320 lbs.
Age: 23
NFL Experience: 2nd season
Drafted 1995 third round (65th overall)
College: Colorado

Noteworthy: Holland, a backup defensive tackle, played primarily as an inside

"Darius has excellent speed, size and overall athletic ability, but he needs to play more consistently."
– Fritz Shurmur, defensive coordinator

"More talent than I cared to think about. He flashed at times, but he wasn't always as consistent as you'd like and that hurt him." – Gilbert Brown, teammate

BERNARDO HARRIS

55

Position: Linebacker
Vitals: 6'-2", 247 lbs.
Age: 25
NFL Experience: 2nd season
Free agent signed January 13, 1995
College: North Carolina

Noteworthy: A quiet, prideful player, Harris was a pacesetter on the Packers' special teams' coverage units. He played in 16 regular-season games and played in each of the post-season games. He led the team with 21 special teams tackles – the most by a Packers player since Jackie Harris' 22 in 1990 – during the regular season.

"He's a physical player, he's got good coverage skills and understands our defense very well, so as a result can manage it well. But I would like him to be more outgoing, more vocal, because he's basically a nice guy and a good kid." – Fritz Shurmur, defensive coordinator

"Bernardo Harris was the biggest, fattest linebacker that I ever saw, and I mean that in a loving way. It was my job to make sure Bernardo Harris did his job by tying up tacklers and so forth. He was a really good player and we have remained close to this day. He always had a smile on his face and that's what you needed." – Gilbert Brown, teammate

55

LAMONT HOLLINQUEST

56

Position: Linebacker
Vitals: 6'-3", 250 lbs.
Age: 26
NFL Experience: 3rd season
Free agent signed January 18, 1996
College: USC

Noteworthy: Hollinquest, a special teams core player, finished second on the team with 15 special teams tackles. He also made six tackles, and had an interception and two pass breakups, during the course of the season.

"He's in a position to either make someone else better or move in and earn more playing time,"
– Jim Lind, linebackers coach

"Lamont was killer on special teams. He loved to get out there and run down and cover kicks and punts. He was crazy. It takes guys like that to win as many games as we won."
– Gilbert Brown, teammate

56

TYRONE WILLIAMS

37

Position: Cornerback
Vitals: 5'-11", 195 lbs.
Age: 23
NFL Experience: Rookie season
Drafted 1996 third round (93rd overall)
College: Nebraska

Noteworthy: Williams played in every game and contributed as the "dime" defensive back and on special teams. He finished second to Mike Prior among non-starters with 22 tackles and also defended six passes. He intercepted a Kerry Collins pass in the NFC Championship Game that set up a late first-half field goal to give Green Bay a 17-10 halftime lead.

Reunion, September 10, 2006

"Tyrone had a great year for a rookie. He became a contributor, especially in the stretch run, the last eight games after Dallas. I don't know where we would have been without him." – Fritz Shurmur, defensive coordinator

"I'll never forget the interception he made against Carolina in the NFC Championship Game. That play showed how much talent T-Dub possessed. I knew it was only a matter of time before he became a starter." – Gilbert Brown, teammate

37

RODERICK MULLEN

28

Position: Cornerback-safety
Vitals: 6'-1", 204 lbs.
Age: 24
NFL Experience: 2nd season
Free agent signed Aug. 29, 1995
Position: Grambling State

Noteworthy: Mullen lined up at cornerback and safety and played in 14 regular-season games before being sidelined with a knee injury. He returned to play in the Packers' post-season.

"He's a big guy with some range and coverage skills. And he's a physical player as well."
– Fritz Shurmur, defensive coordinator

"Roderick Mullen would do whatever had to be done. It didn't matter. Wipe the floors. Clean the lockers. Make tackles on special teams. Step in and play strong in the secondary. Roderick did it all, and he was one of the nicest guys in that locker room." – Gilbert Brown, teammate

Reunion, September 10, 2006

28

Specialists

Desmond Howard 81
Craig Hentrich 17
Chris Jacke 13

DESMOND HOWARD

81

Position: Return specialist-wide receiver
Vitals: 5'-10", 180 lbs.
Age: 26
NFL Experience: 5th season
Free agent signed July 11, 1996
College: Michigan

Noteworthy: Howard was the first special teams player to be voted the Super Bowl XXXI Most Valuable Player after returning four kickoffs for 154 yards and six punts for 90 yards. His 99-yard kick return for a touchdown late in the third quarter sealed the Packers' victory. He returned a punt 71 yards for a touchdown in the Packers' NFC Divisional Playoff victory against San Francisco. In the regular season, Howard returned 58 punts for a 15.1 average and three touchdowns.

"(Howard) took them right out of the game when he took their initial punt for a touchdown. The next time he touches the ball we go in again. It's 14-0 and we've got 9 yards in total offense." – Ron Wolf, general manager, on Howard in the Packers' 35-14 victory over San Francisco in the NFC Divisional Playoffs.

"Desmond was amazing. Those games when we played San Francisco in the mud or the cold or the wind, every time we needed a spark there was Desmond Howard. Every time he touched the ball we felt like he was going to score. He was the man in 1996. He deserved being the Super Bowl XXXI Most Valuable Player. The offense didn't start when Brett and the boys trotted onto the field. It started when Desmond Howard and the punt return team came out. We always felt like we'd be starting at mid-field or better. We had so much confidence in him, and I think that's half the battle on the return units." – Gilbert Brown, teammate

81

PACKERS
81

CRAIG HENTRICH

17

Position: Punter
Vitals: 6'-3", 200 lbs.
Age: 25
NFL Experience: 3rd season
Free agent signed January 14, 1993
College: Notre Dame

Noteworthy: Hentrich punted a team-record 28 times inside the opponent's 20-yard line (the NFL began keeping the statistic in 1976). His gross average of 42.4 yards was the Packers' second-best effort in two-plus decades. His versatility was a tremendous bonus, as he handled the kickoff duties and served as the holder on placements.

"His versatility is just amazing and I think everybody on the team realizes that. He's a team player. If I tell him I want a 35-yard punt, he'll try to give me a 35-yard punt with a lot of hang time to try to take a return man out of the game. He's not selfish in that respect. The other thing, he's really an excellent holder, and it makes for a comfortable situation with the kicker."
– Nolan Cromwell, special teams coach

"Craig was a jack-of-all-trades. He had the hands of a big league shortstop. Whenever there was a bad snap, which was rare, he'd field it clean and get the punt off like no big thing. Sometimes we'd sit around and say, 'Look at them kickers over there.' They're sitting down, walking around, kicking once in a while, and we're out there busting our butt. They'd get to go home early while we're still in meetings, and we'd be like, 'Damn, kickers.' But when it was time and we needed them they were always there for us." – Gilbert Brown, teammate

17

CHRIS JACKE

13

Position: Kicker
Vitals: 6'-0", 205 lbs.
Age: 30
NFL Experience: 8th season
Drafted 1989 sixth round (142nd overall)
College: Texas-El Paso

Noteworthy: Jacke's accuracy and mental toughness made him one of the most reliable kickers in Packers history. He connected on 21 of 27 field goals in the regular season, including a 53-yard field goal to defeat San Francisco, 23-20, on a Monday night game Oct. 14.

Reunion, September 10, 2006

"I think everybody around the league knows how good a kicker Chris Jacke is."
– Nolan Cromwell, special teams coach

"You think of the luxury that the Packers had with Ryan Longwell and it was the same thing with Jacke. You think about a guy like Chris Jacke kicking the ball, kicking off, and it doesn't seem like much. But it's three points that you need, or an extra point that wins the game. I know kickers don't always get the respect that they deserve, but we always appreciated everything Chris Jacke did for us when he was our kicker. He was a great player at his position."
– Gilbert Brown, teammate

Football Fields to Elysian Fields

Fritz Shurmur, Reggie White & Wayne Simmons

BY CHRIS HAVEL

It is difficult to imagine three men being so different as Fritz Shurmur, Reggie White and Wayne Simmons.

So different, that is, yet so much alike.

The Green Bay Packers' 1996 defense was as diverse as it was dominant. Its leaders possessed divergent backgrounds, values and life experiences. Its core players brought a wide range of talent, toughness and tendencies.

Yet somehow, some way, that diversity forced the defense to focus on its similarities. The unit's unselfishness was off the charts. Its football IQ was borderline genius. Its concentration level, attention to detail and work ethic was unmatched.

The weakest link was neither tolerated nor berated. It was elevated. There was a place for everyone, and everyone was in his place, no exceptions allowed.

Shurmur, the 64-year-old defensive coordinator, was the salty veteran with more schemes than a mad scientist and more energy than most men half his age. The Wyandotte, Mich., native wrote more books about football than many coaches read. He was a professor, a taskmaster and a motivator rolled into one.

"I don't think I'd be where I am today if it wasn't for Fritz," nose tackle Gilbert Brown said. "He stuck up for me a lot of times when other people wouldn't. Fritz knew that I had something that he wanted and he found a way to bring it out. I would always do the best of my ability to keep Fritz happy because nobody wanted to be on his bad side. Whatever he told me to do, I would do it to the best of my ability, no questions asked."

Shurmur maintained order in his house with charm, guile and intellect. He could appeal to any player on any level about all things football. There was no BSing Shurmur because he had heard it all before, and it wasn't long before players knew better than to try.

Shurmur doted on his defensive front four.

"He always told us that nothing starts unless it starts with his big fellas up front," Brown said. "He stood over us. He watched us. We were his babies. Nothing was going to start unless that defensive line made it happen."

59
NFL

Riddell
59

Riddell
92

Brett Favre comments on the Reggie White-Wayne Simmons fight minutes before kickoff

"Reggie White and Wayne Simmons.

"Christ. Anti-Christ.

"Reggie loved Wayne like a brother, but he tried his best to change Wayne, too. To change and change and change. Wayne fought it and fought it and fought it. Wayne would never give in to him. They were great teammates on the field, and they got along great in the locker room, but away from football it was another matter.

"They had totally different beliefs and lifestyles and views outside football. It isn't for me to say which was right and which was wrong. Most times they just agreed to disagree and that was the end of it. That wasn't always the case though. In fact, one time it was coming to a fistfight.

"We were playing a December home game in '96. I'm not sure which game it was but I remember guys wearing their long johns and cold-weather gear in the locker room. It was probably 15 minutes or so before kickoff and everyone was getting ready. Some guys were still dressing. Other guys were already dressed and sitting around talking or joking or listening to music on their headphones or what not.

"We had this itty-bitty boom box on a chair in one of the corners and Wayne was playing rap music on it. It wasn't turned up that loud but the language was really vulgar with a lot of f--- this and f--- that. Finally, Reggie said enough's enough and he asked Wayne to turn it off. Wayne told him hell no, so Reggie walked over and shut it off. Wayne proceeded to go over there and turn it back on. This happened a couple of times. By now, it's getting closer to game time and Reggie has had enough. He tells Wayne he doesn't need to listen to this, and Wayne made the mistake of cussing at him.

"Now, Reggie was a holy man but he understood there was going to be some cursing time to time in a NFL locker room. What Reggie would not tolerate was being cursed at directly. To him, that was crossing a line that didn't need to be crossed. He wouldn't take it from anyone, and Wayne made the mistake of crossing that line.

"Reggie starts coming at Wayne, and guys are getting between them, and Wayne is saying, 'C'mon! C'mon!' Of course he's backpedaling while he's saying it. I had never seen Reggie mad like that. We had these wooden garbage cans anchored into the floor, and Reggie's so mad he swings his right arm and knocks the garbage can halfway across the room. I'm sitting at my locker watching this thing work its way across the room.

"Wayne Simmons, a tough guy and a motor mouth, wanted no part of Reggie. Who does? No one had ever seen Reggie like that. I'd seen him get mad on the field but it was nothing like this. Finally, some of the players broke it up and Reggie calmed down. He had this look on his face like, 'What am I doing?' It was amazing.

"The thing is that whole scene sort of built us up. If I'm not mistaken Wayne just absolutely crushed a ball carrier on the first or second play of the game. As he stepped back into the huddle Reggie gave him this big ol' love tap upside the helmet, and Wayne gave him a pat on the shoulder pad and they proceeded to kick butt on the other team.

"It was the only team in my 15 years in the NFL that could have that type of turmoil right before a game, yet nobody worried that we were going to lose. The next day Wayne and Reggie were at their lockers, and Wayne asked, 'Big Dog? You really wasn't going to hurt me, was you?' Reggie smiled, and in that raspy voice of his, he said, 'Wayne, if I had got my hands on you, I would have hurt you. I would have hurt you real bad.' This time Wayne didn't say anything back and that was the end of it."

Shurmur was all about football. Players figured it out or they were forced out because the defensive coordinator, like the defensive leaders, had no time for slackers. However, he always made time for the players that gave it their best and delivered when the game was on the line.

He had a practice of calling players into his office individually the Monday morning after a game. It was only two or three players or four players each week, and it wasn't the same players all the time, but it was a way for him to motivate.

"Fritz made everybody feel special," defensive end Sean Jones said. "You didn't know that he brought three other people in too until you started comparing notes later in the week. He'd say you don't need to be telling everyone this and he'd pull out a film clip. One time we had played Detroit, and Detroit had whipped our butt. It wasn't as bad as they said but it seemed like every run came to the right side. It seemed like Barry Sanders ran every play right at me.

"The next time we played Detroit, Fritz called me in on Monday morning. We hadn't even watched the tape of the game we played that Sunday. He pulled out this film clip, and he always pulled it out like it was a secret. We're in his office, just the two of us, and he's looking around like people are watching. He told me that the Detroit press is telling people that Barry Sanders ravaged the right side of the Packers' defensive line. He said all I want this week from you is to play up the field. They can't blame everything on you. In fact, let me show you something.

"He took every game I played in and every game Reggie played in and teams were averaging 1.3 yards more per carry to Reggie's side. He was telling me what people were thinking, and then he told me what he was thinking. He told me to go out and play a great game because that's what he expected, and so that's what I did."

Shurmur's schemes were legendary, and his game-day play calling was a thing of beauty.

"Fritz had a phenomenal year that year," former GM Ron Wolf said. "He was really good. There's a guy that should've been a head coach at some point in the league but was passed over so many times. Mike (Holmgren) went up against him so many times when he was with San Francisco and Fritz was with the L.A. Rams that he had great respect for how he was being attacked all the time, and the different ways Fritz would change up on him. It turned out to benefit the Pack."

White, still overpowering at age 36, was arguably the greatest defensive player in NFL history.

The Minister of Defense enjoyed a good joke just as much as the next guy, but only if the next guy wanted to win as badly as he did when it was time to get after it. He wasn't the defensive leader because he was the best player. He was the defensive leader because he wanted his teammates to be their best.

White didn't make the players around him better because he was so dominant. He made them better because they didn't want to let him down. He didn't personify excellence, but rather the dogged pursuit of excellence.

Shurmur didn't love White for what his future Pro Football Hall of Fame defensive end could do for him. He loved White for what he could do for his teammates. Shurmur rarely was given to gushing praise, but his comments in the Packers' 1997 media guide demonstrated the high regard he held White in.

"He is a rare football player, a rare individual," Shurmur said. "He is rare in his capacity to play the game consistently. He has tremendous strength and explosiveness to go with speed. He's probably the most unselfish team player I've ever been around and it rubs off. If you could look at one who whose demeanor and whose mode of living is an example for all of us to follow, it's Reggie White."

While Shurmur sang White's praises publicly, he held Simmons in similar high regard. He just didn't make a big deal out of it. Truth be told, Shurmur and Simmons were much closer than some players and most members of the media suspected.

"Wayne and Fritz were fire and ice at one time," Jones said. "At the end Fritz loved him like a son. Wayne was so smart. Wayne was as football intellectually smart as Reggie was gifted as a player.

"We would be sitting in a meeting and Wayne was looking like he wasn't taking notes or paying

59

one bit of attention. Fritz would yell at Wayne: 'You listening to me?' Wayne would say, 'Hell, yeah, Fritz. What you're really trying to say is that you want us to play that Cover 2 like they play down at Tampa. And you want me to run right down the middle and take anything that comes there. That's really 3-Sky, isn't it?'

"Fritz would be like, 'Oh, the hell with it,' and move on to whatever was next."

When Shurmur was fighting cancer in the spring of 1999, Simmons was the first of his former players to call and insist that he keep battling the damnable disease.

"Fritz and Wayne were stubborn and bullheaded and they loved each other to death," Brown said. "You could see the love in those two guys. It was funny because some of the guys were envious of their relationship, not because they didn't like Wayne, but because they wished they were as close to Fritz as he became.

"Wayne had a nickname for Fritz – the old rattler – that Fritz just loved. He also loved Wayne because he was a competitor, physical, fearless. Wayne did things on a personal level that he shouldn't have, and I won't go into it, but on the field he did things so even-keel that Fritz knew he could count on him."

Brown said Simmons' tenacity was legendary. There were many film sessions when players would beg Shurmur to rewind and replay Simmons' exploits repeatedly.

"We'd be sitting there watching film of the 49ers game, and Wayne would be doing a number on Brent Jones, their tight end, and we'd be hootin' and hollerin'," Brown said. "Everybody was like, 'Watch Wayne whoop his butt. Just watch this.' "

Wolf, who drafted Simmons with the 15th overall pick in 1993, never took the rugged strong-side linebacker for granted.

"We had an unsung hero on that defense – a guy that never got credit for anything – and that was Wayne Simmons. He did things to tight ends that just weren't allowed. Brian Williams was our best linebacker. He should have been in the Pro Bowl. He wasn't in the Pro Bowl. (Eugene) Robinson and (LeRoy) Butler were a heck of a pair of safeties.

"But with Wayne Simmons, it was his temperament that set him apart. He had a great defensive temperament and he set the tempo. He really and truly helped an awful lot with what we were able to do defensively because he was tough to run at. He could run. He could cover. He could run with the back. He could actually run with the tight end, which freed up Butler to do some of the things like dogging, which they did."

Wolf called Simmons "a very versatile player, a very tough guy."

"He had issues but who doesn't?" Wolf added. "He was a tough nut to crack and Fritz cracked him. Wayne was really a very, very smart guy. I don't think you could BS Wayne. You had to handle him a little differently than other people, but Fritz knew how and Simmons could play the game of football."

Shurmur, White and Simmons shared an uncommon love of football.

Sadly, they also shared an untimely demise.

Shurmur was 65 when he died of cancer in 1999. To this day, Brown has a difficult time talking about it.

"We all went to see him in the hospital," Brown said. "He was laughing, and he was happy that we were there, but he also was slow. It hurt me bad because I felt like that was a relative of mine."

Brown was a pallbearer at Shurmur's funeral in Green Bay.

"That was a real sad day," he said. "You look at his wife, Peggy, so beautiful and such a nice lady, and you just wish you could take her pain away but you can't. I miss him to this day. I miss seeing that bald-headed man and that white truck with the fishing lures in the back. One day he told us, 'Fellas, I got a couple more years and I'm going fishing and that's all I'm going to do. I love this game, but I've got my (Super Bowl) ring and I'm going fishing and I'm going to have a ball."

Jones was glad to say he was the last player to see Shurmur.

"It was the Wednesday before he passed," Jones said. "We were at his house in Suamico (just north of Green Bay). We went through everything. It wasn't like he was sick. It was teacher and pupil. We talked about football and kids and family and fishing. He had lost some color but he was great. That guy forgot more about football than most people will learn in a lifetime."

Simmons played football with abandon and he lived life on the edge.

He died at age 33 in a one-car crash in Independence, Missouri, on Aug. 23, 2002.

"When I heard the news I cried like a baby," defensive end Sean Jones said. "It was one of the worst days of my life. I don't think anyone was necessarily surprised by it, but that didn't make it any easier to accept. I remember calling Brian Williams, or he calling me, and I cried like a baby with him on the phone. I knew how those guys were and how they liked to have fun and I begged Brian not to let that happen to him."

The tears didn't stop with Simmons' passing.

White died at age 43 of a respiratory ailment at his home near Huntersville, N.C., on Dec. 26, 2004. The shock swept through the NFL and hit hardest among his former teammates, coaches and friends – many of whom were one and the same.

"Reggie was like a big brother," Favre said. "As crazy as it sounds, for me to be a pallbearer for Reggie White – which I never thought I'd even be saying – says a lot. Look at all the people he has known. Look at all the lives he has affected positively. Me? I'm just another player that he played with. I wish he were still here, but I consider it a great honor to be his pallbearer. We were close."

Favre admired White's devotion to his faith. He also appreciated the fact that White never acted like he was holier-than-thou.

"You could be yourself around Reggie," Favre said. "He really took me under his wing. He did a lot for me, on and off the field, that people would never know. He would tell me, 'Go out and play your game. Don't worry about what they're saying because I will take care of it. If you throw a pick I will get the ball back.'

"And I believed him."

Favre smiled when asked about all the times Packers fans would chant, "Reggie! Reggie!" and he would respond with a game-turning sack.

"He made it a little easier on me, that's for sure," said Favre, who spoke with White three days before he died.

"He wanted to know if I would get into NASCAR with him," Favre said. "He said he didn't know anything about NASCAR and I told him, 'Neither do I' and we laughed about that. I was sitting in my truck at the loading dock (at Lambeau Field) and we spent most of the time talking about good times and reliving the memories."

Favre said a photo of White and him is among his most cherished mementos. It depicts White and Favre – with tears of joy running down their faces – walking off Lambeau Field after a 38-10 victory over Minnesota in the regular-season finale

"Today, when I look at that picture of us together – even though he was my teammate and even though he always brought me into a conversation – it always makes me swell with pride to know we were that close."

So were Shurmur, White and Simmons.

The Coach

Staff:

Mike Holmgren, **Head Coach**
Sherman Lewis, **Offensive Coordinator**
Fritz Shurmur, **Defensive Coordinator**
Larry Brooks, **Defensive Line**
Nolan Cromwell, **Special Teams**
Gil Haskell, **Receivers**
Johnny Holland, **Defensive Assistant/Quality Control**
Kent Johnston, **Strength and Conditioning**
Jim Lind, **Linebackers**
Tom Lovat, **Offensive Line**
Marty Mornhinweg, **Quarterbacks**
Andy Reid, **Tight Ends/Assistant Offensive Line**
Harry Sydney, **Running Backs**
Bob Valesente, **Defensive Backs**
Gary Reynolds, **Adinistrative Assistant Football/Offensive Quality Control**
Barry Rubin, **Strength and Conditioning Assistant**
Susan Kluck, **Administrative Assistant (Mike Holmgren)**
Diane Coron, **Secretary**

MIKE HOLMGREN

BY CHRIS HAVEL

Mike Holmgren might describe his seven seasons in Green Bay in a single world.

"Fun," he said. "That's a good word for it."

Holmgren is all about fun, so long as it can be had during the pursuit of excellence. The 12th head coach in Green Bay Packers history attained it in the 1996 season whose pinnacle was a 35-21 victory over New England in Super Bowl XXXI.

Holmgren's Packers returned to play for the world's championship in Super Bowl XXXII, losing to the Denver Broncos. He also guided the Seattle Seahawks to a berth in Super Bowl XL, where they lost to the Pittsburgh Steelers. He is proud on behalf of the organizations to have appeared in three of the past 10 Super Bowls, but he readily admits there is nothing like the first time.

"The first Super Bowl is special because it's the first one," he said. "It was special because it was the Packers. We had built the thing up to go. I don't think many people thought we could do that. The other reason it is special, I would say, is because of all those people that worked for the Packers for so long, certainly long before we got there. The happiness and the joy of seeing their faces getting to the top again, that was special."

The '96 Packers rolled to a 13-3 regular season record and cruised past the San Francisco 49ers in the NFC Divisional Playoffs and Carolina in the NFC Championship Game en route to New Orleans and a January 26 date at the Louisiana Superdome.

That season the Packers had every element in place to be the world's champions of professional football. In general manager Ron Wolf, they had a keen talent scout with a no-nonsense approach to personnel and a facile mind to manipulate the National Football League's salary cap and unfettered free agency.

In the assistant coaches, they had a group of men with the ability to communicate the head coach's wishes to the players, and the knowledge to give their respective position groups an edge over the opposition.

Brett Favre Comments

"My first year everything came pretty easy. I was a little naïve as to how hard it was to play quarterback in the NFL, although there were some games where it would have been different if they'd caught some of those interceptions.

"Then there was my second year. I was struggling. I would have a good game and then a bad game. Or I would have a good game and two bad games. It was up and down. Mike (Holmgren) would always say how you go is how we go. If you play well we'll probably win. If you don't we may not. That was a lot of pressure.

"When I was struggling in my second season, rumors started going around the building that I was going to be benched. I felt like every Wednesday when I came to work I was going to be replaced. It had gotten circulated so much that Mike felt like he needed to address it so he called me into his office. He sat me down and he said, 'Yep, you're struggling. Yep, I expect more out of you. Yep, the team and the fans expect more out of you, and I'm sure you expect a lot more out of yourself. But I want you to know this, and trust me, what I am telling you isn't just hearsay. You are our starting quarterback. You're going to be our starting quarterback. As you go, we go. If we go down then I'm going to lose my job and Ron looks bad, but we're going to go with you. If you mess up this week, we're going to go with you next week.'

"When I walked out of that room it wasn't a free pass so I could go goof off. It was like now I didn't have to play scared and play looking over my shoulder. That was probably the best thing that ever happened to me. Yeah, I got my ass chewed by Mike. Yeah, I played bad at times. Yeah, I've struggled. But I've always known that I can carry this team, and lead this team even though there's going to be tough times. That mentality hasn't changed one bit since the day Mike called me in and told it to me straight."

In Reggie White, they had arguably the greatest defensive player in NFL history. In Brett Favre, they had one of the greatest quarterbacks of all time. In LeRoy Butler, Sean Jones, Santana Dotson, Frank Winters, Edgar Bennett, Antonio Freeman and the rest, they had a deep core group of high-caliber, high-character men.

In Holmgren, they had one of the NFL's best coaches in league annals. He downplays his role in the 1996 team's success, but he agrees that the best teams require each of these elements to reach the Super Bowl.

"Now that I've had the chance to go a couple of times as a head coach, and as an assistant coach with the 49ers as well, you really need that to give yourself a chance," he said. "It's very hard to get there, much less win it.

"As I've gotten older I realize that the combination of front office, coaching staff and players – you have to be working in concert with one another. That was the beauty, as I look back, of that particular time. Ron and I really worked well together. Of course, the chemistry on that team was pretty good, too.

"You had some special players on that team. Reggie and Brett. I could go on and on. The relationship between the coaching staff and the players was real healthy and real good, a real good trust there. That combination was special.

"The teams that go to the Super Bowl have that."

The Packers' locker room featured players that shared a passion for the game. It brought them closer together. In the city of Green Bay, they worked in a place where proximity required they spend considerable time together.

It is why players such as free safety Eugene Robinson would stop in the middle of an interview, tell the assembled media he would be right back and leave to have a quick conversation with a teammate. When a thought regarding that week's game, or that week's practice, popped into Robinson's mind he wanted to share it immediately.

It was all football, all the time.

"I think Green Bay lends itself to that," Holmgren said. "The culture there, as far as things to do for the African-American player, was pretty limited. We brought barbers in and we changed some of the food we served. I believe the players appreciated that. I think they did."

Holmgren also perpetuated the notion that the Green Bay Packers were a special NFL franchise and his team needed to act accordingly on and off the field.

"How we went about it as a coaching staff, and I'm not talking about myself, we really pounded home how important this was to Green Bay. How important it was to approach your profession a certain way because your time is very short in this particular arena. The players bought into it.

"They have to trust you and buy into it. You can't con them and try to be someone you're not or be something you're not. I think the staff understood that and tried to convey that to the players."

In retrospect, the 1996 Packers' coaching staff was among the best ever assembled in team history. It had a nice balance of veteran assistants such as offensive line coach Tom Lovat and eager young men like Andy Reid and Marty Mornhinweg.

"In the beginning, other than Tom Lovat who had coached for a fair amount of years in the league already, for the rest of us – myself included – it was 'The Grand Adventure,' " Holmgren said. "I had young guys on the staff. It was their first full-time coaching job. Andy and (Steve) Mariucci and (Jon) Gruden and those guys were eager and willing to learn. Then you had Tom, very much a stabilizing factor. Later on I had Fritz (Shurmur), who was a tremendous defensive coordinator. I brought Sherman Lewis, our offensive coordinator, with me from San Francisco. I also had Gil Haskell, who I had been with forever, and Harry Sydney, whom I coached when we were with the Niners.

"It was important for me to be able to bounce things off those guys. I thought we had a nice blend of youth and experience. The beauty of it was that we all got along pretty well together. In Green Bay, unlike here in Seattle or a lot of places, you live within five minutes of each other. After the game we went to the Haskell's log cabin and we rehashed the game win, lose or draw and we developed a close-knit group.

Holmgren said his hiring practices focused on teaching.

"As guys would trickle off I tried to hire within and I had a philosophy about the type of coaches I wanted. I wanted teachers. I think we had that.

He also had the players.

Favre became Holmgren's pet project.

At times, the future Pro Football Hall of Fame quarterback resisted.

"At first I was like, 'God, get off my butt," Favre said. "But being a coach's son, I was used to that. But I also would fight it. He found that middle ground. He would use his coaches at times to communicate with me. He also could flip the switch on with his players and himself. We knew when it was time to take it up a notch. I'm sure a few guys may not have liked him or whatever, but he had that hands-on approach, and you need that type of coach."

Holmgren vividly recalls a conversation he had with Favre when rumors were circulating throughout 1265 Lombardi Avenue that the pride of Southern Miss was going to be benched in favor of Mark Brunell.

"I very much remember the conversation," Holmgren said. "It's interesting because we had a staff meeting talking about the quarterback position. We still had Brunell, and Brett was by his own admission a little wild at times.

Sean Jones Comments

"This is the beauty of Mike. As much as he gets heat for being a control freak, he delegates like no other. He allowed Fritz Shurmur, our defensive coordinator, to do what he needed to do with the defense. He didn't interfere.

"The longer I was away from football the more I began to appreciate who Mike Holmgren was and is. Mike is a great football coach. More than that, he is a damn good leader. He doesn't get enough credit for that. The reason I say that is he has very clear rules. You never were confused about what he wants from you. And he's demanding. He makes you accountable. What you have in the league nowadays, young guys get on a team and feel like they'll get a chance to play some time. With Mike you didn't have that liberty. You had to be ready to play all the time. If you were a 12th-round pick, if you were on that team, and somebody went down you better be ready to play.

"There was no excuse. There was no the-dog-ate-my-lunch. No, no, no, no, no. He did not tolerate excuses. That's what I've come to learn. As a player some times, or even in business, you'll hear all the excuses. Mike didn't want to hear any of that shit. There was none of that. You've got work to do. You're here to do a job. Let's get it done.

"Now clearly there's not a more compassionate person. I remember calling him the day before my son was born. I said, 'Mike, my wife just went into labor and I've got to get on a plane.' He said, 'Sean, do you realize it's 3 o'clock in the morning?' I reminded him that he told me I could call any time. He said, 'Well I would hope that you could call me from the hospital and tell me you were already there.'

"Mike was that type of guy.

"He was controlling and there was not a whole lot of down time for the players, and for grown-ass men it was a bit much at times, but that's what he wanted. He was smart enough to let players manage the team. He gave you enough leeway where you realized it was a privilege. It wasn't a right. It was a privilege. He'd say, 'I'm going to let you guys handle it your way but don't let it come back to bite us.'

"We were no choirboys but we had fun and took care of business. I believe a lot of that had to do with the fact that Mike trusted us. We knew that and we didn't want to let him down."

"After going around the room and letting everyone blow off steam as far as coaches were concerned – they all had opinions – I called him in and I told him we're either going to wind up in a dumpster together or at the top of the mountain, but it's going to be together. To Brett's credit he very much worked hard to do things the right way at that position. We went from being a little bit of a gunslinger to I think a very good technician. He worked hard at that.

"You don't have to win the game by yourself. Try it my way. You're going to have five or six plays in every game that I won't believe, but for the most part try to do it my way. So he did that.

"It was a special time. I appreciate that because I love the guy. I think people at times had the idea that there was a problem between the two of us. There never was. I coached him hard but I loved him. Then going through his off-the-field stuff together, which has had a happy ending which I'm glad to say, always brings you closer."

Favre has said he was fortunate to be coached by some of the NFL's finest, including Mariucci, Reid and Mornhinweg. Each brought a different aspect to the position of quarterbacks coach.

Mariucci was Favre's coach, friend and unwavering supporter. He also taught him how to play the position when Favre was still a diamond in the rough. Mariucci helped smooth out the edges and instill confidence.

"Steve was very much an advocate for Brett. There were times I would get upset with Steve because I thought he almost did it blindly. I said part of your job is to be hard on him. Obviously they had a great relationship so that was a good thing.

"When Steve left I had a decision to make. Both Andy and Marty, I'd had such a history with them, from the outside it looked like they were just caretakers of the position because I was very involved with the quarterback myself in those days. But that couldn't be further from the truth. I knew Andy so well, and Marty played for me. He was a smart football guy when he was in high school for pete's sakes. He played the position and understood the position. Andy might be one of the brightest guys I've ever been around.

"When I moved him from a tight end position to a line coach, I thought I was getting him ready to the quarterback thing. In both those cases I knew the communication between the player and the coach would be good."

Favre has become a Holmgren fan. He still watches Holmgren's teams play when possible, and he enjoys trying to call the plays along with his former coach. He even has adopted many of Holmgren's offensive philosophies.

"Mike always said, 'I will never let the defense dictate to me what I do. I dictate to them. They have to stop us. Yeah, if they do all this exotic stuff, if we know what we're doing and we do it well enough – there's hot reads and different places to go with the ball – and we get it out quick, we'll win. We're not going to change on Wednesday what we do."

Part of the Packers' success in 1996 was learning the fine art of practicing efficiently, and at a fast pace, without incurring injuries. The highlight each week was the Thursday afternoon practice that covered the red zone, two-minute drill and short yardage offense.

Players such as Favre and Butler would taunt each other, depending on whether the offense or defense had the better day. Shurmur and Haskell engaged in a heated exchange one day. Afterward, they shook hands and went back to work, no hard feelings.

"It was very competitive," Holmgren said. "I just kept my fingers crossed that no one would get nicked up and hurt, but they learned how to practice fast. What helped that team that year was a healthy respect between offense and defense. We had good players on offense. We had great players on defense. There was a good respect there."

Through the years, the details of Super Bowl XXXI blend together.

"I just remember that there was a certain ebb and flow to that game and momentum changes and the special teams played such a role in that. When we had a chance to make big plays we made them.

"When you have good teams that ability to make the play when it presents itself decides the outcome. When Brett threw the ball to Antonio Freeman it was perfect. The coverage wasn't all that bad. The ball was perfect. When he threw the ball to Andre Rison early, he saw the blitz, he was prepared for it and he did it.

"When we had a chance to make the play, the play that makes the difference, they made it."

That quality to recognize and capitalize on the moment is the difference between champions and also-rans. It comes with preparation, practice and being on the same page.

"That year (1996) was a culmination of every year that came before it. Every year we took another step in building that thing up. It was our time. The time was right. The players really grasped that idea that year."

Holmgren had the right players to win games, and he had the right general manager to get the players.

"I was a first-time head coach. Even though Ron was a first-time general manager, he had a lot more experience in the league than I had. I really respected his opinion as far as players. I wasn't going to do a lot of arguing. The beauty of it was that he always, always asked me about what I thought. That really doesn't always happen, particularly with a first-year head coach.

"We'd go out to dinner. We'd have lunch. He had a great sense of humor.

"The other thing, when we lost a tough game, he was always at his best with me. That's when I could really lean on him. That doesn't happen. A lot of times a management-type person would come in and start asking questions. That's not uncommon. He was not like that. He had a way about him. That's when he was at his best. When we won a game he might come in and ask questions but I didn't have anything to defend then."

Holmgren praised Wolf's draft acumen and his knack for choosing the right veteran player in free agency.

"We had pretty good leadership on that team," he said. "I know when Reggie and Wayne Simmons got into it a couple of times that year right before games there might have been reason to be concerned. But the team understood both those men and what they were all about. They just understood it. That's Wayne being Wayne. That's Reggie being Reggie. OK. Let's go. You had Eugene Robinson, you had Leroy Butler, and you had Santana Dotson. You had Brett Favre. You had (Edgar) Bennett and (Dorsey) Levens. You had some good leadership on that team."

Communication was the key. It began with Wolf and Holmgren's open-door relationship. It permeated the scouting department and worked its way through the coaching staff. Ultimately, it reached the locker room and everyone benefited.

"I think our staff did a great job of coaching them. I'm not talking about me. I'm talking about my staff getting them ready to play. I'd come in and talk to them. I still do.

"You've got 53 guys on your team. Everybody has a role. Your role might be this. Your role might be this. Maybe you're the super star and your role is this. Maybe everyone is counting on you to do this. Everyone has a role and one role isn't more important than the other.

"As long as you're consistently treating players that way, in my opinion, and you're honest with them and you tell them and you show them value in what they're doing – they're reasonable guys – I mean you can't have nut balls, but they're reasonable guys. They'll step up and they'll do it and feel good about it. You never let something good go without a tap on the back and a pat on the back. Ever. That's something I stress with my coaches. You can get after a player at practice. Lord knows I've done it.

"But then the day doesn't end that way. I think players appreciate that."

Holmgren paused.

"It's how teams get to the Super Bowl, and it's why we had so much fun."

LOGOATHLETIC

The General Manager

Staff:

PRO PERSONNEL
Ted Thompson, Director
Reggie McKenzie, Pro Personnel Assistant
John Schneider, Pro Personnel Assistant
Marianne McDermid, Secretary

VIDEO
Al Treml, Director
Bob Eckberg, Assistant Director
Chris Kirby, Video Assistant

COLLEGE SCOUTING
John Math, Director
Bryan Broaddus, Scouting Administrator
Todd Bowles, Scout (East)
John Dorsey, Scout (Southeast)
Shaun Herock, Scout (Midwest)
Scot McLoughan, Scout (Rocky Mountains)
Sam Seale, Scout (Southwest)
John "Red" Cochran, Scout (North)

RON WOLF

BY CHRIS HAVEL

Ron Wolf is a realist.

Black is black, white is white and the rest is just details.

When he became the Green Bay Packers' general manager in November of 1991 the franchise was sagging and the football team was dragging. There was no way to paint a pretty picture, and no sense to try.

The Packers needed a new direction and Wolf pointed the way.

He hired Mike Holmgren to be his head coach. He acquired Brett Favre to be his quarterback. He signed Reggie White to be his defensive stopper.

Those moves grab the attention, and rightfully so, but it was the constant shuffling and reshuffling of the deck that produced a winning hand. Wolf's handpicked coach, and carefully selected players, united in 1996 to be the National Football League's best.

The Packers defeated New England in Super Bowl XXXI at New Orleans' Louisiana Superdome, and Wolf could celebrate the crowning achievement of what became a distinguished 41-year career.

"Absolutely," he said. "When you have a group like that – players that played for each other and with each other – that's something you never forget. Then when you realize that we were the best team in football that year it's special."

The Green Bay Packers' former executive vice-president and general manager set out in 1996 to build a winner. He created a team for all time. The 1996 NFC Central Division champion Packers:

- Earned a fourth straight playoff appearance, a first in team history.
- Captured the franchise's first Super Bowl in 29 years.
- Succeeded in winning 28 of the last 29 games at Lambeau Field.
- Produced the franchise's first 16-victory season.

A decade later the team's achievements are still impressive.

"My goodness, time marches on," Wolf said. "I can't believe it's been 10 years."

Wolf, 68, arrived in Green Bay in 1991 with a five-year plan.

He watched coach Lindy Infante's team struggle to a 4-12 season, and he promptly fired Infante one day after it ended.

Wolf quickly moved to hire San Francisco 49ers offensive coordinator Mike Holmgren as the Packers' 12th head coach. Much of the attention centered on Holmgren's offensive acumen, which Wolf respected, but he also held Holmgren's leadership ability in high esteem.

"Mike's a really good disciplinarian and he's a really good head football coach," Wolf said. "Too many people say great. To me, he was exceptional. What made him special is how bright he is. He's just so smart. He knew how to attack a defense – how to take it apart – and he knew how to get everything he possibly could out of what he had to work with."

A month after Holmgren was hired by Wolf, the GM and head coach elected to trade a first-round draft pick to Atlanta for a third-string quarterback named Favre. Many Packers fans were upset because they didn't understand the math. To them it made no sense until they saw Favre lead their team and throw a football.

"Well, without Ron I wouldn't be here," Favre said. "It all starts there for me. When I was at Reggie White's (Pro Football) Hall of Fame induction last summer, they have us in this small room early in the morning. As soon as I walk in Ron goes, 'There's my other son.' He's a lot more low-key now, he was always under the radar, but he would have never done that before. Now he's kind of letting the proud papa in him come out. And I'm glad to see that.

"Ron was always a little more protective of me than others because I was his guy, but I had to prove myself along the way. He knew that the trade was a big gamble on his part. I didn't know how good I could be but in some ways he probably did. I was confident. I was cocky. But I never had any experience in this style of offense. He saw something in me that maybe I thought I saw in myself but wasn't sure."

Wolf saw a tough, talented and passionate football player – a quarterback with a chance to be

great – and he believed the Super Bowl was within reach.

"I think primarily (we won Super Bowl XXXI) because we had a really good locker room," Wolf said. "We had quality players in key positions. At that time we had the emergence of one of the best quarterbacks the game has ever seen into a top-notch player.

"Furthermore, that defense never got its due. It never got the notoriety it should have and a lot of our defensive players never got the notoriety that they should have. Everybody talks about that 1985 Chicago Bears team. Our guys allowed 19 opponent touchdowns that year in 1996. We broke the record of the 1985 Chicago Bears.

"I believe that these guys never ever got the due that should have been attributed to them. As a group that defense was very good. Even the good players, guys that should have gotten the recognition, didn't get the recognition. But be that as it may they were world's champions and that's recognition enough."

Sean Jones, the Packers' starter at right defensive end, agrees wholeheartedly.

"Don't look at our performance in Super Bowl XXXI, but look at the performance of that defense throughout that season en route to the Super Bowl. Compare it to other defenses. It's a tragedy because there were so many young guys that were with Reggie White and Brett Favre and Santana Dotson and so on, that you never hear of.

"But if you take them collectively and put them on that defense and rank them," Jones continued, "it will rank as one of the greatest defenses to ever play in the NFL. That's where it ranked. Look at the points allowed. Look at the red zone defense. Look at the total yards. Just rank it. Look at the turnover margin.

"People talk about that defense like it's a bunch of also-rans. They say "The Doomsday Defense," "The Steel Curtain," "The Purple People Eaters," "The Fearsome Foursome." The Bears. Put our defense up there and see where we rank.

"We are not even mentioned and it's part of the Green Bay bias. It's part of the whole 'oh, well, it's just Green Bay. They had Brett Favre.' It was that but it was a lot more than that.

"It has been five years and we have only one player from that defense in the Packer Hall of Fame. We have only one player from that defense that is in the Pro Football Hall of Fame. LeRoy Butler needs to go in there.

"Fritz isn't in there. It's a joke. It's crazy.

"Santana (Dotson) has to go in some time. You have a Hall of Fame without Gilbert Brown and what he meant to that era? People forget what these people meant to the team, what they meant to the organization, what they meant to the championship, what they meant to the city. They need to be reminded."

Wolf, unlike many, believes teams can develop dynasties if they know how to work free agency.

"It's like anything else," he said. "Once you get better at that (salary cap) stuff you understand it. You can build a dynasty in this game today under the salary cap if you do it properly. I believe you can. When this (free agency) came in it was one of those things that I wished I was younger, but I wasn't. You can work it."

Sean Jones Comments

"Ron Wolf was a dinosaur. Not in a negative connotation. They don't make them like that any more. His way of thinking is now extinct. The game has changed – and not for the better – Ron was a football guy. Hyperbole aside, all he cared about was football.

"The reason he cared about football and the reason he wanted you to be successful was because he loved football and he loved to win. That's what passed when he left the game. He was a no-nonsense, no bullshit type of guy and he loved the game. He respected the game. He wanted you to respect the game.

"He called you on your bullshit. It isn't about money. It isn't about fame. It's about football.

"He made some great moves, some great decisions. He was the architect. Clearly he was. The Green Bay community as a whole – from Bob Harlan to others in that organization – were great people but they weren't football people.

"Ron was able to respect what Green Bay was all about, educate them about football and not make anybody feel stupid in the process. He made everyone feel like they were part of it. He made every idea seem like it was their idea.

"The reason he wasn't arrogant was because at the end of the day he knew it wasn't saving lives. He knew it was a simple game. He wasn't going to make it more than it was, as important as it was to him, because he had a lot more interests.

"If you were shooting marbles, he wanted more marbles than you. He was a scoreboard guy. However you're keeping score, that's how I'm going to judge myself. But I'm keeping score in other things, too. I don't think there was anything more important to him than his wife and kids. That's why he could walk away.

"When I decided to retire it was not Ron's wish. Since I retired I have had so many positives from him about handling that different and not wanting me to retire. In that moment, it showed me a lot about him in the positive that he respected what I brought to the game.

"My most compelling moments with him were twofold.

"The year before I came to Green Bay we ran into each other and had a very brief conversation. He said: "You're going to be free and you need to look at Green Bay. We'd love to have you."

"I thought he was full of shit. Sure enough the first day of free agency Ron called and said we want you up here and he made an offer that was it.

"When I came up there I replaced a guy that was a pretty good football player in Tony Bennett. But for what they were trying to do they also knew they weren't going to get to the Super Bowl with Tony Bennett. Ron was always looking ahead.

"The next thing I remember about him that tested our relationship and tested our friendship, because I do consider Ron a friend, is that my last year there, two days before training camp he calls me in and says we've got to take some money back.

"I said what? I could have strangled him. He said we were tight and we needed to get some money. My agent said let's find out what they think about you. Do they need the money but want the player? Or do they want the money and don't care about the player? I said OK, take the money but do it in a way where they can give it back. It was $500,000 and I earned it back in playing incentives.

"Before we got to that point, Ron said to me, 'You came here because you wanted to win a Super Bowl, you wanted to play next to Reggie White, blah blah blah. You said you wanted to win a Super Bowl. Well, we're going to the Super Bowl. If I asked you to give up $500,000 to go to the Super Bowl when you were a rookie would you have done it? Do you really want to be a champion? You can do anything you want in your career but there are only a handful of guys that win a championship. There is a bunch of Pro Bowl guys, and guys that are in the Hall of Fame, that haven't won a championship.'

"I believed him and damn well, wouldn't you know, we went out and won it."

Reunion, September 10, 2006

Teams need sharp scouting to rise above. Wolf praised his personnel department.

"They were really good at what they were supposed to do," he said. "They were supposed to find players and they found players. I would mention them by name but I'm afraid I would leave somebody out. They did an outstanding job, no question about it."

Wolf believes part of the secret to that team's success in 1996 was what he called "The Three Musketeers" mentality.

"It was all for one and one for all," he said. "We tried to recognize how important everyone was to the organization. We also tried to do the little things. We had dinners brought in there a couple of nights a week for guys. We had a barber come in for guys. We did those things because it was important to us."

The coaches set the tone and the players responded.

"The only thing we asked our players to do was to play football and act responsible. Be proud to be members of the Green Bay Packers. Act responsible and play the game," Wolf said. "We didn't have any rules other than 'be a player, be a pro,' and fortunately we had a locker room that really benefited us. We had good guys, I mean really good guys, and they were professional in everything they did. They acted and conducted themselves accordingly and for that I will always be grateful."

WOLF COMMENTS ON VARIOUS PLAYERS AND PERSONNEL MOVES:

Gilbert Brown: "His deal was that he could jam up the middle and then make a play down the sideline. The guy could run. He had really good quickness. What he lacked was endurance but Fritz (Shurmur) was able to work some things around to take advantage of that. He had three guys who were superb pass rushers around him. White and Jones and Santana Dotson. The interesting thing about those other three was that they could play the run well. That made Brown better."

The Matt La Bounty-for-Eugene Robinson trade on training camp's eve: "We worked on that for a long time and it finally came to fruition. It was a long, involved process and we finally got that worked out. It's the old baseball adage: You've got to be strong down the middle. When we got Robinson we were very strong down the middle. He was a missing piece. Good football player. Tough. Good tackler. He was very smart. I believe he also led the team in interceptions."

Acquiring receiver Andre Rison on waivers in November: "He was the best pickup right there. We were sitting in Dallas getting ready to play on Monday Night Football and he came through on waivers. I was sitting there with Mike and Sherm Lewis and I said, 'For $100 we have to take a look at this guy.' That was a no-brainer right there. They agreed with that. We had to do something. We had lost to Kansas City, and then we lost to the Cowboys, and then that made it a little easier. That was good fortune."

On running backs Edgar Bennett and Dorsey Levens: "They both fit what we had to do. Mike liked what Bennett brought to the table. The dependability. The good pass catcher. One of the best pass catchers you'll see as a running back. He also was an adequate blocker and runner. With the other guy, Levens, it was one of those things where I would go to Mike toward the end of the year and ask, 'Is there any reason Levens can't play more?' That finally started to happen. They were two really good backs.

On signing tight end Keith Jackson: "That took a while. We had all kinds of problems. I thought I had screwed up our team because we gave up a second (round draft pick) for him and then he didn't show. I almost waffled but I didn't and it paid off. It paid dividends for us at the end when he decided to come in. I would think to me Jackson is the prototypical tight end. He's a great pass receiver. He's a total threat anywhere in the passing game. He's an above average blocker. He was very, very smart. Mark Chmura was a really good blocker. Good short intermediate receiver. He was very dependable, too. I just think Jackson and Chmura really complimented each other tremendously."

On veteran left tackle Bruce Wilkerson stepping in to save the day by protecting Brett Favre's blindside: "I drafted him when I was with the Raiders and he came in and did a tremendous job down the stretch. I do have a soft spot in my heart for Bruce Wilkerson, you bet."

On the offensive line's performance: "Frank Winters held that together. He is really a tough, tough guy. Aaron Taylor's tough. Adam Timmerman's really tough. Again, that team led the league in offense. That's with sending everybody out in pass patterns, too. We led the NFL in scoring, 456 points, which is still a team record."

On receiver Antonio Freeman: "There's a guy that just took advantage of every ounce of ability that he had and he had a lot of ability. That's one of the real good feel-good stories about a guy that comes in, a third-round draft choice, and he gets an opportunity and takes advantage of that opportunity. I always admired guys that did that."

On receiver Robert Brooks: "The guy gives you everything he has and the bottom line he was one of those guys that when he started getting hurt he became more of a liability than an asset. You root so hard for a guy like that because of all he gave."

On punter Craig Hentrich: "I don't think you can overlook the job that Craig Hentrich did. No blocks. Sixty-eight punts. He's just a solid, solid player. He could be your place kicker if need be."

On linebacker George Koonce: "Good player. Another guy that you've got to admire because he stuck it out. A free agent that bounced around a bit and then comes in as a free agent and becomes the starting middle linebacker on the best defense in football."

On safety Mike Prior: "He had great value. He was the fullback on punt coverage. He was the up man on punt returns. He was on all your special teams. He was the fifth defensive back. I know our coaches would have a panic if we were getting ready to take the plane off and he wasn't on it. They would hold that plane up, that's for sure."

On his personnel department: "They did an outstanding job, no question about that. Scott McCloughan, Ted Thompson, I'm going to miss somebody. They were good. They did what they were supposed to do. They were supposed to find players and they found players."

On the importance of having locker room leadership: "Our guys run a traffic light in Green Bay and that's the lead story on the six o'clock news. We had a good core group of guys and they wouldn't allow any of that BS to go on in the locker room. They were very focused and it paid off for us."

On the importance of defense: "In Europe they like soccer. In the United States of America we like scoring. That's the difference. We like to see scoring. People like to sit and watch a no-hitter but how often are you going to see that? Everybody says you win with defense, which is obvious. You do win with defense. You could also win with a not-so-good defense and a really great offense. But if you have a really great defense you're going to win."

On return specialist and Super Bowl XXXI Most Valuable Player Desmond Howard: "That was a hell of a pickup, too. In my 41 years in the game I'd never been around a return guy quite like that, that year. He could've caught the ball with a blindfold on that year. I couldn't envision him being that good. He was that good in college and he ended up that good that year. That was his only year."

On the bottom line: "You get accustomed to winning. The key thing is still W and L. There is no S in there for style points. If you win, it doesn't matter if you win by one or 41, the end result is people remember 13-3."

The Season

Green Bay
PACKERS 34
at
Tampa Bay
BUCCANEERS 3

DATE: Sunday, September 1, 1996
LOCATION: Tampa Stadium (The Big Sombrero), Tampa, Florida
ATTENDANCE: 54,102
WEATHER: Rain & 86°F

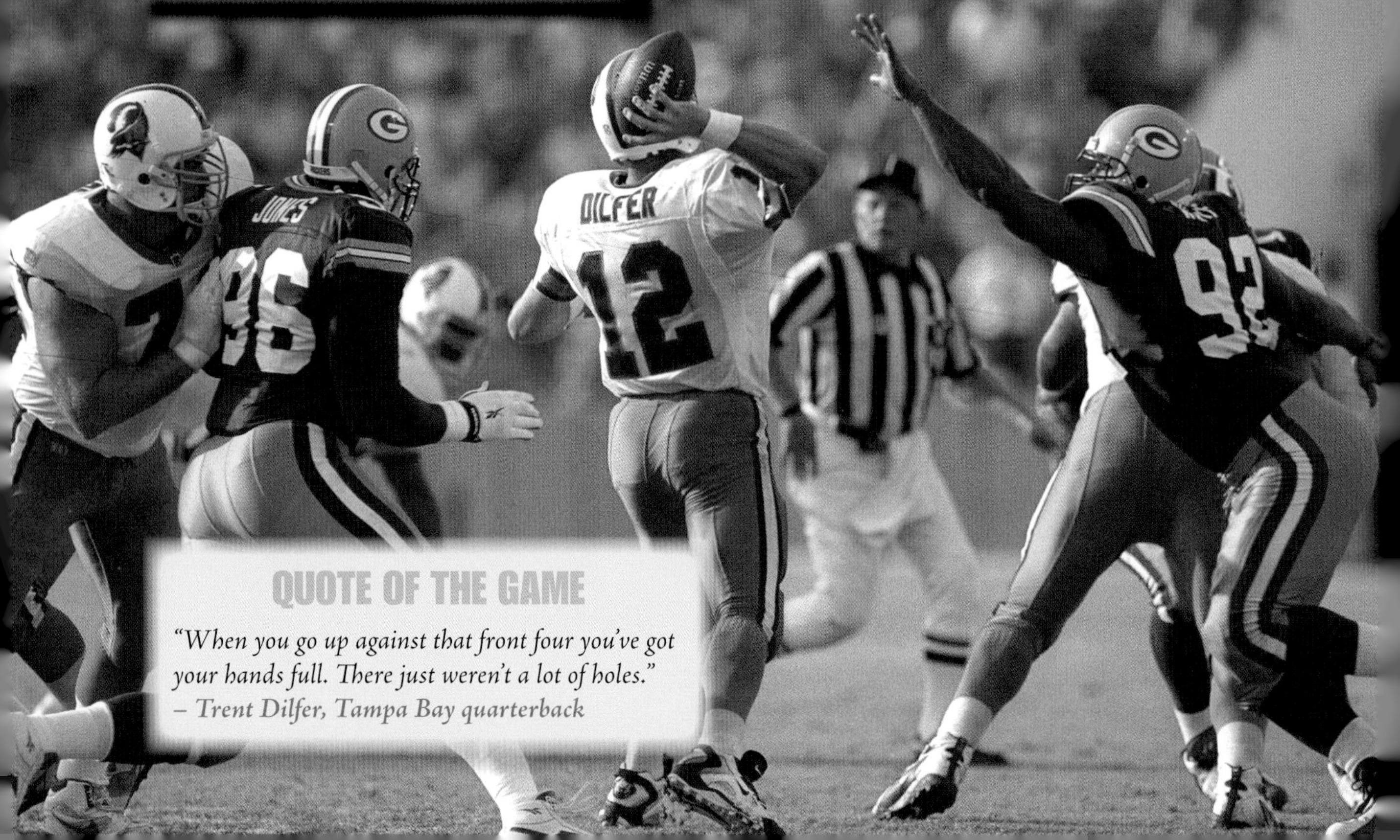

QUOTE OF THE GAME

"When you go up against that front four you've got your hands full. There just weren't a lot of holes."
– Trent Dilfer, Tampa Bay quarterback

GILBERT BROWN REMEMBERS

"We wanted to start our reign of terror throughout the NFC Central Division – the good old black-and-blue division – and what better place to start than on the road against the Tampa Bay Buccaneers. We felt like it was a home game because there were so many Packers fans in the stands. They say bad news travels fast, and in this case, the Packers and their fans were bad news for the Buccaneers.

"When we came out of the tunnel it sent chills through me because this was it. This was the first step in what we believed would be a truly special season. I wiped my eyes before the pre-game introductions and it wasn't because I was sweating so much. I was emotional because I wanted this one for my family and friends and teammates, and because I dedicated the season to my father, LeRoy Brown, who passed on before he got to see me play an NFL game in person. That day I knew he was watching from up above.

"There was another reason we were chomping at the bit. We were sick of hitting each other in two-a-days and we were sick of the preseason games because you only get to play a quarter or two and then you have to go back and kill yourself in training camp.

"We were so confident on defense because everybody knew his stuff, and Fritz Shurmur, our great defensive coordinator, had us so prepared and so keyed up it was unbelievable. We just went out there balling, and the Buccaneers paid the price.

"As a defense, we had some new additions like Santana Dotson and Brian Williams and Eugene Robinson, but we also knew we were tight. We weren't worried about the new guys. We were anxious to see just how dominant we could be with them. We knew our game plan, and we knew we could take over a game.

"The amazing thing for us was to sit back and watch that offense of ours click. To see Keith Jackson explode in that game with three first-half touchdown catches, and to see that offensive line get off the ball, and to see Brett Favre being sharp as a tack, that was something special.

"We forced six turnovers and I don't know how many three-and-outs because we couldn't wait to get off the field to watch the butt-whipping on the JumboTron. It was amazing to see those guys on offense do what they do. We knew in that first game that we might do something big that season."

CHRIS HAVEL COMMENTS

"Sitting in the Tampa Bay press box I couldn't help thinking back to a gorgeous July evening on the St. Norbert College campus in De Pere. LeRoy Butler and Edgar Bennett were casually strolling from the dining hall to the dormitory after dinner. With a pen and notepad in one hand and a tape recorder in the other, I ambushed them in search of a brief interview.

"Too worn out from two-a-days to protest, but not too tired to pause, they politely granted my request. The first question jolted them like a tidal wave of adrenalin: Do you think you can win the Super Bowl? Bennett smiled while Butler took the bait. By the time the loquacious strong safety wrapped up his dissertation, I had enough to write a book. This book. He predicted a trip to Super Bowl XXXI and a victory in New Orleans. He spoke with such passion and conviction the lifelong Packers fan buried deep inside got chill bumps, even while the sports reporter remained placid.

"It wasn't Butler's words that struck me. It was the confidence with which he spoke. By the time the Packers had built an insurmountable 24-3 halftime lead at Tampa Bay, I began to fully appreciate the fact that Butler's comments weren't a prediction. They were a prophecy."

SUMMARY

Keith Jackson caught three first-half touchdowns, Brett Favre was nearly flawless and the retooled defense with Eugene Robinson, Brian Williams and Santana Dotson suffocated the Buccaneers.

GILBERT BROWN REMEMBERS

"The thing about playing on Monday Night Football – especially at home – is that by the opening kickoff everybody, and I do mean everybody, is champing at the bit. We would meet during the day and then go back to our hotel rooms and try to relax. Nine out of 10 times that didn't work so everybody was bolting back to his house to watch TV, lay on the couch and try to keep his mind focused on what we had to do to be ready.

"Nobody could say we weren't ready for the Philadelphia Eagles. We knew they were considered a playoff team, if not a Super Bowl contender, and we meant to put them in their place – at our place. How do you do that? As a player you're trying to find something that could change the momentum of the game, to get it in our favor and to get the confidence going. Usually it started with the defensive line being physical.

"I would look at Reggie and Santana and Sean and I knew what they were thinking: Who's going to be THE GUY that's going to hit them in the mouth and let them know what type of game it's going to be? I pictured their running back, Ricky Watters, and I imagined meeting him head-on in the hole and slamming him to the turf. I pictured their quarterback, Rodney Peete, twisting and turning and trying to get away from me or Santana or Sean, only to come face-to-face with Big Dog. Bam! Lights out. See ya! But I wouldn't want to be ya!

"It didn't take long for us to snatch their hearts out. Doug Evans intercepted a pass right out of the gate on the Eagles' first possession. It did more than put three points on the board. It demoralized them right from the start. Then we forced two more turnovers in the next three possessions.

"Our offense took some time to get going but when Brett and the boys did it was a landslide. When he hit Robert Brooks for a 25-yard touchdown in the corner of the end zone with a minute or so to go in the first quarter the Eagles looked like they had enough. I see that play now and I am amazed at how good Robert Brooks was and how much punishment he absorbed for a guy with absolutely no body fat. He was one of the toughest hombres I ever played with. You know a receiver is tough when guys on his own defense respect the hell out of him.

"Midway through the second half, between series, I just sat back and enjoyed the view while Edgar Bennett, Dorsey Levens and William Henderson tore them up. We finished with a ton of rushing yards and just wore the Eagles out."

CHRIS HAVEL COMMENTS

"After the game, I jokingly asked ex-Packers center Larry McCarren if his presence as honorary game captain influenced the outcome. McCarren, who is now the Packers' radio color analyst and sports director at WFRV-TV in Green Bay, smiled and said, 'Oh, I figure that and Ed West losing the coin toss pretty much sealed it.'

"The Packers' 34-3 victory at Tampa Bay turned heads, but the 39-13 pummeling of the Eagles opened eyes. It was a foreshadowing of things to come."

SUMMARY

The Packers made it 19 wins in their last 20 games at Lambeau Field – a feat unmatched even by coach Vince Lombardi's great teams – and did so with style. It would be inaccurate to say the Eagles never knew what hit them. Sure they did. It was the Lambeau Field mystique, coupled with a dynamic defense and outrageous offense.

Philadelphia
EAGLES 13
at
Green Bay
PACKERS 39

DATE: Sunday, September 9, 1996
LOCATION: Lambeau Field, Green Bay, WI
ATTENDANCE: 60,666
WEATHER: Mostly clear & 65°F

QUOTE OF THE GAME

"What I saw tonight was a team that realized it can be great." – Sean Jones, Packers defensive end

San Diego
CHARGERS 10
at
Green Bay
PACKERS 42

DATE: Sunday, September 15, 1996
LOCATION: Lambeau Field, Green Bay, WI
ATTENDANCE: 60,584
WEATHER: Partly Cloudy & 65°F

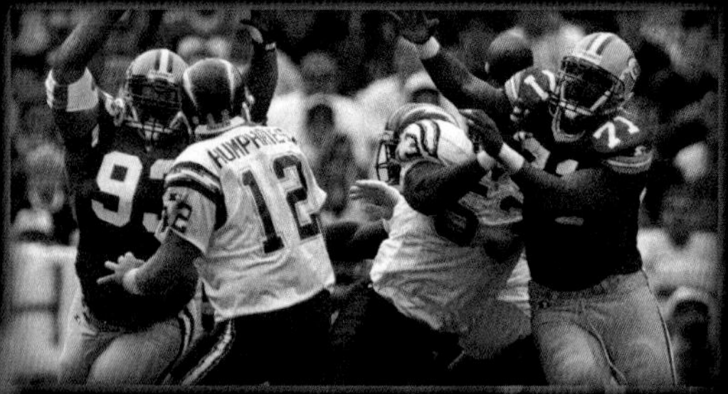

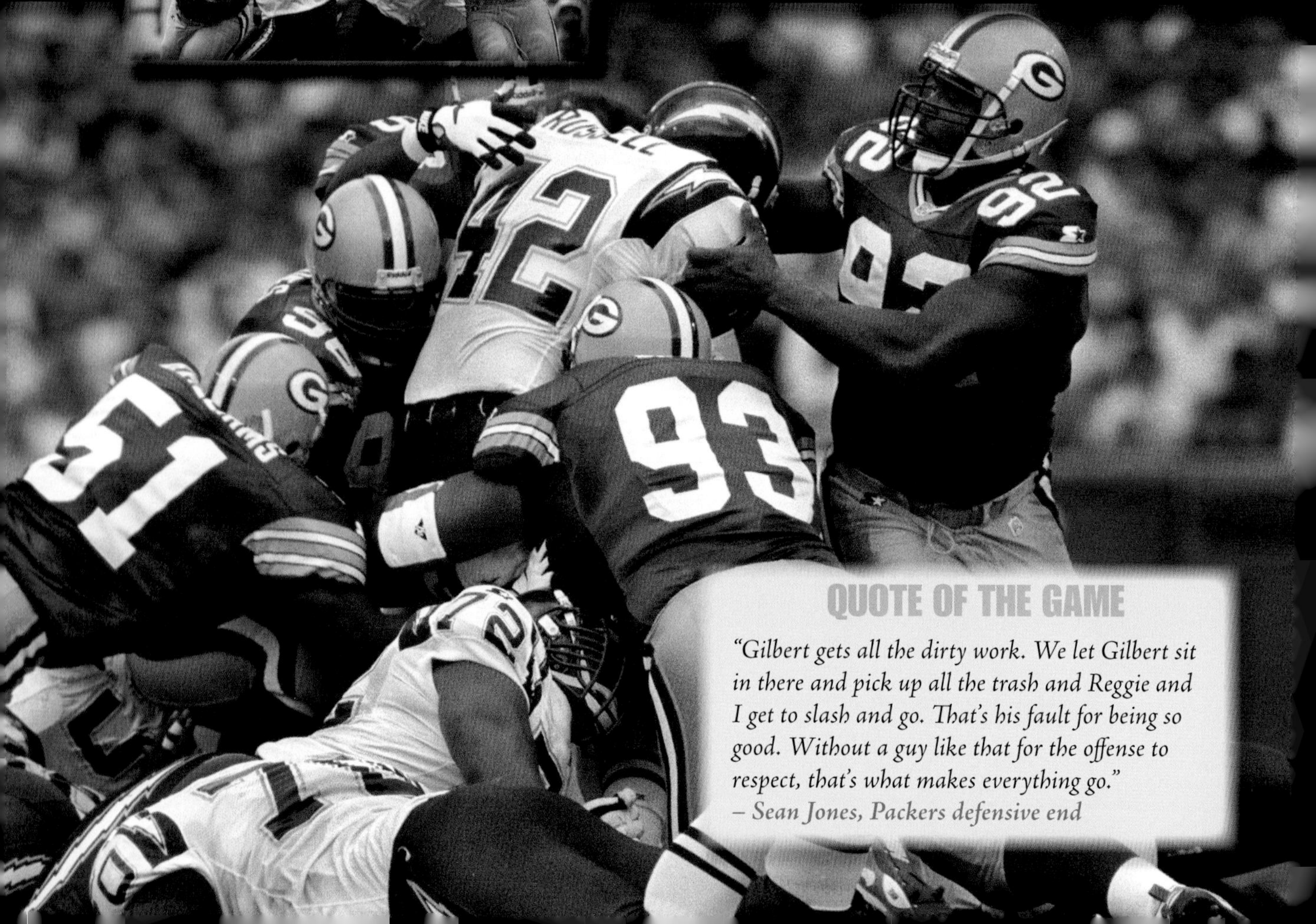

QUOTE OF THE GAME

"Gilbert gets all the dirty work. We let Gilbert sit in there and pick up all the trash and Reggie and I get to slash and go. That's his fault for being so good. Without a guy like that for the offense to respect, that's what makes everything go."
– Sean Jones, Packers defensive end

GILBERT BROWN REMEMBERS

"William Henderson had no fear. He knew all about Junior Seau, the Chargers' great middle linebacker and future Hall of Fame player, but that only psyched him up.

"The bigger, the better, the stronger the guy – the more Will went after him – and the more likely it was that Will would make him pay. It was like Will looked forward to taking the middle linebacker's best shot, just to see where he stacked up against the best of the best, and maybe to remind everyone that Pro Bowl or no Pro Bowl he was one of the best fullbacks in the National Football League.

"If you were a big-time linebacker, and you were standing in the hole, you could be sure that No. 30 was going to put his chest in you. It was hard enough for linebackers to stop Dorsey (Levens) and Edgar (Bennett) behind our offensive line. Throw in the fact that they had to take on Will, who was like a miniature guard, and it was almost impossible. I take nothing away from Dorsey and Edgar, I love those guys and they know it, but Big Will set the tone for our running game. I was so proud of him when he got selected to the Pro Bowl. It's just a damn shame it took so long. And if you don't think he deserved to go, all you have to do is ask great players like Junior Seau for the answer.

"While our offense was running the ball effectively, we focused on shutting down the run on early downs. We had so much confidence in our ability to stop that pass that we did everything we could to get teams like San Diego into passing situations. We had two of the best cornerbacks in the league – Craig Newsome and Doug Evans – and our safeties weren't exactly slouches. We had so many packages and plays and players that we weren't scared of anybody's passing game.

"Against the Chargers, we worked our "thirty-four" scheme. We had the big thirty-four, with me in the middle, and the small thirty-four, with Santana in the middle. Santana and Wayne Simmons would do me-you stunts – they'd decide where to attack as we broke the huddle – and it constantly put different schemes in the quarterback's face. Or we would bring up Doug Evans off the corner, or we would put LeRoy just off Reggie's left shoulder if the offense made the mistake of lining up the tight end on the other side of the formation. It wasn't all that complicated, but it was effective. Me? I'd usually just shut it down in passing situations and enjoy the destruction from the bench."

CHRIS HAVEL COMMENTS

"Through the first three games the Packers' average margin of victory was 29 points. That's more than four touchdowns a game. The thing I remember more than the blowout victories to start the season was the way the team handled the success. The big wins didn't pull the team apart. It brought it closer together.

"When players weren't teasing one another in the locker room, they were giving each other props. They didn't throw teammates under the bus. They threw them bouquets, often with a playful reminder to not let it go to their heads.

"Players knew their roles, did their jobs and appreciated their teammates. Mike Holmgren was a master motivator, and he did everything in his power to promote cohesiveness, but a head coach only can do so much. The players took pride in their work. Not only because it meant a shot at fame and fortune. But because it meant there was less of a chance they would let down the guy next to them.

"Demolishing San Diego was one thing. Finding it in themselves to stay together was quite another. It is amazing that something so simple can be so rare."

SUMMARY

The Packers smacked the Chargers so hard the entire AFC woke up sore the next morning. Chargers quarterback Stan Humphries completed just 16 of 30 passes for 130 yards and two interceptions. San Diego got behind by so much so fast it had no choice but to throw and still managed just seven passing first downs.

GILBERT BROWN REMEMBERS

"We had some classic battles with the Vikings. We also had some not-so-classic battles like this one. It was tough because we were in the dome, so the noise factor was through the roof – some people said they would run it through the P.A. system – plus you were playing people that hated your guts.

"Most of the time we went up there and beat ourselves, but I will give credit where it is due, starting with Warren Moon. He was the guy that made everything happen as far as being knowledgeable and being schooled on the game. We would watch what he was doing with the hard count, or pre-snap keys, or whatever, but Moon was a really good veteran – a future Hall of Fame quarterback – that could mask those things.

"Randall McDaniel, their All-Pro guard, was no joke either. Usually I can get a good push on somebody. Not with him. A lot of that was because of the time I spent going one-on-one with him in the Vikings' training camp. He liked going against me because he was using me as a gauge to figure out how to play other big nose tackles. He would let me think I was getting a great push against him, but all the while he was feeling me out and thinking about ways to hunker down and slow me down.

"Now that's a smart player."

"Robert Smith, their running back, was better than most fans gave him credit. You thought he was soft, but he kept coming and coming and his speed was outstanding. It was our job to stop him up front, but if he got past us you better send the dogs because there was no catching him. He didn't put the fear of God into us the way Detroit's Barry Sanders did, but Robert Smith had a very good offensive line and he know how to use it.

"Was there anything positive about getting whipped at Minnesota? Yeah. It made us tougher, and losses like these helped us win a championship. But that didn't make it any fun while you were going through it."

CHRIS HAVEL COMMENTS

"Same old, same old, for the Packers up in the Metrodome. Mike Holmgren proved to be the better coach, but the Vikings' Dennis Green definitely had his number. The Vikings were a strong team, and the victory improved their record to 4-0 to move them into sole possession of first place in the NFC Central. But the Packers' misery in Minneapolis seemed to go beyond the fact that the Vikings were a talented team.

"Brett Favre fumbled three times on sacks, and the Vikings recovered two of them. The reaction in the press box was, "What's new?"

"The post-game interviews in the visitor's locker room in the Metrodome were pure hell. The locker room was cramped and hot. The Packers' players were ticked off and in no mood to talk. The head coach conducted his interview atop a makeshift podium in an adjacent – and even smaller – locker room. The Packers' annual trouncing here became business as usual. The only surprise was that the atmosphere didn't lead to any ugly exchanges between the media and the players. It was almost as if the Packers were resigned to the fact that it was going to be a long game."

SUMMARY

Too many penalties, too many turnovers and too much Minnesota Vikings were the Packers' undoing in their first loss of the season. At one point, it got so ugly that Packers GM Ron Wolf could be heard shouting, "Hey, protect the quarterback!" Wolf was referring to the officials, whom he felt were letting the Vikings get away with murder, but he might as well have been talking about the offensive line.

Green Bay

PACKERS 21

at

Minnesota

VIKINGS 30

DATE: Sunday, September 22, 1996
LOCATION: Metrodome, Minneapolis, MN
ATTENDANCE: 64,168
WEATHER: Indoors

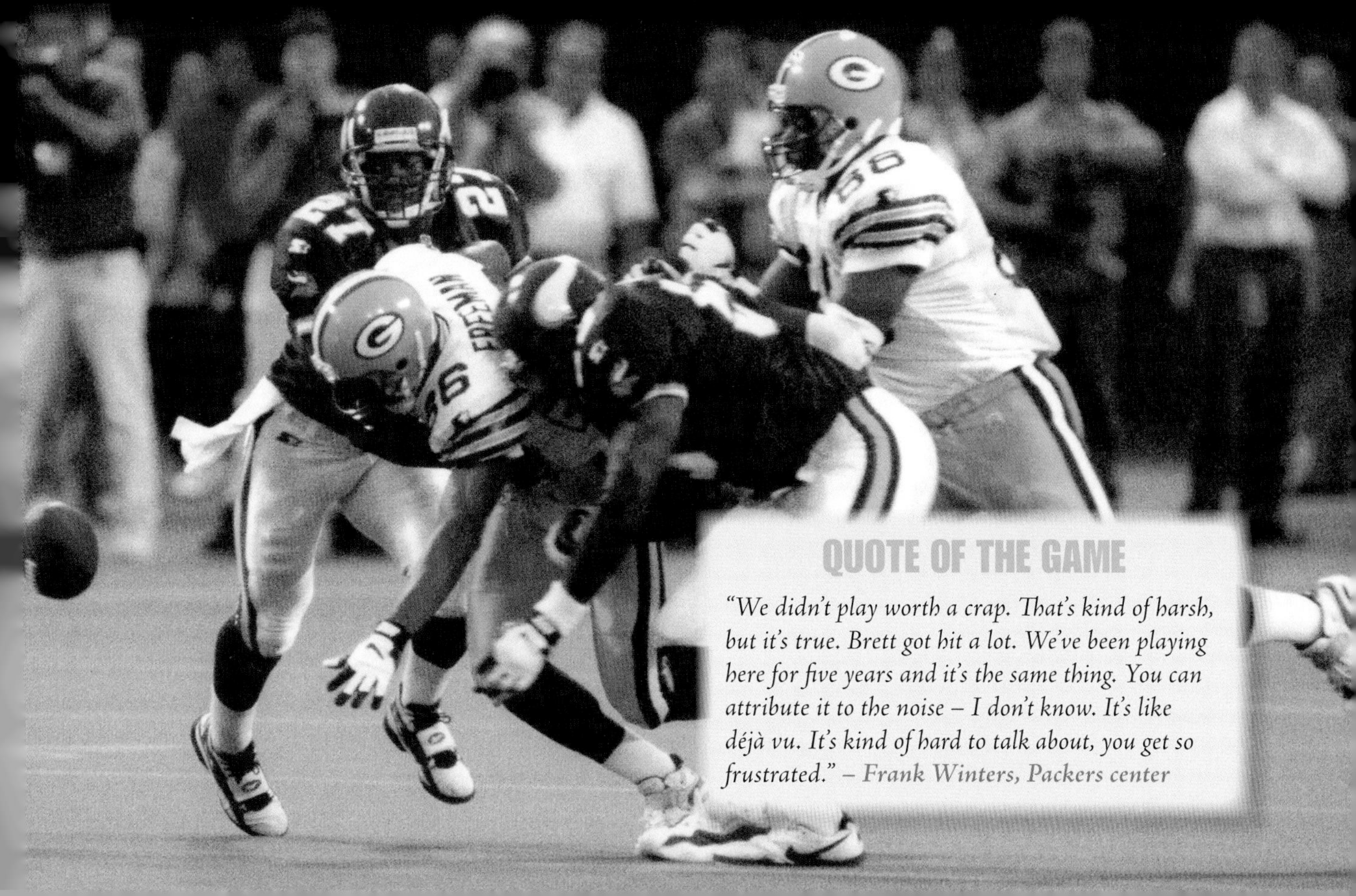

QUOTE OF THE GAME

"We didn't play worth a crap. That's kind of harsh, but it's true. Brett got hit a lot. We've been playing here for five years and it's the same thing. You can attribute it to the noise – I don't know. It's like déjà vu. It's kind of hard to talk about, you get so frustrated." – Frank Winters, Packers center

Seattle
SEAHAWKS 10
at
Green Bay
PACKERS 31

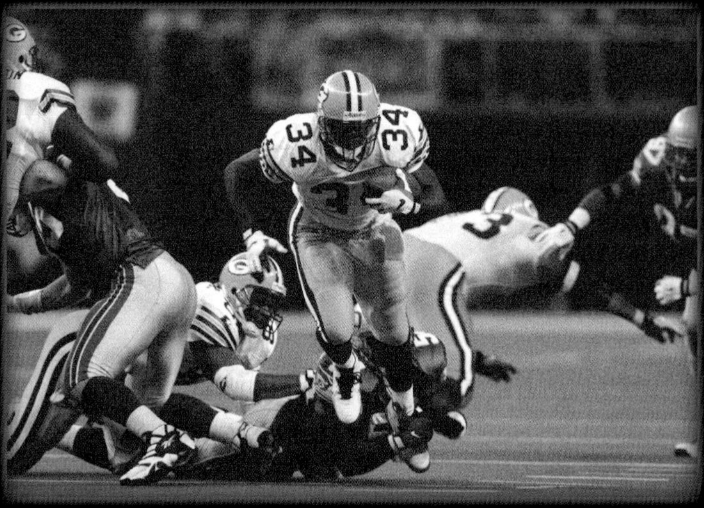

DATE: Sunday, September 29, 1996
LOCATION: Lambeau Field, Green Bay, WI
ATTENDANCE: 59,973
WEATHER: Indoors

QUOTE OF THE GAME

"I want that to be the headline of every paper in the country. 'Holmgren does it on turf.' "
– Mike Holmgren, Packers head coach

GILBERT BROWN REMEMBERS

"This is what I like to refer to as our ninth home game of the season. We had enough fans in the stands at the Kingdome to fill all of De Pere and Ashwaubenon, too. There were so many Packers fans in the stands it was unbelievable. We were 2,000 miles away from home – clear across the country from Lambeau Field – and you would have thought the Seahawks were dressing in the visitor's locker room.

"I glanced up in the stands just before the National Anthem and I thought, 'I have yet to see a Seattle Seahawks fan.' That kind of loyalty means a lot to players. I know it did to us. We would talk about it and joke about it in the locker room. We felt like we didn't need the team charter to get home. We could just hop in our vehicles and drive home. It's games like this that make Packers fans the best in the world.

"The other great memory I have from this game involves Big Dog. Our defense had so many interceptions it was crazy, so I guess Reggie felt like he needed to get into the act, too. He picked off a Rick Mirer pass – I teased him about jumping the route – and he returned that thing something like 50 yards (actually 46 yards).

"You talk about funny. Reggie gets the pick, makes like Eric Dickerson, sprints down the sideline and finally gets tackled (at Seattle's 21-yard line). Reggie's giving high fives and hugging everybody as he's coming off the field. Then he's on the sideline sucking all the oxygen tanks he can hold, and wouldn't you know it? The offense goes three and out, so we have to settle for a field goal. We're telling (holder) Craig (Hentrich) to try to stall in the huddle, or to take a 5-yard delay of game penalty, or to do something so Big Dog can catch his breath. We were teasing Reggie that he needed a TV timeout, but the truth is we were laughing so hard WE needed it to catch OUR breath.

"As hilarious as it was, it also reminded everyone what a great athlete Reggie was, not that anyone needed to be reminded. That play showed the basketball skills that he was always talking about. He was a tight end in high school and that interception showed his good ball awareness. I love reminiscing about Reggie. I just wish he was here to reminisce with me."

CHRIS HAVEL COMMENTS

"This game served to remind everyone of general manager Ron Wolf's prowess. On the eve of training camp, Wolf traded Matt LaBounty, a reserve defensive end, to the Seahawks in exchange for free safety Eugene Robinson. LaBounty, a solid player, would have seen little if any playing time in Green Bay. Meantime, Robinson became a mainstay in the secondary and a key replacement for the departed George Teague.

"Robinson's contributions manifested themselves in many ways. On game day, because of his diligence in film study, it was almost as if he knew what play the offense was going to run. After practice, he implored the defensive backs to stay longer and catch football upon football at close range off the Jugs machine. It is one reason the Packers' interception total soared, and the defensive backs dropped fewer would-be picks.

"Furthermore, Robinson and LeRoy Butler clicked almost immediately. I remember countless times when either player – in mid-interview – would halt the proceeding because he remembered a key element regarding the upcoming game. Both safeties were constantly thinking football, an attitude that became pervasive throughout the entire locker room. Robinson and Butler made it cool to talk football 24-7, as opposed to debating what new video game was the most fun, or which nightclub was the hottest.

"That mindset went a long way toward fostering the defense's tremendous success. Of course, defensive coordinator Fritz Shurmur's constant teaching, encouraging and harping didn't hurt."

SUMMARY

The Packers managed to win for only the second time in 14 games on the road, in a dome, and on turf. The Seahawks didn't put up much of a fight in the Kingdome, and their five turnovers proved to be too much to overcome.

GILBERT BROWN REMEMBERS

"This was the real black-and-blue game right there, buddy. Even though you talk about the Packers-Bears rivalry, and the fans understand what it's all about, there's nothing like playing in one of these games to really appreciate what it's all about. It's a cliché but it's true: Regardless of the records it's going to be a dogfight. This is one pro rivalry that's the real deal. There's no fake hoopla. We were out there to get after each other. It was serious business, and it didn't matter if they had a mediocre offensive line.

"There were two games every season – the Bears games – that we knew Monday morning we would wake up aching from head to toe. That is unless you played them on Monday Night Football. Then you'd wake up hurting on Tuesday morning.

"This was the game that Brett (Favre) connected with Antonio (Freeman) on the Hail Mary touchdown pass at the end of the first half. It also was the game that the Bears' Alonzo Spellman connected with Brett along the sideline after he let the pass fly. We were jacked because 'Free' made a circus catch for the touchdown, but we were pissed because Spellman did Brett like that. It was a cheap shot to say the least. It was like when we would watch Brett and Warren Sapp go at it. We knew it was competitive and we couldn't come out on the field even though we wanted to, but we also knew that our offensive linemen wouldn't let any BS go on. We saw that in practice every Thursday when it was good versus good (No. 1 offense versus No. 1 defense).

"Frankie Winters was the ringleader of dirt. If I was on another team, and I had to line up against Frankie, I would make sure I had knee braces on, elbow braces on, ankle braces on, whatever braces I could find. You knew he would do whatever he had to do to get the job done. And if somebody messed with his boy (Favre) there was going to be hell to pay because he wouldn't stand for it.

"It's a lot of the reason why Brett has been able to play so long, and it's why we loved Frank Winters so much, even if he was a SOB to practice against. I didn't mind so much though. He never took cheap shots in practice, not serious ones, anyway. And I always felt like I'd rather be on his side than on the other team. You need tough guys to win in the NFL, and they don't come much tougher than Frank Winters."

CHRIS HAVEL COMMENTS

"The Packers committed just four penalties for 25 yards. Think about that. In a hostile environment on the road against its chief rival, Green Bay played with poise and precision. This game began a remarkable three-game stretch where the Packers committed just 10 penalties for 69 yards. That is as many penalties as some teams are flagged for in four quarters, let alone 12.

"It is a testament to the concentration level – and the level of professionalism – head coach Mike Holmgren and his staff instilled in the team. Holmgren was a stickler for doing it right all the time, not just some of the time, and no one ever heard a player or a coach say, 'That's OK. We'll get it next time.' No. That wasn't acceptable. Holmgren was a perfectionist and a detail guy, as were his coordinators and his special teams coach.

"Nolan Cromwell, the special teams coach, received scant praise during the course of the season. Looking back, Cromwell probably deserved better from the media, and that includes yours truly. The special teams units were highly organized, immensely skilled and exceedingly well coached. Don Beebe's 90-yard kickoff return for a touchdown in the third quarter of the 37-6 victory over the Bears illustrates the point.

"There is nothing glamorous about coaching special teams. When a player such as Beebe, or Super Bowl XXXI MVP Desmond Howard, makes a scintillating return, or the kicker or punter do their job to a T, the players get the credit. But when there is a mistake on special teams, especially if it is costly – they usually are – the coach gets the heat. Here is hoping Cromwell graciously accepts this belated compliment."

Green Bay

PACKERS 37

at

Chicago

BEARS 6

DATE: Sunday, October 6, 1996
LOCATION: Soldier Field, Chicago, IL
ATTENDANCE: 65,480
WEATHER: Sunny & 68°F

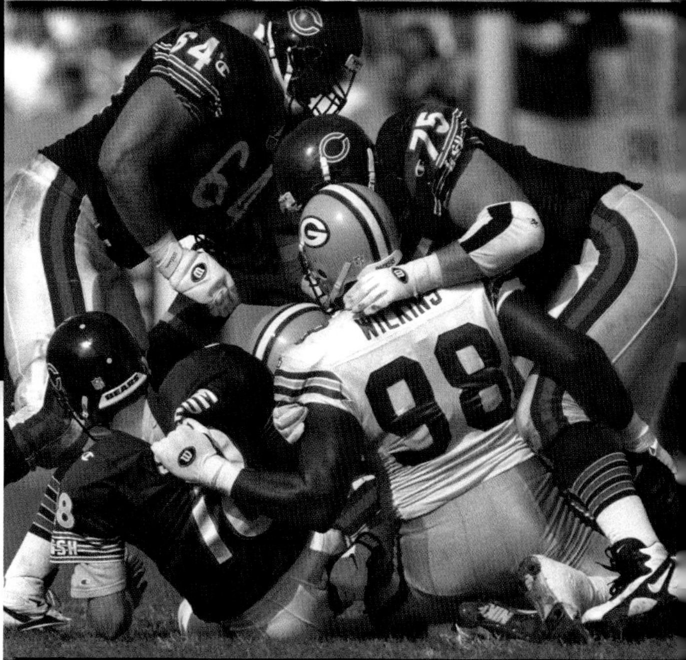

SUMMARY

The Packers led 7-3 late in the first half of a typical tug-of-war with the Bears at Soldier Field. In the two-minute offense, Brett Favre and Antonio Freeman played catch to connect on three passes for 42 yards. That set up Favre's 2-yard touchdown pass to Keith Jackson with 35 seconds in the half. While the Packers' offensive coaches were making their way from the Soldier Field coaches' box to the visitor's locker room, Doug Evans intercepted a pass with 20 seconds on the clock. With 11 seconds and the ball at midfield, Favre improvised on coach Mike Holmgren's third down call, rolled right, and hit Freeman on a 50-yard Hail Mary touchdown with no time left. In the span of 35 seconds, a close game became a 20-3 blowout.

QUOTE OF THE GAME

"Ever since I got here, we've been told by Mike (Holmgren), 'Try to dominate. Try to put yourself in a position to dominate. Try to get good enough where you can dominate.' We've gotten good enough to do that."
– Sean Jones, Packers defensive end

San Francisco

49ERS 20

at

Green Bay

PACKERS 23

DATE: Monday, October 14, 1996
LOCATION: Lambeau Field, Green Bay, WI
ATTENDANCE: 60,716
WEATHER: Partly cloudy & 44°F
NOTE: Final score in overtime

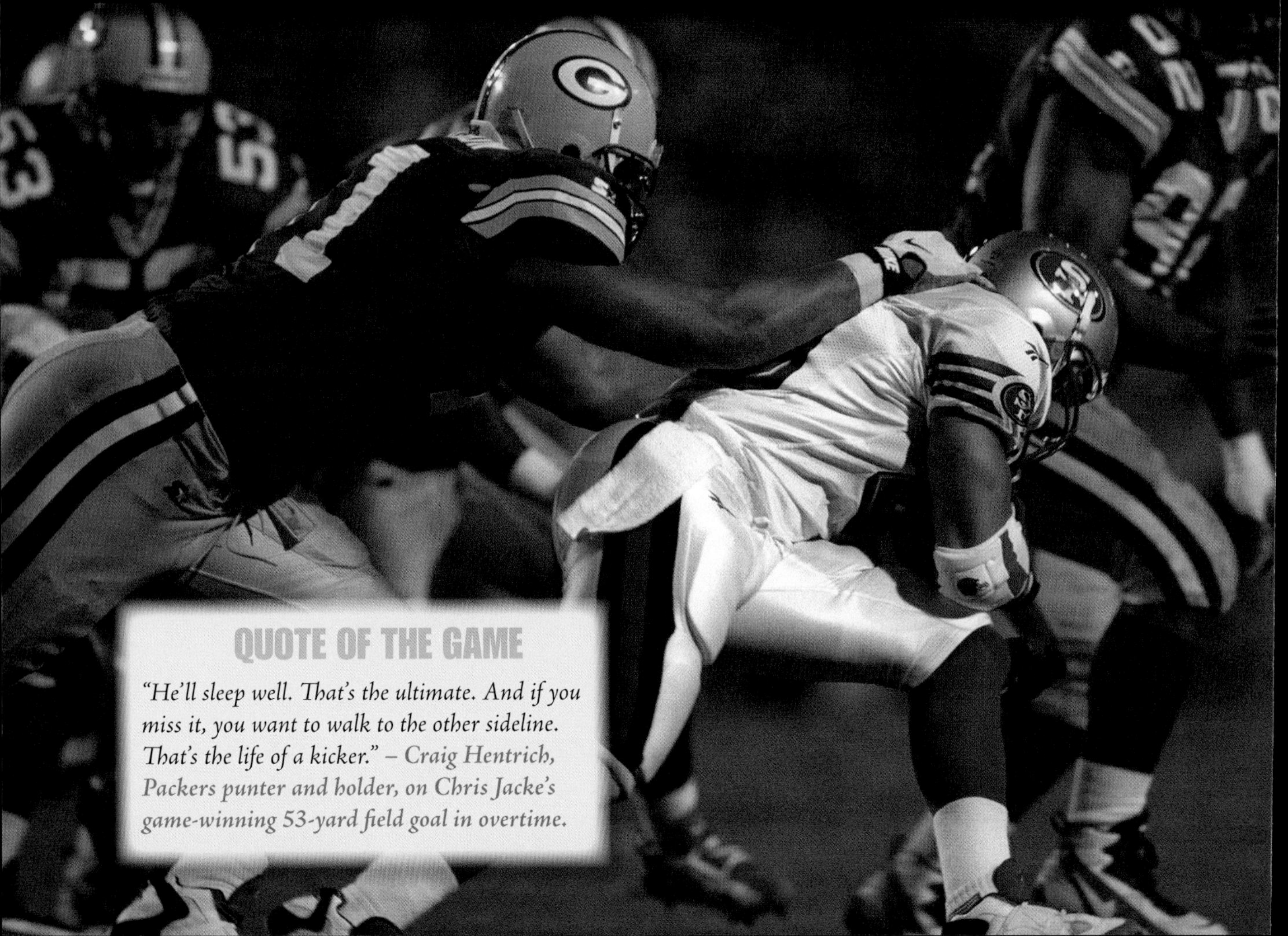

QUOTE OF THE GAME

"He'll sleep well. That's the ultimate. And if you miss it, you want to walk to the other sideline. That's the life of a kicker." – Craig Hentrich, Packers punter and holder, on Chris Jacke's game-winning 53-yard field goal in overtime.

GILBERT BROWN REMEMBERS

"When Robert Brooks went down with the knee injury I was seriously upset. When Don Beebe stepped up and made huge play after huge play I can't say that I was surprised. For two guys that come from totally different backgrounds, Robert Brooks and Don Beebe were so much alike it was scary. They were deeply religious. They took great care of their bodies. They were excellent teammates.

"That's why I was sad for Robert when he got hurt, because I knew if we went on to do great things it would be really tough on him not to be playing. And that's why I was happy for Don Beebe because he was a true pro, and one of the guys – like Reggie White and some others – that deserved to be on a Super Bowl champion.

"That win over San Francisco, at home on Monday Night Football, really started the fans and media thinking we could win it all. It showed how tough we were and how resilient and how we weren't going to settle for being second best.

"When Chris Jacke made the 53-yard field goal to win it in overtime, we celebrated like there was no tomorrow. What we didn't know was that in terms of football, at least for the season, Robert Brooks didn't have a tomorrow. When we saw him in the locker room after the game we knew he was hurt but we didn't think he was out for the season. He never showed that when we got back to the locker room. When we found out it really dampened our spirits because he was our go-to guy, he was one of the guys that make the world go 'round at 1265, and we knew what we were capable of. It threw us off – not because we thought we wouldn't be as good – but because we wanted him to be a part of it.

"The thing about Mike Holmgren was if a player goes down, the next guy has got to step up, and he didn't care who it was. That's how we practiced. Don Beebe was the next guy. I remember growing up watching all the things he had done in Buffalo and knowing that he didn't get that Super Bowl ring. I hear he is an excellent high school football coach in Illinois, and his team is awesome, and I'm not surprised.

"He'll tell you like it is. He won't be cussing or ranting or raving. He'll go on the field and show you. You love him for that. You want him to succeed. He was one of the guys that I played hard for because I loved him, and I'm sure his players feel the same."

CHRIS HAVEL COMMENTS

"Chris Jacke showed his mettle by nailing the 53-yard field goal while knowing that a miss would mean the 49ers were only a couple first downs away from winning. Don Beebe was another mentally tough guy. He was ready when Robert Brooks went down, and it showed the way he played. He caught 11 passes for 220 yards – the third-most yards in team history – and the offense didn't miss a beat.

"I admit that I felt bad for Robert Brooks, who was lost with a season-ending knee injury on the first play. By the time the game ended Edgar Bennett and Earl Dotson were also out with injuries and had joined Brooks in the training room. If they felt sorry for themselves it didn't show. They were so happy they had won. When Jacke made the kick, Bennett, with his left shoulder in a sling, said, "I was high-fivin' with my good arm!"

SUMMARY

Don Beebe's clutch performance, and Chris Jacke's clutch kick, catapulted the Packers to the forefront of NFL fans' consciousness. Not just in Green Bay, but around the entire league. After this game, the Packers were considered a Super Bowl XXXI contender, if not the favorite.

Game 8

GILBERT BROWN REMEMBERS

"The Buccaneers had a big, bruising fullback in Mike Alstott, and we wanted to prove that you weren't going to come up to our house without a hall pass. All you heard on ESPN and the NFL highlight shows was "Alstott this" and "Alstott that" and how he could run over any defense. Errict Rhett was pretty good at what he was doing, too.

"We didn't care.

"Mike Alstott, the big bruiser, finished with four carries for 8 yards and a whole lot of punishment. He didn't give it out. He took it. We took him out of the game before it even began. We had the linebackers to do it. George Koonce, Wayne Simmons and Brian Williams didn't get the pub that they deserved, but that only drove them to be better.

"Whenever anyone talked about or wrote about Koonce it was that he was a guy that wasn't good enough to make it in the NFL, so he had to play in the World League. With Simmons, it was all about how he was such a bad dude, an underachiever, and not worth the first-round draft pick (GM) Ron Wolf spent to get him. With B.W., it was about how he took so long to develop and that he almost didn't make it as a rookie.

"I'll tell you what. I'll take those three linebackers over any three you can name for two reasons. First, they could flat-out play. They didn't take nuthin' from nobody. When the game started

they were all about doing whatever it took to shut down the other team. Second, they didn't give a rip what anybody else thought about them. They weren't looking to win awards. They were looking to win games. They loved to hit, and to play.

"We had a great defensive line, but a big part of what made it work was that we had great linebackers behind us. We could take chances that you just wouldn't take if you didn't really believe the linebackers had your back. They were always in position to make plays, and that allowed us to get after it and dominate without worrying about giving up a big play and having Fritz's butt all over us. If we missed a tackle, and that didn't happen very often, we knew Wayne or Koonce or B.W. would be there to finish the guy off."

"It was Shutdown City."

CHRIS HAVEL COMMENTS

"The Packers' defense came in two sizes: Gilbert and Brown. It was larger than life, led by characters that were almost mythical figures.

"Reggie White – in my opinion – was the greatest defensive player in NFL history. He was the most feared pass rusher, an immovable object against the run and a tremendous leader in the locker room, in practice and in games. He took pride in his work. He took tremendous care of his body. He played injured. He played hurt. He had an awareness of who he was and what he meant to his teammates, and he used that stature to quietly, constantly motivate the men around him.

"Fritz Shurmur, the defensive coordinator, was old school. To him, the only substitute for hard work was more hard work. He thought about football 24-7. He believed that you only get what you demand, and if what you demand is reasonable, the truly professional players will respond. If they don't, they aren't worth a lick anyway.

"Gilbert Brown was the epitome of the word "teammate." He sacrificed self-glory for the greater good of the team. He understand Vince Lombardi's

Tampa Bay BUCCANEERS 7 at Green Bay PACKERS 13

DATE: Sunday, October 27, 1996
LOCATION: Lambeau Field, Green Bay, WI
ATTENDANCE: 60,627
WEATHER: Cloudy & 56°F

No. 1 concept without the benefit of playing for the legendary coach. He took on double-team blocking with enthusiasm. He didn't care if the fans or the media appreciated the sacrifice. He knew that Shurmur, White, Simmons, Santana Dotson, LeRoy Butler and the rest appreciated it. That was all he needed. If he had the love and respect of his teammates and coaches – the men that he relied on and vice-versa – what else was there.

"When the Packers throttled Tampa Bay in this game, they did so because Mike Holmgren cared more about winning than being considered a great offensive head coach. If he had to beat you 13-7 so be it. The best game plan wasn't the one that produced 40 points and 400 yards in total offense. It was the one that magnified his team's strengths, diminished its weaknesses and was flexible enough to adjust to circumstances."

QUOTE OF THE GAME

"Buddy Ryan used to have a saying: 'The best thing that some guys have going for them is they don't have to play.' We don't have any guys like that on this team." – Sean Jones, Packers defensive end

SUMMARY

The Packers' 13 points was a season low, but this six-point victory didn't seem that close. Trent Dilfer's receivers were blanketed from start to finish, and the result was two costly interceptions. The Green Bay offense was dealt a blow when receiver Antonio Freeman suffered a broken left forearm on a hit by Tampa Bay's Melvin Johnson. The hit was helmet-to-helmet and Freeman's ulna snapped when Johnson's knee landed on it. Freeman telephoned Robert Brooks, who was at home with a season-ending knee injury, from the locker room during halftime. Brooks was compassionate and encouraging, although Freeman admitted he was heartbroken. It wasn't the end for Freeman though. He returned Dec. 1 with a cast on his forearm, and he caught 10 passes for 156 yards in a 28-17 victory over the Bears. Talk about toughness.

Detroit

LIONS 18

at

Green Bay

PACKERS 28

DATE: Sunday, November 3, 1996
LOCATION: Lambeau Field, Green Bay, WI
ATTENDANCE: 60,695
WEATHER: Mostly sunny & 43°F

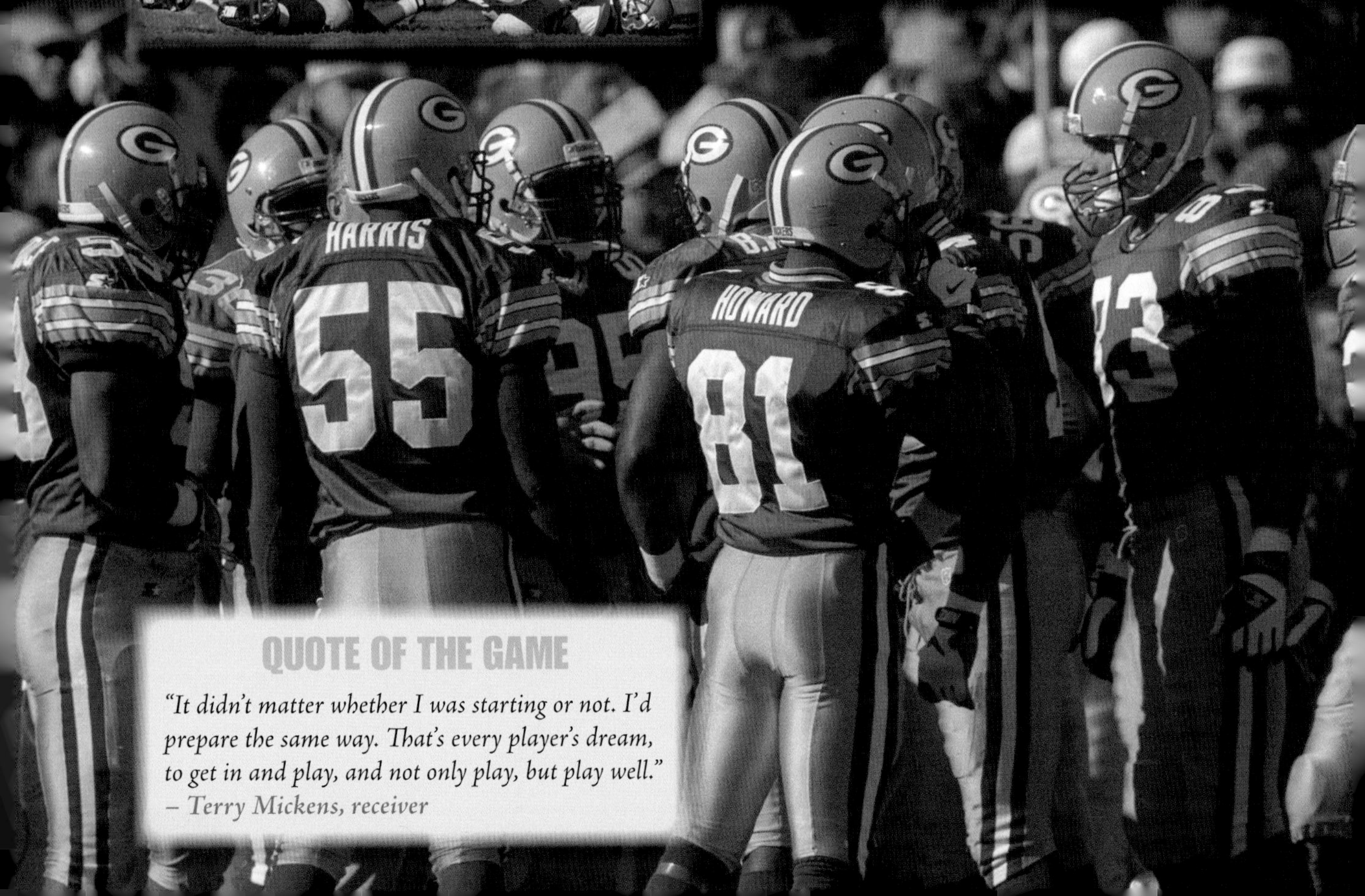

QUOTE OF THE GAME

"It didn't matter whether I was starting or not. I'd prepare the same way. That's every player's dream, to get in and play, and not only play, but play well."
– Terry Mickens, receiver

GILBERT BROWN REMEMBERS

"Barry Sanders had a Cadillac commercial on TV at the time. All week leading up to the game the guys on defense kept saying, 'We don't want to be on that Cadillac commercial.' I'm guessing NBA players felt the same way about the Chicago Bulls' Michael Jordan. They didn't want to be the guy in the highlight film, or the life-size poster, getting dunked on by Michael. Nobody wanted to be THAT GUY. We didn't Barry Sanders to do us like that, and we could play now, but he still got 152 yards.

"When it's Barry Sanders saying and doing are two different things. You would have him stuffed for four plays, five plays, six plays ... and then BAM! He'd be gone and you weren't sure what hit you. Then you would turn around just in time to see him handing the football to an official in the end zone. He never really had an offensive line. It didn't matter. He would still find a way to get the Lions' offense some big-time yards, even if he had to do it by himself.

"Everybody was a fan of Barry Sanders. Reggie even said he loved Barry Sanders. He thought he was great and that's saying a lot coming from him. Growing up in Detroit my favorite running back was Eric Dickerson but you can't even compare the two. Dickerson was great in his own way, one of the all-time greats, really, but Barry was Barry. I saw the Chicago Bears' Walter Payton on TV when I was a kid, and I thought the world of him, but getting to be on the field with Barry Sanders in real life? C'mon. It's like getting a chance to play with Reggie White or Brett Favre. It's something you can't wait to tell your grandchildren about some day."

CHRIS HAVEL COMMENTS

"One of the true privileges of being a sports columnist and getting to cover an NFL team on a full-time basis is seeing the great players do their thing. Brett Favre. Reggie White. LeRoy Butler. Those guys are special. What makes it even more so is getting to watch great players from other teams, and Barry Sanders topped the list. He could make a 3-yard loss look like the second coming of Gale Sayers. By the time the defense finally corralled him, they weren't the only ones gasping for air. The guy was simply breathtaking, and I remember the great anticipation I felt knowing the Packers' tremendous defense was going to get after one of the greatest backs of all time. It reduced football to its simplest terms: Here I am. Catch me if you can. And the Packers did. Well, most of the time, anyway.

"Barry Sanders was the best running back on the field, and a terrific neutralizer, but the Packers were the better team. They had a superior defense, a staggering array of offensive weapons, exceptional special teams and rare quality depth. While Sanders was dodging defenders, a beat up Packers receiving corps got a boost when Terry Mickens come off the bench to catch seven passes, including two for touchdowns. The Lions weren't going to beat the Packers, but it was fun watching Barry Sanders try."

SUMMARY

Terry Mickens' heroics off the bench garnered headlines, but Don Beebe's stellar play kept a battered offense dangerous. Beebe's 65-yard touchdown catch on a play the coaches drew up specifically for this game, gave Green Bay a 28-10 lead late in the third quarter. Beebe's four catches gave him 25 receptions through nine games, the second-highest total on the team.

Game 10

GILBERT BROWN REMEMBERS

"The Chiefs were better than we thought. OK, they were a lot better than we thought. It isn't easy admitting something like that but it's true. Arrowhead Stadium was the loudest stadium, other than Lambeau Field, that we played in all season. I felt like I was back at Kansas playing against the Nebraska Cornhuskers in Lincoln.

"We had reeled off five straight wins – and we had survived a game and a half without 'Free,' – but we were hurting. Physically and mentally we were spent by the time we got to Kansas City. It was an AFC opponent, and even though it was being hyped as a possible preview of Super Bowl XXXI, we were pretty much shot. We lost by a touchdown but I still remember the headline, 'Chiefs Crush Packers!' That hurt almost as much as the game, but that's how high expectations were running in Green Bay.

"Greg Hill, the Chiefs' running back, wasn't a very big dude. But he really ran hard and busted it up in there a couple of times, and they had a really good O-line, too. We felt like we needed to pick it up for our offense, and believe me, we tried. But it was one of those games that there wasn't anything left when we reached for a little extra. Give the Chiefs credit, though. They were good. Damn good."

CHRIS HAVEL COMMENTS

"This game reminded me of the time I watched Ken Norton break Muhammad Ali's jaw in a heavyweight title bout on ABC's Wide World of Sports. I saw it, and I blinked, and I still couldn't believe it. Just like Norton, the Chiefs had dismantled a champion with cold, calculated precision. The Packers lost by a touchdown but it seemed like three touchdowns. For the first time all season, I wondered if the Packers might be in serious trouble because of the injury situation at receiver.

"Still, the Packers had several things going for them. They had Brett Favre at quarterback, a strong running attack led by Edgar Bennett and Dorsey Levens, and a defense that could dominate if necessary.

"The Packers also had a head coach, Mike Holmgren, that knew how to coax his team into giving everything it had to give. If that meant throwing the ball sparingly, or utilizing the short passing game to give a weary running attack a much-needed breather, he would find a way. Whatever it took, Holmgren would make it work, and excuses simply weren't tolerated. Neither was losing.

"I was certain better days were ahead. I just didn't know how far ahead."

SUMMARY

The Packers' numerous injuries at receiver and tight end finally caught up with them. Already without Robert Brooks and Antonio Freeman, the Packers lost starting tight end Mark Chmura to a sprained arch. The Chiefs' cornerback duo of James Hasty and Dale Carter smothered the receivers while defensive ends Derrick Thomas and Neil Smith did likewise to quarterback Brett Favre. The Chiefs notched four sacks and constantly harassed Favre into errant throws.

Green Bay PACKERS 20 at Kansas City CHIEFS 27

DATE: Sunday, November 10, 1996
LOCATION: Arrowhead Stadium, Kansas City, MO
ATTENDANCE: 79,281
WEATHER: Overcast, cold & 30°F

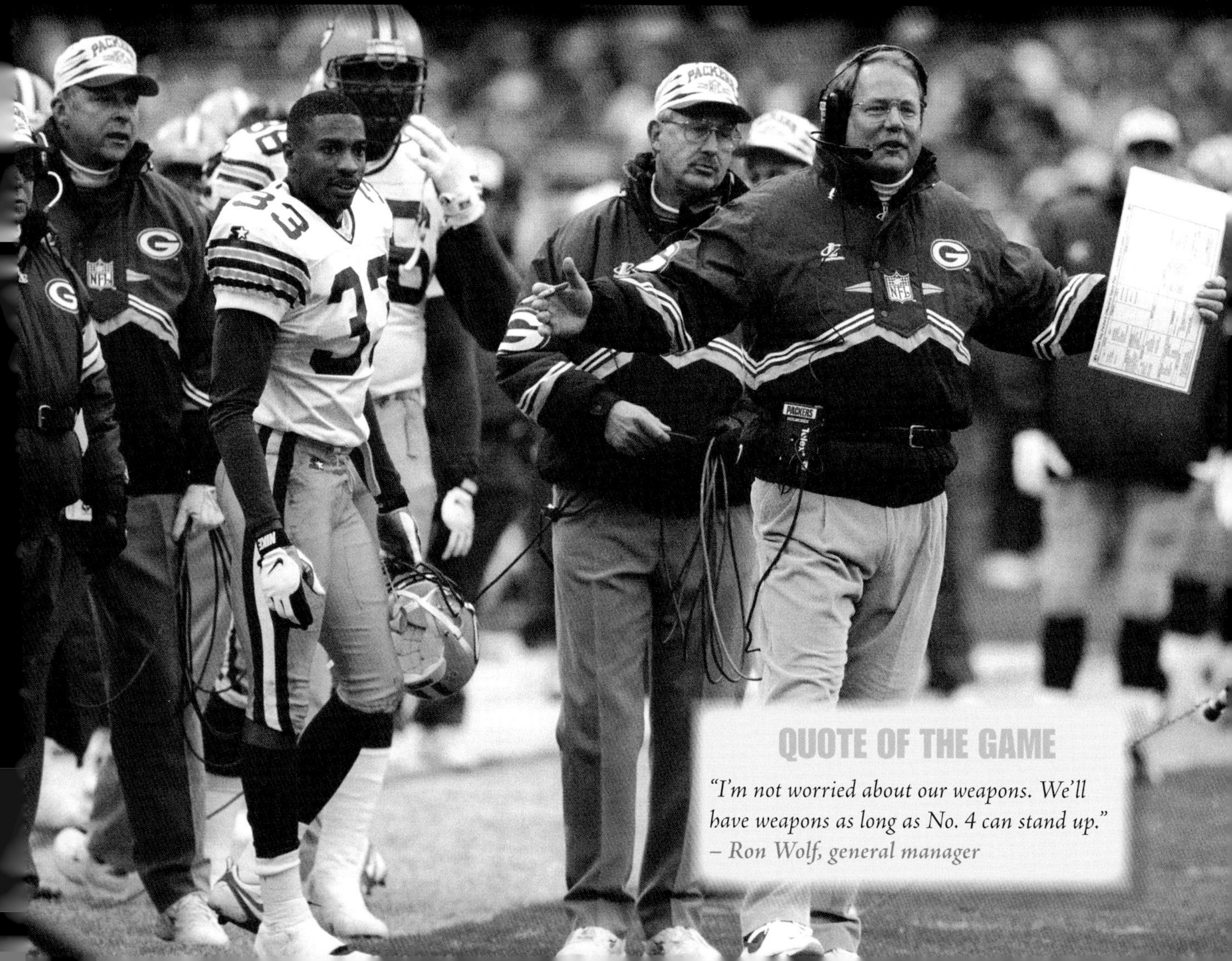

QUOTE OF THE GAME

"I'm not worried about our weapons. We'll have weapons as long as No. 4 can stand up."
– Ron Wolf, general manager

Game 11

GILBERT BROWN REMEMBERS

"That was the game that broke our hearts because we were determined not to lose to them. Before the game, Wayne Simmons and I promised each other we would die on the field tonight before we would let the Cowboys in. We were fighting and scratching to win, and we didn't let Dallas cross our goal line, but the damn kicker bailed them out. It may look good for the record books to have a kicker make seven field goals, but who wants any record broken against them? Not us. That's why Reggie got so upset. The Cowboys could have taken a knee. That put a bad taste in our mouth. If you're a competitor and you don't like to lose it's going to tick you off. We had Reggie's back on this one. When he ran over there we all ran over there with him.

"We were more ticked off after the game than we were before it. I didn't like the fact that Barry Switzer, their coach, didn't respect us. He was an a-hole anyway, and this just proved it.

"After the game, we were in the locker room and the media started talking about how the Jacksonville Jaguars released Andre Rison. Right away, we were wondering if Ron (Wolf) and Mike (Holmgren) would bring him in. Our receivers were hurting, and we needed the help, but some people thought it might be the final nail in our coffin. I disagreed. I was all for signing Rison. We had great leaders on that team. We had Reggie White, Sean Jones, Brett Favre, LeRoy Butler. Bring him on in. We've got the guys here that will make sure he's going to do what he is supposed to do. And "Bad Moon" knew it. We weren't going to let him come in and mess up our chance to win a championship.

"Well, we signed him and it turned out to be a great move. He played hard, did what he was supposed to do and kept his mouth shut. He was a great teammate for that stretch run. After it was all said and done, and we won Super Bowl XXXI, Andre told the team that he only had one regret: That he wasn't with us from Day One of the season."

CHRIS HAVEL COMMENTS

"The most notable aspect of this loss, aside from it prompting the Packers to sign Andre Rison, is that Green Bay didn't lose the rest of the season. The Packers won five straight to close out the regular season, and followed it up with three post-season victories and a Super Bowl championship. What stood out in the visitor's locker room at Texas Stadium was the team's grim resolve. This was a group of very proud men, and they had come too far, and worked too hard, to let it slip from their grasp.

"The emotions of losing back-to-back games, and watching Dallas coach Barry Switzer smirk while sending out the field-goal unit in the closing seconds, pushed them over the edge.

"I remember Sean Jones collecting himself afterward, and saying, 'It's only the third game we've lost. There are a lot of teams, including Dallas (7-4), that wish they only had lost three times.' That is why the Packers were a championship team. No matter how upset they were in the heat of the battle, eventually they could step back, see the big picture and realize that things aren't never as bad as they may seem.

"Some of that came from the coaching staff, to be sure, but a majority of it came from the team leaders. In defeat, perhaps when it matters most, the Packers' leaders came shining through. They wouldn't be denied a berth in Super Bowl XXXI. It was almost as if they willed it to happen. The one thing they wanted most – other than a Super Bowl ring – was a chance to get the Dallas Cowboys up at Lambeau Field. That wouldn't happen until Nov. 23, 1997, when the Packers tore them apart, 45-17. In this case, revenge was sweet. It just took longer than the Packers had hoped – and the schedule makers would allow – to exact."

Green Bay
PACKERS 6
at
Dallas
COWBOYS 21

DATE: Monday, November 18, 1996
LOCATION: Texas Stadium, Irving Texas
ATTENDANCE: 65,032
WEATHER: Clear & 55°F

SUMMARY

This was the Packers' seventh straight loss to Dallas at Texas Stadium in the past three-plus years. It marked the team's first back-to-back losses, and while it came into the Monday night game as the NFL's top-scoring team, it left having averaged just 13 points in the two losses. The Packers' frustration peaked when the Cowboys' Chris Boniol was sent out to attempt – and then convert – an NFL-record tying seventh field goal. Reggie White went to the Cowboys' sideline and admonished Cowboys coach Barry Switzer for rubbing it in and disrespecting the Packers.

QUOTE OF THE GAME

"This will be a huge test. I think we'll be fine. We're down now, sure. This is a tough loss. But this team has had a knack of putting things behind it and moving on." – *Don Beebe, receiver*

Green Bay
PACKERS 24
at
St. Louis
RAMS 9

DATE: Sunday, November 24, 1996
LOCATION: Trans World Dome, St. Louis, MO
ATTENDANCE: 61,499
WEATHER: Indoors

GILBERT BROWN REMEMBERS

"This was the turning point of the season. It took two losses, and we were already ticked off because of the Dallas game, and now we got a chance to show people what we were made of in a Sunday night game. I was sick but it had nothing to do with Dallas. I was throwing up all night long in my hotel room the night before the game. Gabe Wilkins, my roommate, finally runs out of the room, gets our trainer, Pepper Burruss, and tells him that it sounds like I'm dying in there. Pepper did what he could for me and I finally got some sleep.

"I wake up the next morning and Fritz (Shurmur) is right in my face. He tells me that I don't look that bad to him, that he doesn't want to hear

it, and that I should grab a Snickers bar and some water and let's go. I knew I had to go, and I'm just not talking about playing in the game, if you know what I mean. It didn't matter how sick I was, and Fritz really didn't have to tell me that he needed me. I sucked it up and played because we couldn't afford a three-game losing streak, and I wasn't going to make any excuses.

"I really hated that dome in St. Louis, and the Rams started off with a 9-0 lead. It seemed bleak. Then we got a field goal right before the first half ended and as minor as that may sound it was huge to us. We knew we needed to have this game, and we needed somebody to give us a spark. We talked about it in the locker room at halftime. The field goal was nice, but we needed more. It turned out to be Doug Evans to the rescue.

"The Greyhound made the play of the game, maybe the play of the season, when he stepped in front of Tony Banks' pass and returned it 32 yards for a touchdown. The interception was vintage Fritz Shurmur. He had LeRoy fake the blitz, and he sent Eugene Robinson instead, which surprised the hell out of Banks. He hurried his throw – a slant pass to J.T. Thomas – and The Greyhound read it all the way. In a flash that awful first half was forgotten. The loss at Dallas was forgotten. The injuries and the loss at Kansas City were forgotten. We were ready to roll ahead and never look back.

"That season could have kept sliding, and sliding, and sliding, but we needed to refocus starting with St. Louis and that's what happened. We always divided the season into four quarters – four games – and this game was the final one before the season's fourth quarter. We had Chicago at home the next week, and we didn't want to risk having to play a division opponent, even at our place, with so much on the line."

CHRIS HAVEL COMMENTS

"Gilbert Brown showed why he was such a valuable member of the Packers' great defense. On the Rams' first play from scrimmage in the second half, Tony Banks handed the ball off to Lawrence Phillips, who promptly came face-to-face with The Gravedigger. Nobody has to ask how that turned out. Brown, who was taking fluid intravenously after being sick the previous night, drilled Phillips to the turf.

"It prompted safety Eugene Robinson to say, 'Talk about giving out the game ball, it should go to that guy over there (pointing to Brown). He threw the center out of the way and smacked the hell out of Phillips. I think that was the play of the game."

"Brown was a warrior in every sense. His resounding tackle set the tone for the second half, and Doug Evans' nifty and timely interception sewed it up. That was why this defense was exceptional. The players worked in concert, they did what they were told and they had the knowledge to know when to deviate if necessary. Fritz Shurmur, like many defensive coordinators, can draw up the most exotic plays in the world. But if LeRoy Butler doesn't execute the fake blitz, and Eugene Robinson doesn't hustle like crazy to get in Tony Banks' face, and Doug Evans doesn't read, read and react it is meaningless. The Evans interception is a wonderful illustration of why football is the ultimate team sport. It takes great talent to win games, but without commitment and communication all the ability in the world doesn't mean a thing."

SUMMARY

This was the springboard to Super Bowl XXXI. With their backs to the wall, the Packers were able to erase a 9-0 deficit on the road in a dome on national TV. It was ugly, especially when the Rams' Kevin Carter sacked Brett Favre for a safety, but Green Bay never blinked.

QUOTE OF THE GAME

"I read the quarterback, read the receiver and looked for the ball. It wasn't that hard. Read, read, ball: It's everything we work on in practice."
– Doug Evans, cornerback

GILBERT BROWN REMEMBERS

"After a rugged three-game stretch on the road this was our homecoming game. Lambeau Field is the best place in the world to play a football game. You've got the elements. You've got the fans that will sit outside in all the elements. You've got the players that will defend their backyard at all costs. It's like you're at a college game. After losing at Kansas City and at Dallas, and getting off to a rough start at St. Louis, we were anxious to get back on our home turf. We came into the game wanting to shut out the Bears completely. We wanted to remind everyone which team had the best defense in the league. We didn't force a single turnover, which was disappointing, but Chicago still only had 10 points going into the fourth quarter. We controlled the game.

"Offensively, Antonio (Freeman) couldn't wait to get back in the lineup. He was out four games with a broken left forearm. We missed him. We were 2-2 in that stretch. I give credit to Don Beebe and Andre Rison and Terry Mickens for stepping up, but now it was like, 'Daddy's home and he wants to recapture his throne.' Free caught 10 passes for 156 yards and it was a great game. We lost Robert Brooks earlier in the season and everyone was hoping Free would come back because we needed another weapon. Free showed what kind of player he is, and how tough he is, by playing so well with a cast on.

"Free's first catch of the game, a 14-yard completion, ended badly. The Bears' Marty Carter hit him and forced a fumble. I'm guessing some fans were thinking Free was going to be in for a long day. It turned out the Bears were the ones in for a long day. The amazing thing to me is that Free came back from a serious injury and didn't miss a beat. It's a credit to the trainers and strength coach for keeping him in such great shape. It's also a tribute to the relationship between Free and Brett. It was like Free never left. The timing was perfect on the routes, even in practice the week before the game. Free would come out of his breaks and wham! The ball was right on the money. Brett didn't worry about throwing it too hard, or taking it easy on Free. He threw it just like he always did because he knew his main man would catch it just like he always did."

CHRIS HAVEL COMMENTS

"Antonio Freeman was drafted primarily to be a punt and kick return specialist. It didn't take long for general manager Ron Wolf to realize he got much more in return. Freeman brimmed with confidence from the first day he arrived in Green Bay. When Freeman was a rookie, assistant coach Gil Haskell told me that Freeman was constantly pestering him about playing time. He wanted to be in the starting lineup, or at least have a key role in the game plan, and he never let up on Haskell. Did it bother Haskell? Hardly.

"Haskell explained how difficult it is to start in the NFL, especially as a rookie receiver in coach Mike Holmgren's offense. Haskell added, 'But if anyone could do it, Free could. He's going to be really good for a long, long time.' Haskell was right.

"Through the years, particularly toward the end of Freeman's career, we had our differences. He thought I was overly critical of him, and I thought he was too good to be getting suspended for showing up late for practice. We were both right to a degree, but I will say this: Freeman was one of the toughest, smartest and clutch receivers that I have ever seen in the NFL. He didn't take any guff from anyone. He wasn't the fastest receiver, and he wasn't the tallest, but he always seemed to find a way to make the play. He was a body catcher, but he rarely dropped a pass.

Chicago
BEARS 17
at
Green Bay
PACKERS 28

DATE: Sunday, December 1, 1996
LOCATION: Lambeau Field, Green Bay, WI
ATTENDANCE: 59,682
WEATHER: Scattered flurries & 29°F

"Freeman was well-liked in the locker room, and his chemistry with Brett Favre – like his double-move – was second to none. It was as if Freeman and Favre could read each other's mind. Freeman picked up where Robert Brooks left off. I cringe whenever I hear someone say they wonder what Brett Favre would have done if he'd had a great receiver. Actually, he had two of them. Robert Brooks and Antonio Freeman."

SUMMARY

The Bears tried to play it close to the vest and succeeded for a half. It was 7-7 going into the third quarter, but Desmond Howard's 75-yard punt return for a touchdown gave the Packers a much-needed jumpstart and Green Bay was on its way. The Bears scored a late fourth-quarter touchdown to make it 28-17 but it wasn't really that close.

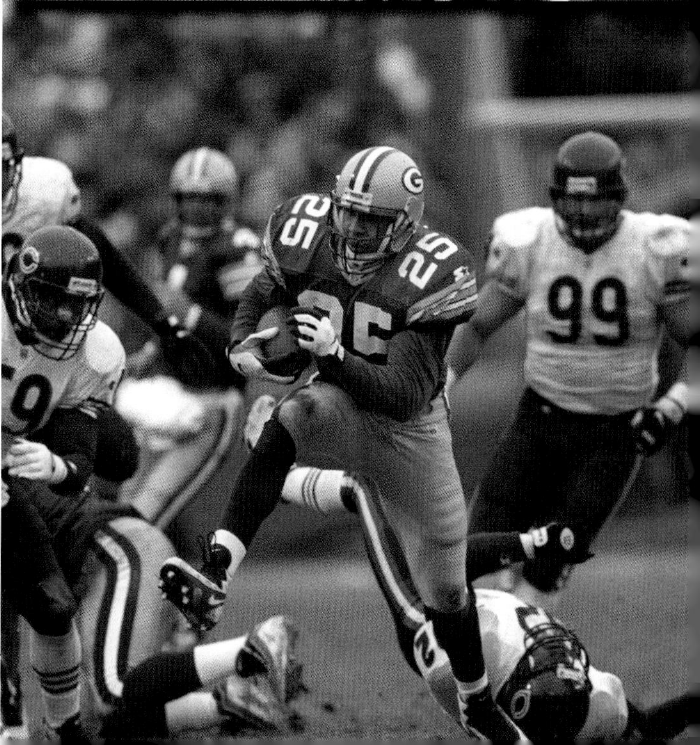

QUOTE OF THE GAME

"The Kansas City game – Mike Holmgren will tell you the same thing – is about the only game in the three years I've been here where a team played more physical than we did. The Bears executed and ran their plays, but it wasn't like they were winning the physical battle." – Sean Jones, defensive end

Denver

BRONCOS 6
at
Green Bay

PACKERS 41

DATE: Sunday, December 8, 1996
LOCATION: Lambeau Field, Green Bay, WI
ATTENDANCE: 60,712
WEATHER: Mostly cloudy, windy & 31°F

GILBERT BROWN REMEMBERS

"We didn't expect to blow out Denver, but we did expect to win. The big storyline going into the game was that John Elway wasn't going to play. He had a sore hamstring or something but we weren't listening to that stuff. We looked at it like football is football. One guy doesn't change the whole outlook of any game. We prepared as if Elway was going to play. Then, if he didn't, it was a bonus. No disrespect to Bill Musgrave, who backed him up, but he wasn't going to get it done against our defense.

"We played hard even though Elway wasn't out there because we knew they liked to throw the ball and we wanted to see how we matched up. We did our best to mow them over because they were an AFC team – and we didn't care much for the AFC – and because we wanted to let everyone know that we meant business from here on out.

"Fritz (Shurmur) was a task master. He kept riding us all week about how a really good defense would hold the Broncos – Elway or no Elway – to less than 100 yards passing. Everybody from LeRoy (Butler) to Reggie (White) to me took that as a challenge. We figured they couldn't run on us because our defensive line was so much bigger and stronger

than their offensive line, plus we were just as quick. Terrell Davis finished with something like 50 yards (actually 54) they never got that part going.

"When the game was over we got Fritz's attention and pointed to the scoreboard. We weren't pointing at the final score, 41-6. We were pointing at the total yards passing. The Broncos had just 83. All Fritz could do was smile.

"We also looked forward to seeing someone other than an NFC Central Division opponent. Back then, when there were five teams in the division, half the schedule was against teams in the division. It was rejuvenating to go up against a team that you didn't see every other week. We wanted to match up against one of the AFC's best and see how it played out. We were curious more than anything, and we were right: Elway wouldn't have made a difference. This game also clinched the NFC Central Division title. We were 11-3 and we felt good about it, but we also knew we had a bigger prize out there: Home-field advantage throughout the playoffs. We didn't want to go back to Dallas. It wasn't because we were scared of them. It was because we were sick of playing there. We also knew if we had home-field advantage we were going to the Super Bowl because nobody was going to beat us at Lambeau Field. It just wasn't gonna happen."

CHRIS HAVEL COMMENTS

"The Packers were as impressive in the locker room after the game as they were on the field during it. They had just clinched the NFC Central Division title, but they weren't celebrating as much as they were looking ahead to Detroit. They meant to have the home-field advantage throughout the playoffs and they weren't about to be derailed or denied. After an injury-plagued season the offense was beginning to hit it's stride. The Packers scored 70 second-half points in the past three games, which was more than they had scored in the preceding four games (67) combined.

"They spared coach Mike Holmgren the customary Gatorade bath, choosing instead to save it for a more appropriate time and place, such as the NFC Championship Game at Lambeau Field, or Super Bowl XXXI in New Orleans, or both.

"The Packers weren't without their problems at this stage. John Michels, the rookie left tackle, was struggling to replace the retired Ken Ruettgers. Teams weren't able to take advantage of Michels' inexperience mostly because Holmgren game-planned to help the young left tackle, and because Favre's ability to escape and make plays out of the pocket kept defenses on their heels.

"Quietly, behind the scenes, Holmgren and general manager Ron Wolf waited to see if Michels would find a groove. When that didn't happen they decided to go to Wilkerson in the regular-season finale. They knew what Wilkerson could do and they didn't want to risk losing their only viable alternative at left tackle to injury. They figured Wilkerson could get ready with one start under his belt, so that's the way they went."

SUMMARY

The Packers were in full strength and they made Denver pay for it. For the first time a month, coach Mike Holmgren had both tight ends healthy and he used a liberal dose of the "tiger" or two-tight end formation. Mark Chmura, coming back from an arch injury, caught four passes for 70 yards. Keith Jackson, his running mate, caught three passes for 20 yards and a touchdown. The dynamic duo at tight end was back in full force, and so was the Packers' top-rated offense.

QUOTE OF THE GAME

"When we went with two tight ends, especially when we were lined up on the same side, we got a lot of attention over there. We tried to throw a pass over there early and they had four guys trying to cover two. That helps out the guys on the weak side." – Keith Jackson, tight end

Game 15

GILBERT BROWN REMEMBERS

"Barry Sanders made us look bad that first game. He tore us up (20 carries for 152 yards) and we wanted to make sure it didn't happen again. We went out there with an attitude and it was like, 'Don't return to the scene of the crime.' Regardless how many times you face Barry, you better not get comfortable because that's when he'll get you. If you did something good, you better do it again. You can never relax when he's around.

"We proved that we were top dogs in the NFC Central, that we were the division champions, but we still had work to do. That's the thing people don't realize sometimes. It was mid-December, and we were a veteran team, but we still felt like we needed to improve each practice, each game, each week.

"We had 11 penalties for 75 yards that day on the road in a dome and we still overcame that. You don't want 11 penalties, ever, especially with Mike Holmgren standing on the sideline. It struck fear in guys to commit a penalty and then have to come to the sideline and look him in the face. He hated penalties. He harped on us all the time that most penalties happen because you're tired or you're not focused. I wasn't tired, and I was focused, but I might jump offside if I wasn't watching the ball. Now, I wasn't the guy to get in trouble very much, but if coach Holmgren did yell at me it was mostly about my weight. He yelled because he wanted me to know he was looking after me, and he wanted me to be able to help the team in my role. If I was a little overweight he yelled at me because I wasn't preparing myself to help the team.

"Coach Holmgren would have Earl Dotson, Paul Hutchins and me in the training room late on Thursday nights. Sometimes we would be in there until 10 o'clock, 11 o'clock, in the steam room trying to make weight for Friday morning. I don't know exactly how much weight I may have dropped, but I know I dropped $1,000 in fines every so often. It wasn't the money that scared us the most. It was letting coach Holmgren down, having to see his face and explain why we were five, six pounds overweight. When that happened he would send for me, and I would be like, 'Oh, god.' It was like the Blues Brothers. That door would open by itself and there'd be hell to pay, not to mention a fine."

QUOTE OF THE GAME

"It was a magnificent effort today. We had to control the run but also, with as many threats as they have, to stop them in the passing game. That was a magnificent effort ... on turf."
– Fritz Shurmur, Packers defensive coordinator

CHRIS HAVEL COMMENTS

"This team was thrilled after every victory but especially following a victory on the road, in a dome and against a NFC Central Division rival. The visitors' locker room was cramped inside the Pontiac Silverdome – perhaps one-third the size of the home team's locker room – but the Packers weren't in a hurry to leave. While other players would do post-game interviews at their lockers, LeRoy Butler would methodically take his time getting dressed. He was always one of the best-dressed players – nothing but suit and tie for this guy – and when the Packers won on the road he was brimming with satisfaction. After a majority of his teammates wrapped up their interviews, Butler would cinch up his tie – the telltale signal that he was now ready to talk. And talk. And talk some more. Butler's dimples, like his words, were illuminating.

"Butler was loquacious and animated. The Pro Bowl safety would point to teammates while making

Green Bay

PACKERS 31

at

Detroit

LIONS 3

DATE: Sunday, December 15, 1996
LOCATION: Silverdome, Pontiac, MI
ATTENDANCE: 73,214
WEATHER: Indoors

his point, and occasionally engage them in the interview in an effort to bring home the point. The pure joy and passion with which Butler played, and talked afterward, was magnetic. Some players felt obligated to speak with the media. Butler embraced it. Often, he would reveal insight that wasn't common knowledge. If a player was sick as a dog the night before, or a coach emphasized a point and then it proved to be critical to the outcome, Butler was the player most likely to spill the beans.

"If a reporter didn't have an especially strong story angle entering the post-game locker room session, he could figure there was a 90-percent chance they would have one if they made it a point to stop at Butler's news conference. Other players had different styles. Gilbert Brown, for instance, spoke in soft tones – almost under his breath – but he could say a lot in a few words. Wayne Simmons, like Brown, wasn't talkative but he was graphic. Simmons could give a writer that certain something that brought home to a reader the intensity of the game, often couched by the disclaimer (expletive deleted).

"Sean Jones was an extremely articulate athlete that seemed to sense exactly what the media was looking for, and sometimes before the media realized what it was looking for. Jones would draw on his experience and weave in tales of Buddy Ryan, Warren Moon or the Oilers' legendary collapse against the Bills in the 1992 AFC playoffs. Jones also had a social conscience and used his platform, his stage, to make not-so-subtle points about the world we lived in.

"While covering the '96 Packers, the post-game interviews weren't merely informative to the readers on Monday morning. They were informative to me, and I still find them fascinating a decade later. Much like the 1960's Packers, the 1996 team was replete with well-spoken, highly educated and incredibly passionate men that took their profession and all that came with it quite seriously. Then they framed it in the perfect context: Football is supposed to be fun, and few teams had as much fun as the '96 team."

SUMMARY

The Packers' first touchdown came on an electrifying 92-yard punt return by Desmond Howard. The Heisman Trophy winner from the University of Michigan relished the fact that he was able to prove he could still play. The Washington Redskins, who had return specialist Brian Mitchell, discarded Howard after the 1995 season. He went on to become the MVP of Super Bowl XXXI. Howard's ability to set up blocks, make the first would-be tackler miss, and then burst through the hole without fear were keys to his punt return success. He also was sure-handed in any type of elements.

Minnesota
VIKINGS 10
at
Green Bay
PACKERS 38

DATE: Sunday, December 22, 1996
LOCATION: Lambeau Field, Green Bay, WI
ATTENDANCE: 59,306
WEATHER: Overcast & 31°F

QUOTE OF THE GAME

"(Andre) Rison's catching the ball, our two running backs are humming and you have Desmond Howard, he's going to get you field position. People have to be a little concerned when they play the Green Bay Packers."
– Tom Lovat, offensive line coach

GILBERT BROWN REMEMBERS

"We came into this game ticked off because we had lost to the Vikings (30-21) earlier in the season. If we lost to them at Lambeau Field it would have crushed us. We wanted to prove to the Vikings, and to ourselves, that we were the best team in the NFC Central. We had the better record (12-3 coming into the game) but if they had swept us home and away, they could have said, 'Yeah, but we got you twice.' We weren't going to let that happen. We were the division champions, and that made our season sweeter, but the next-best thing was sending the Vikings' butts home so they could watch us on TV. There was another bonus, too. We got the bye week because we had home-field advantage throughout the playoffs.

"I had personal reasons for wanting to destroy the Vikings. Cris Carter tormented me when I was a rookie in Minnesota. It was good to see him walk off the field a loser. When I was a rookie he hazed me to death. He would stand up at dinner during training camp and look around the dining hall and say, 'Let's see. What rookie should sing for his supper?' And then he would point at me, tell me to get up and make me sing. It was always me that they made sing and I began to hate having to walk into that dining hall. Here I was a grown man trying to make it in my profession and I had to deal with this foolishness. I was shy so that made it even worse. There were times I couldn't concentrate during two-a-days because I was so upset about the hazing.

"Now, as a member of the Packers, I had my revenge. I'm not a vengeful guy and anyone that knows me will agree. But what Cris Carter did to me, and (Vikings coach) Denny Green allowed to happen, hurt my pride and hurt my chances to make the team. That isn't right. Cris Carter never said a word to me on or off the field until after we won Super Bowl XXXI. I don't remember what I said to him but it wasn't much. For years, if I saw him I would go the other way. I didn't even want to speak to his ass. I can get past that now because it was all growing pains, but it bothers me that Cris Carter and Denny Green never apologized, never said they were sorry, and I don't think ever even realized the hurt that they were putting on a guy that was supposed to be a teammate, a player and a friend."

CHRIS HAVEL COMMENTS

"The Packers dominated the Vikings from start to finish in a game that reasserted their dominance and reaffirmed Green Bay as the odds-on favorite to win the NFC Championship. The fans at Lambeau Field celebrated like I'd never seen them celebrate. I think a great deal of that was because their team had home-field advantage. They didn't want to let go of the 1996 season. The only fitting farewell, and acceptable sendoff, would be the one that sent the Packers – and a lot of their fans – to New Orleans.

"The Vikings were trash-talking the Packers at the start, and cornerback Corey Fuller took it to a new low when he eye-gouged Packers center Frankie Winters at the bottom of a pile. Winters' vision was blurry for several days, and his eye was swollen and bloodshot. Winters said he was glad he didn't suffer permanent damage to the eye. Before the game, ex-Packers linebacker Jeff Brady said he was going head hunting. Brady's big talk didn't amount to much because he was too busy taking a pounding from Packers fullback William Henderson.

"LeRoy Butler, a player that can dish it out as well as take it, didn't have much to say to the Vikings on the field. He was enjoying their destruction with quiet satisfaction. When he did speak to them, he offered a sarcastic suggestion: "I told them to look at the scoreboard." Enough said."

SUMMARY

The Packers' defense, which held the team together while the offense fought through numerous injuries to its receiving corps, was at its very best. The offense, finally healthy, churned out its best performance of the season. Edgar Bennett rushed for 109 yards to become the first 100-yard ball carrier of the season. The Packers rushed for a season-high 233 yards, their best single-game performance since they rushed for 257 yards against Chicago in 1994. Desmond Howard returned four punts that included runbacks of 47 and 25 yards, and his lone kick return went for 40 yards.

GILBERT BROWN REMEMBERS

"The Mud Bowl. That was the most fun I have ever had playing in a game. It was like we just got out of school, it's recess, and the teacher said, 'Go have fun.' So that's what we did. We had San Francisco's number for a long time. I think we beat them mentally and physically. My college roommate, Dana Stubblefield, was a really good defensive tackle with the 49ers. When they were winning Super Bowls he would show off his ring and tell me that San Francisco was the greatest, just to rub it in.

"Now it was my turn. We called each other whenever the Packers and 49ers played, and once we got the upper hand, I would make a point to tell him, 'Adam Timmerman told me to tell you that he's going to kick your ass.' That would get Dana fired up, but I think it worried him, too. Timmerman was handling him and he knew it. Adam Timmerman's nickname was The Brawler, like a pro wrestler, and he was whooping Dana's ass up and down the field.

"I love Dana Stubblefield to death. We had a lot of good times at Kansas. But when the 49ers won the Super Bowl, and you'd try to talk to him, he was Mr. High Heaven. Then when we won the Super Bowl and got our Super Bowl ring, I tried to be Mr. High Heaven back to him but I couldn't do it. It just didn't feel right. I'd start laughing or joking about the good times we had and we'd end up reminiscing.

"The reason I told Dana that stuff about Timmerman was to gain an edge. Adam Timmerman was my go-to-guy to get inside Dana's head. I knew what kind of player Dana was – a damn good one – and I didn't want him to get loose on us because he could cause a lot of trouble for an offense. I would call Dana and say, 'Hey, let's get together when you come to Green Bay. I'd love to see you. And oh, by the way, Adam Timmerman says he's going to whip your ass.' Dana would say, 'We'll see.'

"Another guy that got inside the 49ers' heads was Desmond Howard, Mr. Michigan, the Heisman Trophy winner. He was the spark that we needed and you could tell the 49ers just hated having to kick it to him. That year our offense didn't begin when Brett and Edgar and the guys took the field. It began when Desmond dropped back to field the punt. He was always good for at least 10 yards, which got our offense one first down closer to the goal line, and he was so sure-handed it was sick. The weather could be downright awful and Desmond would just drop back, smile and catch it like it was 80 degrees and sunny. No big deal. Then he'd make a guy miss, all the while keeping his eyes on what was happening up field with the blocking, and he'd pick his hole and go. He was Mr. Excitement, Mr. Spark, and whenever there was a lull he'd make a big play.

"Desmond Howard reminds me of Kansas City's Dante Hall, who is a great return man but not as great as Desmond for one reason: Desmond helped us win a championship."

CHRIS HAVEL COMMENTS

"The Packers' 17th straight win at Lambeau Field possessed all the elements, including the elements, that make Green Bay one of the National Football League's most storied franchises. The San Francisco 49ers were the perfect foil in this drama.

San Francisco
49ERS 14
at
Green Bay
PACKERS 35

DATE: Saturday, January 4, 1997
LOCATION: Lambeau Field, Green Bay, WI
ATTENDANCE: 60,787
WEATHER: Rain & 34°F

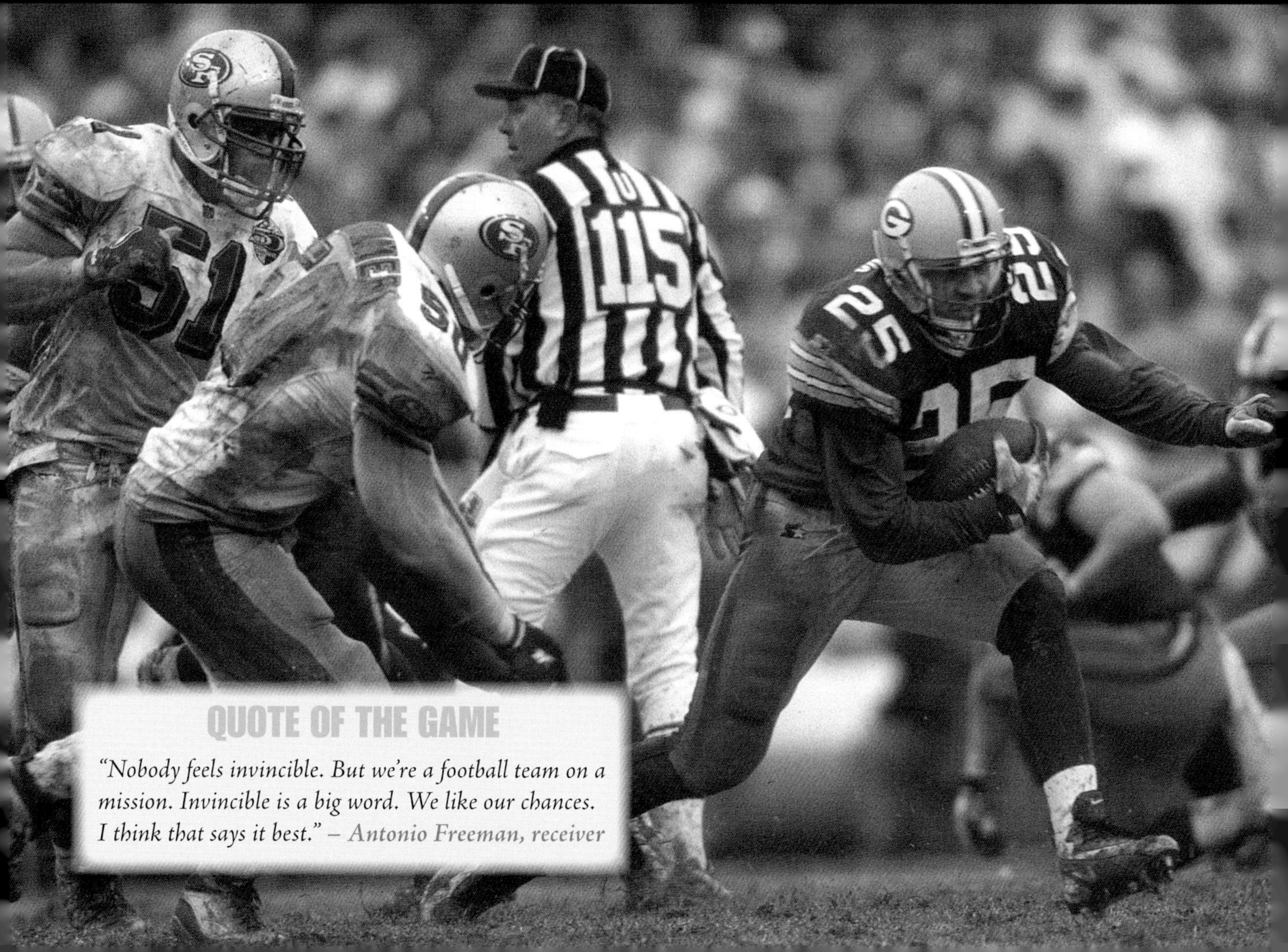

QUOTE OF THE GAME

"Nobody feels invincible. But we're a football team on a mission. Invincible is a big word. We like our chances. I think that says it best." – Antonio Freeman, receiver

They were West Coast cool, a team whose best days were behind it, but whose greatness was recent enough to make the Packers' conquest all the sweeter.

"Packers coach Mike Holmgren had gone from being the 49ers offensive coordinator to being the captain of his own ship. Brett Favre had played in the shadows of Steve Young, who once snubbed him at the NFL's Quarterback Challenge, but the tide had turned. Reggie White could have gone to San Francisco, a team with a rich tradition and a wealthy owner, but instead chose Green Bay and the Midwest. White could have accentuated the 49ers' greatness, and prolonged it, but instead charted his own course. The path of least resistance lost out to White's desire to blaze his own trail.

"What began in the 1995 NFC Divisional Playoffs – a 27-17 victory by Green Bay over San Francisco – ended in the 1996 NFC Divisional Playoffs with the Packers' rout of the 49ers. The torch was passed. Green Bay had replaced San Francisco as top dog. The one-year transformation was staggering. The Packers had pulled off an upset in San Francisco in 1995. Now, their victory over the 49ers was no surprise at all.

"The country's fascination with Green Bay, and its Packers, soared like it hadn't since the 1960s. Green Bay's charm captivated the nation. Its colloquialisms made it smile. Its self-effacing personality, coupled with its grinding blue-collar work ethic, led the national media to tell one homespun story upon another. To outsiders, Green Bay's shot-and-beer persona with its Friday fish fries, frigid temperatures and fun-loving folk was a slice of football nirvana. To Green Bay, it was everyday life."

SUMMARY

The 49ers' Steve Young tried to play despite extremely sore ribs. He lasted long enough to complete two of five passes for 8 yards before giving way to Elvis Grbac. On a blustery, rainy day – many say it is the coldest game they ever played in or sat through – the 49ers didn't have a chance. Grbac completed just 19 of 36 passes for 125 yards with three interceptions. Meantime, the Packers' two-headed monster of Edgar Bennett and Dorsey Levens combined to rush for 126 yards in 32 carries. The Packers committed just one penalty for 5 yards, and although they fumbled five times, the 49ers recovered just one.

Carolina
PANTHERS 13
at
Green Bay
PACKERS 30

DATE: January 12, 1997
LOCATION: Lambeau Field, Green Bay, WI
ATTENDANCE: 60,216
WEATHER: Cold & 3°F

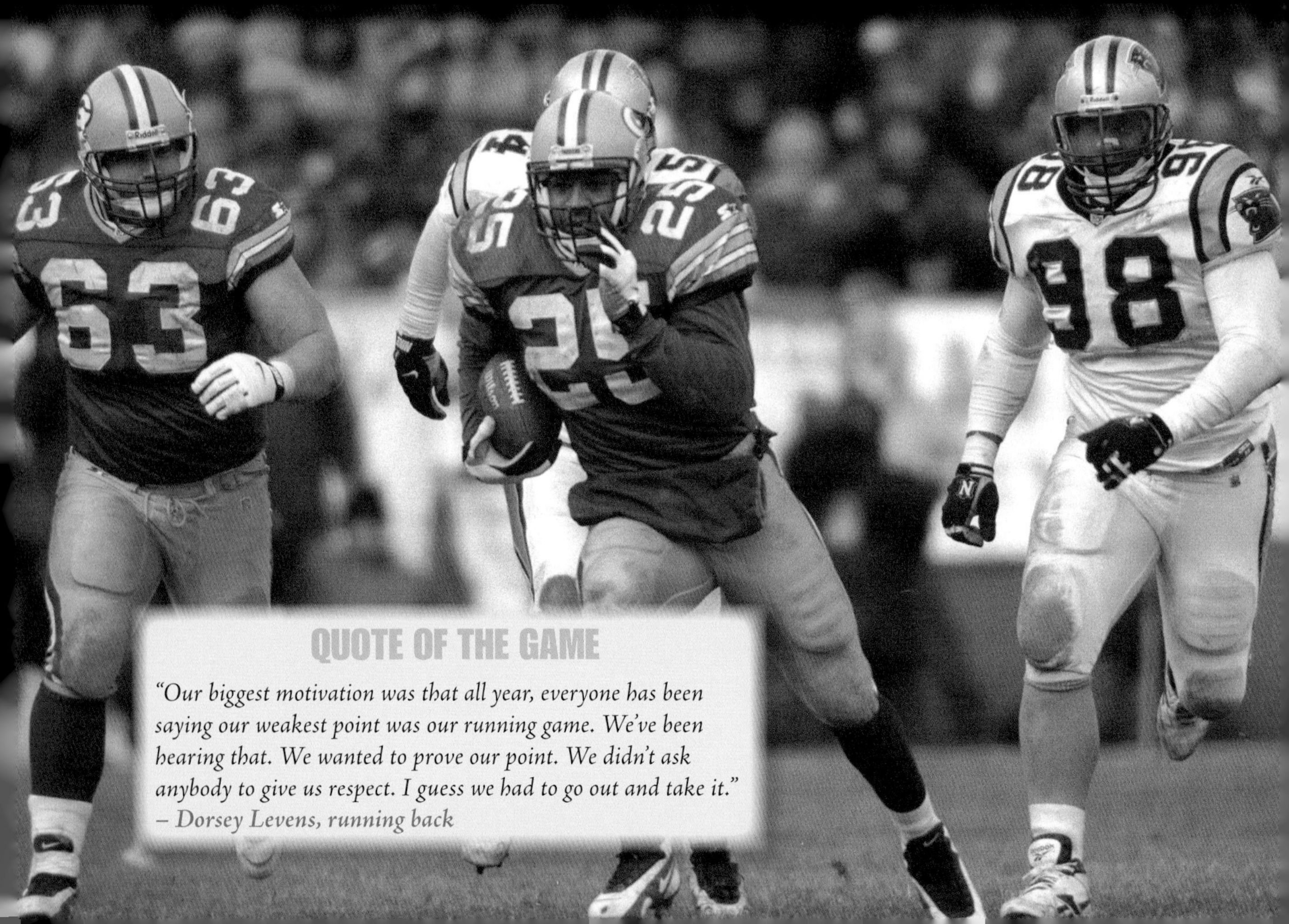

QUOTE OF THE GAME

"Our biggest motivation was that all year, everyone has been saying our weakest point was our running game. We've been hearing that. We wanted to prove our point. We didn't ask anybody to give us respect. I guess we had to go out and take it."
– Dorsey Levens, running back

GILBERT BROWN REMEMBERS

"We could hear the Carolina Panthers trying to psyche themselves up during warm-ups. Their players would be saying things like, 'Oh, it's not that cold.' When I hear guys saying that, I know that deep inside they're really thinking it's cold as hell. We knew anybody coming to Green Bay in January was going to feel it. That's why we worked so hard all season to get home-field advantage. Us? We were immune to the cold. We would purposely step on players' toes because we knew it hurt. We didn't try to pretend it wasn't cold. We knew it was cold, and we used it to our advantage.

"Coming into the game, we knew Carolina had a great defense. The Panthers had an NFL-best 60 sacks that year, and guys like Kevin Greene had a reputation for being tough and getting the job done no matter what. Well, we had tough guys, too. We had Reggie White and Santana Dotson and Wayne Simmons and LeRoy Butler. We weren't going to take a backseat to anybody. The Panthers had a very good defense, but the best defense showed up that day.

"When the game ended, I just sat back and watched like I always do. I saw Reggie White's excitement, and joy, and relief that he was finally going to The Big Dance. I didn't understand it at the time because I hadn't gone through all the years of trying like he had, but 10 years later I understand. While I was watching Reggie I was telling myself that this is why you play football, and I was happy that he was happy.

"I looked at Fritz (Shurmur), a guy that put his heart and his soul into whatever he did, and to see him so happy and going around hugging players was a thrill. The first guy that Fritz went to was LeRoy, that's the first guy he hugged, and it might've made me jealous except Fritz always let the defensive line know that we were first all the time. Watching Fritz and LeRoy hug and share tears of joy was like seeing your Dad and your older brother sharing something special. That was the first time, the only time, I saw Fritz cry. I tried to fight back my own tears but I couldn't do it.

"I looked around the locker room and I saw Keith Jackson and Don Beebe and Andre Rison – guys that never got a shot, or wanted one more shot – and it was like a Who's Who of the NFL. They were hugging and crying and having such a good time. I remember Reggie going around the whole stadium to shake hands with the fans to hug the fans, and the rest of us were right behind him to do the same. That was cool.

"It's been 10 years but I still get emotional just talking about it. I've always been sort of tenderhearted but that doesn't mean I'm weak. It means I cared so much for all those guys in that locker room, and for the coaches, that it just hits home. Those memories and the feelings I still have are as real as it gets."

"Green Bay, I hope you're proud of us, because we're proud of you"

-Reggie White, defensive end

CHRIS HAVEL COMMENTS

"Lost in the Packers' delightful dominance of Carolina was the fact that the Panthers actually led, 7-0, when Kerry Collins hit Howard Griffith for a 3-yard touchdown pass. It came after a Brett Favre interception deep in Green Bay territory. The amazing thing is that nobody really seemed too concerned. The Panthers scored to take the lead, and the Packers went back to work as if nothing happened.

"It says a lot about coach Mike Holmgren's steadying influence, and Favre's ability to persevere and stick with it, and the defense's unflinching confidence. The defense gave up that early touchdown, but when Carolina drove deep into Packers territory in the second quarter, Green Bay's defense made a terrific goal line stand. It sucked the life out of the Panthers, and it energized the Lambeau Field crowd.

"The image of Favre's chest pass to Dorsey Levens, while the Panthers' Kevin Greene was trying to drag down the quarterback, remains vivid. So does the image of Levens' 29-yard touchdown catch in the back of the end zone. Levens, a sensational athlete, outmaneuvered Panthers cornerback Eric Davis on the play. In the third quarter, Levens turned a well-timed and well-executed screen against a Panthers blitz into a 66-yard catch-and-run that set up the decisive touchdown. The Packers capped the drive with Edgar Bennett's 4-yard blast off tackle to make it 27-13. In a single, overpowering drive, Carolina went from being one play away to tie the game, to being two touchdowns behind and having no realistic chance to come back.

"The post-game celebration remains the most electrifying scene I have ever witnessed at a sporting event. The columnist in me tried to soak in every word, every detail, every moment, while the small-town boy from Adams-Friendship, Wisconsin, that grew up as a Packers fan felt wave after wave of pure bliss. After so many seasons, and so many Sundays, of watching my Packers lose, the team that I was being paid to cover for a living, the Green Bay Packers, were going to the Super Bowl.

"It doesn't get any better than that."

"This is an unbelievable setting. If this doesn't move an individual, nothing will. To witness all that happened, particularly after the game ... The crowd stayed and the crowd cheered and the crowd has always given us magnificent support."
– Ron Wolf, general manager

SUMMARY

Brett Favre's day began about as awful as imaginable. He completed just three of his first nine passes, including an interception that set up Carolina's offense for the game's first touchdown. Favre was unfazed. After all he had been through in regards to being treated for an addiction to painkillers, this was far from insurmountable. Favre went on to complete 16 of his final 20 passes to finish with 292 yards and two touchdowns. Favre proved why he was the NFL's Most Valuable Player, and why GM Ron Wolf and coach Mike Holmgren stuck with him through good times and bad. Now, he was getting a chance to go home – New Orleans was just 60 miles from Kiln, Mississippi – and he was going to make good on his promise to win Super Bowl XXXI.

New England

PATRIOTS 21

VS

Green Bay

PACKERS 35

DATE: Sunday, January 26, 1997
LOCATION: Louisiana Superdome, New Orleans
ATTENDANCE: 72,301
WEATHER: Indoors

QUOTE OF THE GAME

"There's an old saying that the cream always rises to the top. I was just another strong link in this very, very strong chain. You have such talent on this team, you just want to contribute." – Desmond Howard, Packers return specialist and Super Bowl XXXI Most Valuable Player

GILBERT BROWN REMEMBERS

"It was a blur.

"That's the only way I can describe the time between the pre-game warm-ups and the pre-game introductions. I remember putting my uniform on, going out onto the field to warm up, and walking back to the locker room. The rest is a blank.

"I don't remember Mike's speech. I don't remember if any other players said a few words. I don't remember if I stood or sat at my locker. I don't remember if I prayed, or if I tried to pray but couldn't remember the words.

"I vaguely remember filing out of the locker room, and slowly making my way down the hallway toward the tunnel, and thinking, "It's OK."

"Our defense was going to be introduced and we had a routine, except there was nothing routine about playing in the Super Bowl. Our routine was always Sean Jones first, then me, then Santana Dotson, then Reggie, and then the rest of the defense. I'm walking behind Sean and all I can see his jersey number and it's cool until we reach a point where the tunnel opens onto the field. Suddenly, all I can think is, 'Wow!'

"I see the crowd, but I don't see Sean anymore even though he's in front of me. All I see is cameras and fans and lights and smoke, and I'm thinking what the hell am I doing here? Then I'm thinking that I've got to play. I've got to back it up. I've got to do what I've got to do because I have to pull my end, and that was just so we could all come through the line and get the game started on time.

"It seemed like it took forever. It was in slow motion. Then the PA announcer said, "Number ninety-six, Sean Jones!" I was already crying by that time. I didn't know I was crying until I looked down and saw the tears. I'm thinking this is no way for a grown man to act in front of 70,000 fans and a worldwide TV audience. I still don't know how I got out there, but I'm guessing Santana got tired of waiting and gave me a shove.

"When everyone was introduced we huddled up, looked at each other and waited until Big Dog came in and said, "Dominate." It was time to go.

"Just about everyone predicted we would win, and we did, but by no means was it easy. When it was time for the coin flip everybody wanted to be out there on that first snap. I don't mean the Packers' offense and the Patriots' offense. I mean everybody.

"The coin's in the air and my guys are saying, 'Defense first, defense first,' and Brett's saying, 'Offense first, offense first, c'mon, c'mon, c'mon.'

"The Patriots won the toss, which meant our defense won the coin flip. By now I was like a glass of water boiling over. It's like you've got a powerful headache, and then you get that first hit and 'Bam!' it's like swallowing a magic pill, and it feels so good.

"We did our job. We got the ball back for our offense. They took it from there. Brett hit Andre Rison for a 54-yard touchdown on the second play, an audible of all things, and there was never a doubt in my mind whether we were going to win. We had so many weapons. We had so much confidence.

"When our offense scored we turned to each other and said, 'Now it's our turn.'

"We had the number one defense in the National Football League. We felt that people feared us. We knew offensive linemen feared us. We knew it because when we would break that huddle, and we were standing there waiting on them, the offensive linemen would turn and be like, "Oh, brother."

"They couldn't see my face because I've got my shield on, but I could see theirs and I had a pretty good idea what they were thinking: Damn, we cannot move these dudes. They turn around and look at me, and Santana who is six-foot-five, and Reggie White who is, well, Reggie White, and then they see Sean Jones' tall ass. They're thinking: They didn't look that big on the tape."

"That isn't to say New England couldn't play. That offensive line worked its ass off trying to keep us off Curtis Martin's back and out of Drew Bledsoe's face. Like I said, it wasn't going to be easy and we knew it. Our defensive line looked bigger on the field than we did on the tape, but that works both ways. Keith Byars was a lot faster than we thought and Ben Coates, their tight end, was pretty damn good, too.

"The Patriots double-teamed me on early downs, which I expected and actually looked forward to. I've got 600 pounds, give or take, of offensive linemen leaning on me. I love that. I love getting into that contact. When I'm getting that type of attention, and I'm hearing guys struggling and grunting and groaning while they're trying to move me, and they can't do it, that makes me go even harder. I've got two grown men trying to push me out of there and they can't do it.

"That was my role. I knew it and I loved it. I wasn't the only one. Each of our guys knew what was expected and what they had to do to get it done. We had a tough defensive line, athletic linebackers and a couple of really smart safeties.

"When Eugene Robinson told you something, you knew that he knew what he was talking about. You didn't ask questions. You just did it. When you see that guy in the film room studying all the time, and he tells you to do something on the field, if you don't you're dumb as hell. We didn't have any dummies.

"LeRoy Butler was our other safety. Eugene put us in position to make plays and LeRoy usually was the one that made them. Offenses spent the better part of their practice time trying to figure out how to stop The Butler. It didn't matter.

"The Patriots tried to work their tight ends in the passing game, and they tried to get Curtis Martin loose in the running game, but it didn't amount to much. New England actually led, 14-10, after the first quarter but nobody was panicking. Reggie made it a point between quarters to let us know it was time to get serious. We shut out the Patriots in the second quarter and led 27-14 at halftime.

"New England kept coming at us, though, which I would expect of a Bill Parcells team. But Desmond Howard was slicing them up with kick and punt returns, and our defense was too talented and too disciplined to let this game get away. We were up by two touchdowns going into the fourth quarter, and Big Dog decided it was time to seal the deal. Reggie had three sacks to set a Super Bowl record, two of which came in the fourth quarter when the Patriots never crossed midfield.

"You could tell there was no stopping him. He knew that he had to shut the game down. He knew he had to turn it up or he wasn't winning the game. Big Dog took over. I'm still amazed today because the game was there and somebody had to close it out. No problem. He was like an executioner with a guillotine and he pulled the lever. Lights out.

"We had the NFL's top-ranked defense and everyone took pride in it. Our reward was to know it made Fritz happy. Fritz told us he was going to get everybody a football because we were the No. 1-rated defense. I still have that football in my case and it's the best memento I could ever want. It's great to know we made it through some really good teams – teams like New England – and that we won Super Bowl XXXI.

"But it's extra-special because we were the league's best defense."

CHRIS HAVEL COMMENTS

"The Green Bay Packers hadn't been to a Super Bowl in 29 years. I hadn't been to one at all. Imagine the thrill for this Wisconsin native and Packers fan, born and bred, to be covering the Packers in Super Bowl XXXI. Many a sports writer lists the event among their career highlights. In January of 1997 I discovered why.

"I spent 10 days in New Orleans leading up to kickoff. By day, I wrote a sports column on behalf of the Green Bay Press-Gazette and Gannett News Service. By night, I pondered the next day's column topic while getting acquainted with The Big Easy.

"I wrote about a voodoo shop, a cemetery that was situated above ground and below sea level, and a creepy mansion owned by horror novelist Ann

> *"I look at the faces of my players and my coaches and ownership in the locker room and I'm humbled by that, overwhelmed by it. There is a great sense of accomplishment. I'm so happy for these guys. They've worked so very, very hard for this." – Mike Holmgren, Head coach*

"A lot of guys questioned our heart and our ability, so it's good to finally win this game and shut a lot of people up. We're not flashy. We're not flamboyant. But we won it. And the rest of them were sitting home." – Sean Jones, defensive end

"I think maybe I added some confidence. I think it might've been stripped some because of (the Packers') losses to Kansas City and Dallas, but Green Bay knew it was getting a bona fide receiver. To the rest of the world I wasn't a bona fide receiver. But to the Packers I was, and I'd like to take my hat off to them for giving me a chance to become Andre Rison again, but this time it's Andre Rison as a better person." – Andre Rison, Packers receiver

Rice (at least I think that's what the cab driver was asserting in his native Cajun). After four days, I was lacking in sleep but overflowing with material. It was a sportswriter's nirvana.

"New Orleans is the perfect site to accommodate a Super Bowl.

"The ancillary venues, and that includes the watering holes along Bourbon Street, are within walking distance of one another. Rue Bourbon was colorfully adorned like the thousands of football fans – many of whom were equally lit – that partied day and-or night. The steamy, seductive street sported a fresh coat of paint for the occasion: It was Patriots blue-and-red up one side and Packers green-and-gold down the other.

"Super Bowl XXXI possessed as much charm as its site. The Packers played the rare role of heavily favored underdog. The Patriots played the perfect foil. The storylines were compelling and the game was equally so.

"The coaching match-up featuring New England's Bill Parcells and Green Bay's Mike Holmgren was a keen contrast in styles. Parcells was old school all the way. He had earned his stripes with the New York Giants and he had been there before. He also was embroiled in a battle of wills with Patriots owner Robert Kraft, and the east coast media made sure it stayed in the headlines. Holmgren was a disciple of Bill Walsh and the "West Coast" offense. His ties to the San Francisco 49ers drew attention, but it was his masterful handling of MVP quarterback Brett Favre and the offense – coupled with a terrific defense and an unwavering attention to special teams – that won games.

"Favre and Patriots quarterback Drew Bledsoe couldn't have been more different. Bledsoe was a former top draft pick with immense talent and expectations to match. Favre was the wild-eyed Southern boy, a gunslinger that could tame any NFL defense with a flick of his wrist, and a quarterback that played with a linebacker's mentality.

"Favre was out to prove that he could defeat the Patriots, and that he had won a stalemate in his fight to overcome an addiction to painkillers. He also wanted to help Reggie White, his good friend and teammate, succeed in his quest for a Super Bowl ring.

"Other subplots swirled.

"Could White and the Packers' No. 1-rated defense suffocate the Patriots' offense? Would Favre stand up under the pressure of New England's defense and New Orleans' proximity to his hometown of Kiln, Mississippi? How would NFL castoffs such as receiver Andre Rison and return specialist Desmond Howard perform in the spotlight? How would left tackle Bruce Wilkerson, the reliable relic, hold up against the Patriots' pass rush? Could the Patriots' interior offensive line block Santana Dotson and Gilbert Brown? Would talented veterans such as tight end Keith Jackson and defensive end Sean Jones bask in sweet Super Bowl success at day's end? Could safety LeRoy Butler and receiver Antonio Freeman finally make a national TV audience realize just how immensely talented they were?

"What of small-market Green Bay? Could it succeed in conquering the NFL, especially in the era of free agency and salary caps? Would general manager Ron Wolf's gutsy personnel decisions reap a football scout's ultimate lifetime achievement award?

"The suspense built to a crescendo inside the Louisiana Superdome, and Super Bowl XXXI maintained it throughout one of the most riveting games in its history.

"The Packers scored first. The Patriots answered to take the lead. The Packers responded with a barrage of big plays. Howard, the diminutive return demon, gave Green Bay the lead for good on a 99-yard kickoff return. White, the Minister of Defense, sealed the deal by hurrying, harassing and sacking Bledsoe in the final quarter.

"Packers 35, Patriots 21."

"The most intriguing question of all – could the Packers regain their place as world champions – was answered with a resounding yes. The Vincent T. Lombardi Trophy was coming home courtesy of the 1996 Green Bay Packers.

"What a story it would make, and what a thrill to tell it."

SUPER BOWL XXXI SUMMARY

It took the Packers 29 years to return the Vincent T. Lombardi Trophy to its rightful owner. It was worth the wait. The Packers' high-powered offense struck pay dirt on its first series when NFL Most Valuable Player Brett Favre called an audible on the second play from scrimmage, faked a handoff and threw a 54-yard touchdown pass to Andre Rison. Favre later connected with Antonio Freeman for a then-Super Bowl record 81-yard touchdown pass to give Green Bay a 17-14 lead and the Packers never trailed.

Green Bay's top-ranked defense registered five sacks of New England quarterback Drew Bledsoe, including three sacks by Reggie White to set a Super Bowl record. The Packers' Doug Evans intercepted a Bledsoe pass to set up one Green Bay field goal, and the defense swarmed 1,000-yard rusher Curtis Martin while limiting him to just 42 yards rushing on 11 attempts.

The Packers opened a 35-21 lead when Desmond Howard returned a kickoff 99 yards for a touchdown late in the third quarter, and the Patriots never threatened. In fact, the Patriots failed to cross midfield in a scoreless fourth quarter.

Super Bowl XXXI was a perfect example of a NFL team having each of the three phases (offense, defense and special teams) working in concert and feeding off each other. The offense got the Packers an early lead with the big play to Rison, and it retook the lead with the big play to Freeman. The special teams units didn't surrender any big plays, and broke open the game with Howard's big kick return. The defense set up the offense with excellent field position and didn't allow New England to rally in the fourth quarter. That's the way the Packers won Super Bowl XXXI: All for one, and one for all.

"There are no individuals on this team. It feels good to be on a team that works toward the same goals. To be with guys who are unselfish. This is probably the first team that I've been on where you actually enjoyed coming to work each day."
– Reggie White, defensive end

"After 43 years, and that's a pretty long time, this moment is the highlight, but it's hard to describe. I'd search for the words, but I don't think I'd do it justice."
– Fritz Shurmur, defensive coordinator

"I think the Packers' weapons now in the 19th week of the season speak for themselves. The have the highest-scoring offense in the league. It's usually done with weapons, so they don't need me to speak for them. I think they've made their own statement here this month." – *Al Groh, Patriots defensive coordinator*

THE GRAVEDIGGER

THE GILBERT BROWN STORY

CHAPTER ONE

"GROWING UP GILBERT"

Most nights, mama and me would sit on the front porch until it was dark.

While everybody else was sitting in the back yard, I would go around to the front and sit next to mama, and we would talk about all kinds of different things. Sometimes we just sat there and didn't talk much at all. It didn't matter. I guess I liked being near her because no matter how good or how bad my day went she always made me feel better.

OK. I admit it. I am the biggest mama's boy there's ever been. It's been like that ever since I can remember, and I wouldn't have it any other way.

There was one evening when I was probably 13 that I told her, "Mama, you know what? One day I'm going to buy you this big house and I'm going to buy you a nice car. I'm going to play pro football. What do you think of that?"

Mama just smiled and said, "OK, son. I can't wait 'til that day comes."

I know in the back of her mind she was thinking, "Yeah, right, whatever. That's nice, but it's probably not going to happen."

Nobody believed me. I couldn't say that I blamed them.

I was 13 and I hadn't played football yet, and I really didn't even like football. But I was dead serious. I was going to play pro football. That night when I told my momma, I made up my mind. I was going to make it happen.

To this day I tell mama, "Remember that night when we were sitting on the porch and I told you that?" She just smiles. She remembers. Looking back, I still don't know how I did it, but I did it. I became a pro football player. I got to play for the Green Bay Packers, and what's more, I got to help them win Super Bowl XXXI.

You should have seen mama's face the day I gave her the keys to her new house. She lit up like a Christmas tree and then she began to cry. It was tears of joy. Then I started to get emotional, too. That's just the way I am. I've always been big, and people say I have a big heart, too. I guess I do have a big old soft spot. The funny thing is when I stepped onto the football field, or whenever anyone messed with my family or me, that big old soft spot disappeared real fast. Then I would become a big old bad guy.

That's not something I'm necessarily proud of. It's called survival. You will understand it better when you hear where I came from, what it was like for me as a kid and how I grew up while living on Detroit's west side.

When I was 12, 13, 14, all I wanted to do was sit by my mama, eat whatever we had to eat in the house and play basketball. I didn't want to play football. There was too much running around and the coaches made you do all kinds of crazy stuff out there.

I admit it. I was kind of like a punk.

I grew up at Griggs and Schoolcraft. That was the busiest intersection there was closest to my house, and that was the name of our neighborhood.

It had another name, too. Cambodia.

It was a rough area – inner-city Detroit all the way – and times were tough. We didn't have much to eat and we never had any money. At least it seemed like we never had any money, and we knew better than to ask for something if we didn't work to get.

It was tight. I would go to school and I would bet the guys that I had one hundred and ninety-two ways to eat bologna. That was one of the main course meals. It was bologna because it was so cheap. It forced mama to be creative. We would have bologna fried, baked, boiled, with one piece of bread, with two pieces of bread, with mayonnaise, with mustard, with catsup, with cheese if we were lucky.

That's how it was, man.

It wasn't easy for my mom and dad. If we got fried chicken, mom would have to cook four chickens so we'd have enough to go around. She would cut them up and try to make every little bit count. Growing up I wasn't going to eat just three pieces of chicken. When we had chicken I wanted to enjoy it, and the rule was if you weren't there when it hit the table, then you went hungry.

I never knew people eat chicken backs – there's no meat – until I got old enough to know sometimes you take what you get. My brother Carlos was so slow getting to the table that's all he got to eat. He'd have two or three chicken backs for dinner. After a while, Carlos started to like chicken backs, and I'm thinking to myself that he's the only person in the world that likes chicken backs. I'm not even sure there's such a word as chicken backs.

But after mama cut up the chicken, she'd slice off the back and cook that up, too. That's all my little brother got. I'd say, "Go ahead, you chicken-back eater." He'd just laugh and sit there and smile and eat his chicken backs.

The thing we did have a lot of was the most important thing of all.

We had a lot of love in that house.

Of course a lot of that came from my mama, Mrs. Ann Brown, the best mom a son could ever ask for. She was sweet and sort of quiet but you didn't want to cross her. She had rules, and she was strict, and if you didn't follow them you were in trouble. Of course, she did it for our own good. She had seen too many children hurt because they didn't listen to their parents, or because they really didn't have parents at all.

We had mama to look after us kids, and we had dad to look after us all.

My dad was LeRoy Brown, Jr. He was bad, bad LeRoy Brown, the baddest man in the whole damn town. He was a big man, and a strong man, and his weight fluctuated between 240 and 270. Once it got up to 300 pounds. He wasn't tall. Maybe five-foot ten, but he was tough inside and out.

Dad was around most of the time, and he was always around on holidays or when mama needed him or if it was one our birthdays. He worked in an auto assembly factory for Chrysler, and he did odd jobs, too. He loved his cars, and he loved working on them with my uncle. That's where I get my love of cars, and every time I think about cars or see a certain make and model, I think of him. My dad wasn't perfect. Nobody is. But I always knew he loved us and he was there for us when mama needed him.

The details don't matter. All that matters is he did the best he could.

Dad managed a gas station for a while that wasn't far from our house.

Mama helped him at the gas station once in a while. She also did cleaning for people in their homes, and she did cleaning in office buildings in her spare time. Most of the time she was at home raising us kids and trying to keep us out of trouble.

That alone was a full-time job.

Mama wouldn't let us go anywhere in the neighborhood after dark. We couldn't set foot out of the yard. I love her for being that strict. I didn't understand it at the time, but it makes sense now. If she could keep an eye on us, she knew we were safe and she didn't have to worry. I thank her for that. If we came home from school we had to stay in the yard. We had to ask wherever we went. We couldn't even go in the streets. It was taboo and I didn't like it.

Now I'm glad. So are my brothers and sisters.

I have an older brother, LeRoy III, who was a tough character. He played football and he didn't take any crap. He was two years ahead of me in school. Everybody knew him, and most everybody liked him. Nobody wanted to get on his bad side.

I also have a brother, Carlos, and a sister, Carla, who are four years younger than me. They are twins, even though they don't look like it. Carlos was a very good athlete, too, and real smart. He was no pushover, either. He's just friendly by nature like me. Carla was an excellent basketball player. She played with the boys since she was little, and I was always proud of how good she could play, not that I ever told her.

Then there is Joann. She is the baby. Joann is six years younger than me, and she was the family news reporter, which means she was the tattletale. Everything we did, every time we set one foot out of the yard after dark, Joann would run and tell mama.

I had my own secret weapon.

I was always a big kid, and I would get teased about it. Finally, I decided to fight fire with fire, so one year I asked for a tape recorder for Christmas. I was going to make sure that my brothers and sisters would think twice before they started to tease me.

I had my tape recorder, and I labeled my tapes. I put the names of my brothers and sisters on the tapes, and when I knew one of them was going to get a whoopin' I would run upstairs to my bedroom, grab my tape recorder and whichever tape I needed. Then I would run down to the basement, hide the tape recorder behind a bookshelf or underneath some clothes, and I would hit the "record" button.

That way I had the whole whoopin' on tape. I would have tapes of my brothers and sisters begging for their lives, saying, "Please, mama. Don't whoop me. I won't do it again, I promise. Don't whoop me!"

They would carry on and on, and it got to the point where it was almost ridiculous and I would have it all on tape. The next time we were out in the yard or on the playground and they would start teasing me about being fat or whatever, I would say, "Wait just a minute. Let's hear how you got spanked the other day." Then I would run up to my room, grab my tape recorder from its hiding place, run back outside and turn it on. It got to be where they were so humiliated because they didn't want their friends to hear them begging and crying like a baby that they would beg ME not to play the tape.

Needless to say the teasing stopped. The spankings continued, though.

Everyone that knows my family knows about the green belt. It's nailed to the wall next to the steps leading down to our basement. Whenever us kids got in trouble or did something wrong my mama would say, "Go get the green belt." We had to get it. Man, I hated that. It was like having to walk to your own executioner's table.

Before I go any further, I have to say that this wasn't child abuse. It wasn't even close. There were times when it hurt, and I didn't think it would ever stop, but it wasn't anything that was going to leave scars of any kind, physical or mental.

It's different nowadays.

Too many parents either ignore their kids, or they're way too philosophical. You don't have to beat your children, but you have to let them know in no uncertain terms what's right and what is wrong. Giving them a timeout or making them sit on top of a step for 15 or 20 minutes just isn't going to get it.

I wasn't brought up that way and my kids aren't going to be brought up that way. When you mess up and you disobey your parents they have to let you know it's serious. If it wasn't for that green belt there's no telling what would've happened to us kids. I can say honestly that I'm not so sure we'd all be alive if we hadn't listened to our mama.

This one time LeRoy was hanging out with the wrong crowd and my mama – who warned him about it already – drove to school. She stopped by the playground, rolled down the window and yelled, "I'm going to fix you. If you don't beat us home, when you get home I'm going to spank your tail. Now get moving."

LeRoy took off running like the wind. We took off, too. He was hauling butt, but we got caught by the stoplight and I'm yelling, "Run the light! C'mon, mama, run the light!" She was trying to give him a chance but it wasn't working. She could have stopped the truck and she still would have beaten him home.

While she parked the truck, I jumped out and ran upstairs to get my tape recorder. This was going to be good. I hid the tape recorder and was standing on the stairs with my arms tucked. "You're about to get it now," I said, as they walked down to the basement.

When he came up, I went down to get my tape recorder. He was ticked off. If he could have found my tape recorder – and believe me I caught my brothers and sisters trying to find it more than once – he would have destroyed it.

Gilbert's Family

Sheryl Cherry and Jamal Brown

Jesse Brown, Carla Haun, Jada Brown

Gilbert, Joann (Jab)

Coach Dozier, Gilbert

Gilbert, Leroy III

Gilbert - 1989

Carlos, Mom, Gilbert, Willie Mae, Aunt Jessie, Leroy III

Leroy Jr., Ann Brown- 1968

Carla Brown

Leroy III,
Baker U, Kansas

bert's

Gilbert, Leroy III

Mom, Gilbert - 1992

Gilbert, JoAnn, Leroy III, Carla, Carlos

JAMAL PHILIP BROWN 90

Vitals: Six feet, 290 pounds
Age: 13
Position: Nose tackle/offensive line
Grade: Eighth
Honors: Selected as Pop Warner all-league at nose tackle

"Jamal had the first article written about him this season. He made the Pop Warner all-league team at nose tackle. Jamal is a big kid who is very well mannered, gets pretty good grades and loves his mama to death.

"Everybody knows that Jamal loves to joke and loves to play around. If you joke on him, he's always quick with a comeback. When I look at Jamal it's like I'm looking at myself. I think he is exactly like me in so many ways that it's scary. I wasn't as big at 13 as he is now, but I see me every time I see him doing something. His mannerisms. The way he talks. I can tell he opens up when he's around his friends a lot more than he does when he's with everyone else. He likes to have fun all the time.

"I don't try to spoil him. I want him to get a taste of the real life. I do take care of him though. I'm very proud because that's my son and he does a lot of things right."

– Gilbert Brown, father

I would still have that tape recorder to this day, except when I went off to college I was too stupid to take it with me. Eventually they found it and destroyed the evidence.

One time LeRoy got this bright idea to get some crayons and draw all over our room on the wall. Like a dummy I did it with him. Then I get another bright idea. I said, "We'll get our shoes and put them in mud outside and we'll decorate the ceiling by making it look like someone walked on it."

Between the crayons and the mud footsteps I don't know which was worse.

We were so proud of our handiwork that we had to get mom right away to come see our room. I said, "Hey, mom, pretty cool, huh?"

She looks around, shakes her head and says, "Go get the belt."

That might have been the worst whoopin' I ever got. I didn't think it was ever going to stop. While we were scrubbing the walls and the ceiling, I turned to my dumb brother and said, "Don't ever ask me to draw another thing in my life."

I try to sound mad when I'm telling the stories but it doesn't work. The truth is it's always great when you have brothers and sisters growing up. I still laugh when I think of all the stupid stuff we would do.

Christmas was always special, and I don't know how my mama and daddy did it, but we always had something for Christmas. It may not be a whole lot of stuff, and it may not be very fancy, but there was always something under the Christmas tree.

In so many ways what you remember isn't the toys or the gifts, it's being with your family.

I used to get so excited I couldn't sleep the night before Christmas. Come to think of it, I couldn't sleep the night before Super Bowl XXXI, either.

I guess some things never change.

I do remember my favorite toy though. I love toys. I still collect figurines and I'm a comic book collector, too. I love Spider-man. I love all that stuff.

One year, the thing I wanted most for Christmas was a Tyco train set. It was futuristic and it had the tracks going up and down the walls. Well, I couldn't believe it but I actually got it for Christmas that year.

I ran upstairs to my room and I put it all together and I plugged it in and I hit the switch. Nothing. It didn't work.

I redid the wiring. I checked it twice. I plugged it back in. Nothing. I said, "No! No! No! It can't be." I re-hooked it up about 85 times. Still nothing. I cried. I tried pushing it around the tracks but it wasn't the same thing.

I ran downstairs and said, "Mama, my train set doesn't work. We've got to take it back right now." I knew if she didn't take it back right then it would never get taken back. Well, she never took it back. I'm thinking she probably bought it at a rummage sale or from someone's garage because it probably cost too much brand new, so she may not have had any place to take it back. I never did ask and it really doesn't matter.

I got the Tyco train set that I wanted and I still have it to this day. It's sitting right in the basement of our old house. I bought that house we grew up in, and my brother LeRoy still lives there. Whenever we go back home I say, "Mama, my train set's still sitting down there. It's right by the steps. It still doesn't work." My mama smiles at me and says, "I know. And the green belt is still there, too, nailed right to the wall."

We both laugh about it.

Like I said, there was love in the house, and I don't know how my mama and dad did it but they always found a way to have the right things at the right time.

During the week it was rough trying to feed everybody, and we would be saying, "Why can't we have this? Why can't we have that? Why do we have to eat bologna all the time?" I get embarrassed about the way I complained. I should have known better.

But on special days, it was special.

I was a good student. I didn't like school because I was always the big kid and I was always the kid that everybody wanted to tease, or I was the kid that everyone wanted to try and fight, so I just hated going to school for a while there.

Through the third, fourth, fifth and sixth grade it was rough.

In the sixth grade my principal called me. I wondered what I did wrong because I didn't really get into trouble much at all. He said, "Gilbert, I have a favor to ask. How would you like to play Santa Claus for the kindergarten students?"

That's how big I was. I was in the sixth grade and the principal was asking me to play Santa Claus. At the time I thought it was pretty cool. To this day I get teased about it. Well, I asked the principal what I had to do and he said, "Just put on this Santa hat, say ho-ho-ho, ask what they want for Christmas and give them a piece of candy."

I thought, "I can do that."

So I went down to their wing of the school, acted like Santa Claus, passed out candy and had a great time. It even led to me playing Santa Claus in a school play, which was great because my mama and daddy were there to watch me. I was sweating my butt off in that Santa Claus suit, but I loved it because they were there to see me.

I wasn't just Santa Claus. I was the head of the safety patrol.

I was in charge of the crossing at the busiest intersection and everybody knew they didn't have to check on Gilbert Brown. Why? Because everybody knew that Gilbert Brown never abandoned his post. Rain, sleet, ice, cold it didn't matter. I was like the mailman. I always delivered. It was my job and I was proud of it and I took it serious.

Well, one day I'm in the seventh grade, and I've got my safety patrol belt on, and I see this really big kid coming at me. It turned out LeRoy beat up his little brother in a fight the day before. I didn't mind that except LeRoy didn't bother to tell me about it. He probably thought I'd tell mama and he'd get the green belt and I'd get my tape recorder.

This big kid comes up to me – he was the size of a grown man, a high school kid – and he tells me that he's there to settle the score.

I've got my safety patrol gear on and I look stupid and this guy looks like a really mean mother. He keeps getting closer to me and closer to me and I'm thinking, "Oh, God. Oh, God. Here we go." All of a sudden he takes a big swing at me and it's like I can hear it coming. Whoosh! I ducked. He missed. I was going to come at him and knock him down, but the dude was too big for me.

That's when Gilbert Brown, for the first time in his life, abandoned his post.

I turned and started running and running and running. I ran the whole mile and a half home and the dude finally got tired of chasing me and gave up. I didn't want to fight that dude, but when I got home I wanted to fight my brother for not telling me about his fight and for making me leave my post.

My brother was always doing dumb stuff like that.

We had a neighbor, a guy by the name of Louis, who was a bit odd. I would cut his grass or shovel his sidewalk to make a few bucks. The work was always hard so I would have my brother come with me and give me a hand. Then we'd split the money.

One time we were feuding with these guys a few blocks over. They were too big for us, though, so we tried to steer clear of them. That worked for a while.

My brother and three of his friends were on the porch while I was cutting the grass, and they were just hanging out and talking, but I noticed that the shrubbery was moving. I didn't think much of it and my brother and his friends left.

When I finished cutting the grass, about 15 minutes later, I noticed that there were 100 dudes hanging out down the street. OK, maybe not that many, but it sure seemed like it. After I got paid, I took my lawnmower – it was one of those hand-push mowers, nothing fancy with an engine – and I started to walk home.

I got a block or so away when I saw that those dudes had one of my brother's friends up in the air and they were kicking the hell out of him. I couldn't do anything about it so I kept walking and minding my own business. Or so I thought.

I don't know where all these dudes came from but there about eight of them. They had me surrounded and there I am holding my push lawnmower looking like I'm about to get my butt kicked something fierce.

One dude slips out a knife and takes a big swing at me. He caught me in the face but it could have been a lot worse. So I'm standing there with this raggedy lawnmower and I'm really starting to get mad. I grab the mower and start swinging it like my life depended on it. I caught three of them with it right away and they backed off. Then I looked up and I saw mama and my aunt with their blue van. Man, that blue Dodge van looked as long as Lambeau Field right then, and my mama cut off the alley.

Then she got out and started shouting at those dudes and wouldn't you know it? They took off running. I got in the van and mama drove to where they lived. She got out and the dudes were sitting on the porch acting all innocent. Their mom comes out and starts shouting at mama about how she's bothering her kids.

Mama wouldn't hear it. She got in that woman's face and told her off and said she didn't want those boys bothering her sons again or else. We never did have any trouble from them again, and I couldn't have been more proud of my mama and my aunt.

Mama was always there for us. We were her babies. She wasn't going to anything happen if she could help it. She couldn't shelter us when we went off to school, but when we were at home or in the neighborhood she did her best to see that we were OK.

Years later, when I finally made it to the NFL, I tried to return the favor. I moved my mama from that house. I bought her a home between Six Mile Road and Seven Mile Road. There's a golf course nearby and it's really beautiful. As soon as you cross Six Mile it's back to Cambodia. On one side you've got Aretha Franklin, and on the other side you've got my old teammate, Keith McKenzie, and his rough neighborhood. He grew up in Highland Park, and when we'd visit each other, we always put the word out that it was OK for either of us to travel in the other's neighborhood. That's the way it was, even when we were playing for the Green Bay Packers. You still needed a pass to get through each other's 'hood.

Well, even though I bought mama that big beautiful house she didn't want to leave. She had too many memories, and after my dad passed, I don't think she liked the idea of living anywhere else. In a way, she still wanted to be near him.

I did the only thing I could. I bought the house we grew up in. My brother, LeRoy, still lives there. It's a rough neighborhood but he can handle it.

I hated to make mama leave. The nice thing is she can visit whenever she wants. That's how much I love her, and how much respect I have for my dad's memory, and how much I loved growing up at Griggs and Schoolcraft.

YEAH, IT WAS A ROUGH NEIGHBORHOOD. BUT IT WAS HOME, AND THAT'S NEVER GOING TO CHANGE.

CHAPTER TWO

A Nose Tackle Is Born!

One day during the summer before my freshman year at MacKenzie High my brother LeRoy pulled me aside for a serious conversation.

You have to understand that LeRoy is a hard ass. He's bad, bad LeRoy Brown III, and that's no joke. He's a bad man. He still lives in the house we grew up in. It's a rough neighborhood, but it's his home turf. It's his 'hood. He doesn't need permission to be there. He's from there. He's part of it just the same as the houses, the concrete, the alleys, the graffiti, the poor, the homeless … even the Baptist church across the street.

Well, LeRoy put a hand on my shoulder, stared me straight in the eye and said, "Look, I'm tired of you sitting by mama all day. You're going to high school this fall and I don't want you cramping my style. I've got a reputation so when you come through there you've got to be right. You've got to play football."

I've got to do what? Play football? No way.

Now, I know I told mama I was going to be a big NFL star and that I would buy her a fancy car and a nice home, and I meant it with all my heart. I really WAS going to be a football player some day, just not today.

I had been to LeRoy's practices and I didn't want any part of it. They had Pepper Johnson, who went on to become a great NFL linebacker with the Cleveland Browns and the New York Giants, and they had a lot of other big dudes that went on to play Division I football for college powerhouses like Notre Dame, Michigan and Michigan State.

MacKenzie High has an awesome football coach, Bob Dozier, and a tremendous history of producing top-notch football players. It was a feeder system, like baseball's minor leagues, for the best college football programs in the Midwest.

That part I understood. What I didn't care for was the running and the crazy stuff that went on in football. I told LeRoy that. Now my brother is looking at me and I can tell that he is thoroughly disgusted. Finally, he shakes his head and says, "Man, don't you get it? I want you to play. I want you to be good. I want to be proud of you. Just go out for football and give it your best. That's all I want you to do. Then, if it doesn't work out, we move on. You can say you tried, and I can say I've never seen you before in my life."

I had no choice but to go out for football, which meant I had no choice but to get a physical exam. That made two things I wasn't crazy about – playing football and having a doctor tell me to turn my head and cough.

Actually, the physical exam went great. I failed. My blood pressure was too high. It might have been because of something I ate, or because I was so nervous, but I wasn't thinking about that. I was thinking about not having to play football. So I went home, walked in the front door, acted real sad and plopped down on the couch. LeRoy was already home when I got there and I couldn't wait to tell him the bad news.

"I can't play football, dog," I said, sounding truly heartbroken. "High blood pressure. We got any chips in the house?"

It was about then that mama walked into the living room, took one look at me and asked what was the matter.

I told her about the high blood pressure and that I failed my physical and how disappointed I was that I couldn't play football. My bottom lip even quivered a little bit. She listened to what I had to say, looked at me real close and after a long pause said, "Go get a couple of lemons from the kitchen and start sucking on them."

Mama has old-fashioned remedies for everything. She has so many she could write a book about it, and she probably should do just that. Up 'til then I always thought of mama's home cures as a good thing. Now I wasn't so sure, and my worst fears came true because I sucked on those lemons, re-took my physical the next day and passed.

Football wasn't pretty at first.

I remember putting the pads on for the first time, waiting for our first practice to start and thinking all the while, "I must look like a big old dummy in this uniform."

Practice was worse. I didn't like the running, I didn't like playing on the offensive line and I didn't like being teased about my weight. I literally told my coach, "My head hurts, my stomach hurts, my whatever hurts just to get out of practice."

Care to take a guess as to who isn't happy about this? I mean, besides me? You guessed it. LeRoy. He didn't say anything. He didn't have to. He just gave me this look like he was trying to figure out one question, "Why is my big baby brother such a punk?"

I hated football. I hated it with a passion. I guess I didn't hate it as much as I cared about wanting to make LeRoy proud of me.

So I stuck with it even though I was a freshman, which also meant I was a practice dummy, a big fat practice dummy for the No. 1 varsity offense. The varsity had a dude named Willie Jones. He was a big guy. He was a pretty good player, too. I lined up across from him and I was thinking, "Willie might be going somewhere (to college)." He was going somewhere, all right. He was going straight for my gut.

I don't know if Willie Jones was mad at me, or he just didn't like freshmen very much, or maybe he wanted to teach me a lesson. Whatever the reason, Willie hits me dead in the stomach. HARD!

I'm rolling around on the ground like I was gut-shot, and coach Dozier comes over, looks at me and shouts, "Get your sorry butt on the sideline."

I'm mad. I mean REALLY mad.

For the first time since I started playing football, I'm sitting on the sideline and all I can think about is getting back out there and kicking Willie Jones' butt. Finally, I get up and start jogging to the defensive huddle. Coach Dozier sees me and shouts, "What are you doing?" I told him I wanted back in. He says, "For what?"

Coach Dozier saw for what on the next play.

When Willie Jones came at me I got real low and hit him with everything I had. I flipped him. I literally flipped him over. He landed on his stomach. Willie Jones was on the receiving end of the meanest flip of my soul. I flipped Willie Jones, and it was the turning point of my football career.

After that I wasn't just a freshman. I was THE man. I would catch rides home with the senior offensive linemen after practice, and we'd see LeRoy walking home, and I would smile and wave at him as we drove by. That still kills me because I know he was mad that I was in tight with the seniors so quickly, but he was proud of me, too.

I played offensive line on the varsity team, and LeRoy and I were the right side of the line for a couple years. I was the right tackle and LeRoy was the right guard. We clicked and it wasn't long before everybody knew the Brown Brothers were whipping butt and taking names. When we played teams with a strong right defensive end or outside line-backer, LeRoy and I would line up on the left side and we'd run that way.

We had some really good backs, including a future Pro Football Hall of Fame running back by the name of Jerome Bettis, and we tore up defenses. We tore up a lot of offenses, too, because LeRoy was a linebacker and I was a nose tackle.

We won six of nine games my sophomore year, and we held offenses to an average of just 9.4 points per game. Our nickname was the Stags. We felt like Studs.

I had 89 tackles and 10 sacks my senior year, and I earned all-state honors. I also ran the 100- and 200-meter dashes and was a shot putter in track. My best time in the 100 meters was like 10.6 or 10.7. I would be at a track meet, and Jerome Bettis and I were part of our 4 x 100 meter relay team, and guys in the next lane would be smiling at us. We would look at them and say, "Go ahead, keep smiling, but this is no joke."

Then we would blow their doors off.

Track was something to do to stay in shape when I wasn't playing football, and it was a lot of fun, but by my senior year I planned to play Division I college football. That was my thing, and I got a lot of recognition for it, but it wouldn't have happened without LeRoy. Those couple of years in high school that I got to play with him, and alongside him, is as good as it gets. All the things that he did for me, I owe it all to him.

Without him, I wouldn't be here. I wouldn't have played college football, much less pro football, if he hadn't pushed me.

Of course, Coach Dozier is another reason why I was able to play pro football. Detroit's MacKenzie High School has a great tradition and he was the driving force. He produced several players that went on to the NFL and I'm proud to say I'm one.

Coach Dozier was a father figure to all his guys.

He was the type of coach that would make you get your progress reports on Friday. If you came in with an F, he would hold a public flogging in the middle of the gym. He wouldn't let us slide on the grades or on the field.

He was so proud of MacKenzie High football, and he would get so into the games, that he would play the University of Michigan fight song on the loudspeakers in the gym. We're taping our ankles and he's cranking up the UM fight song. Unreal. He wanted to get us fired up because he was so fired up.

He was a coach that got us in the mood, and he cared so much about his players. He

Mrs. Ann Brown

talks about Gilbert trying to cope with his father's death in February of 1992. Gilbert was a junior at the University of Kansas but that didn't keep him from being at his father's bedside day and night:

"Gilbert had it rough because he came home from Kansas the second day his father was in the hospital. The doctors told me it was best to have the kids come, so Gilbert and his brother LeRoy, who was attending Baker University in Kansas, came home right away. For the next several days, every time I went to the hospital, which was four times a day, Gilbert would go with me. Finally, Gilbert was so worn out I told him to stay home, get some rest and let LeRoy go.

"When LeRoy walked in that day, and he saw all these needles in his father's arms and a tube in his throat, he went down in a heap. He passed out. The nurse and I tried to catch him to keep him from hitting his head. Well, I took LeRoy home and put him on a plane back to Kansas, where he stayed until the funeral.

"Gilbert stayed in Detroit the whole time, about nine days in all, and he went to the hospital every day. Gilbert's father was a big man, and he was built a lot like Gilbert across the shoulders. When the doctors and nurses tried putting a tube down his throat he fought them so hard they had to paralyze him.

"There was this skinny little X-ray technician, and she needed to prop up Gilbert's father so she could slide the X-ray film behind him, but none of the interns standing around the desk offered to help her. Finally, she asked Gilbert if he would help her, which he did of course.

"When Gilbert came out of the room he said, 'Mama, that's not my Daddy in there.' I'm thinking he was already dead and Gilbert felt it. His father finally passed the next morning. His father didn't show a lot of emotion to anyone when he was younger. It just didn't happen. If he felt it, he hid it. Well, after his second stroke that changed. That's when he started showing emotion. By that time, LeRoy and Gilbert were already in college so there was a lot that they didn't see.

"Once, right before Gilbert went back to college for the fall semester, his daddy let him know how he felt. He also said it once when Gilbert was in Kansas, I was in Detroit and his father was in West Virginia. I put us on a three-way call, and he told Gilbert, 'Always listen to your mama.' Then he told him, 'I love you son' and hung up the phone right away.

"After his daddy died, Gilbert didn't want to go back to school but coach (Bob) Dozier, his high school football coach at MacKenzie, and several other friends made sure he got back. They weren't going to let him quit even though he felt like it. That isn't what I wanted, and it wasn't what his daddy would have wanted, either. He was still enrolled at Kansas when the Minnesota Vikings drafted him the following spring."

cared more about everybody else than he did himself.

Going into my senior year, I always had trouble getting to my first-hour class. It was Biology. I had to get there before first hour started, by 8:05 a.m., and he would come to my house every morning and pick me up to make sure I made that first-hour class.

The way I rewarded him was a trip to Super Bowl XXXI in New Orleans. He was the only person that I got a ticket for to that game. I didn't want any distractions. It was down in New Orleans, which was a distraction enough. I didn't give tickets to anybody. I was focused. I was determined. I was going to do whatever it took to win that game.

The only person I gave a ticket to was Coach Dozier. I didn't give my mama, my brothers, my sisters – NOBODY – a ticket. They understood that I wanted to be focused, and they knew that I wanted to treat Coach Dozier first class. Besides, he was like part of the family anyway. I got him a room, everything he needed, and that was my way to thank him for getting me where I was supposed to be."

I still get asked about Jerome Bettis all the time. What's he like? What was it like in high school together? Who was the better athlete?

I don't mind. I'm proud to know him and to have played with him in high school.

JB was a nose tackle at the time. He stumbled into being a fullback, a running back, and then a linebacker. I was in the 10th grade when JB transferred from Henry Ford High School. We were handing balls off and JB gets the ball and starts bowling everybody over. Boom! Boom! Boom! He really didn't get his opportunity though because we've got two all-world running backs. But it didn't take long to see that he was something special. By the time he got to the 10th grade, and everybody started hearing about JB, it was only going to be a matter of time before he started.

JB also played basketball. I did track. My coach didn't want me playing basketball. I was the big man, and he didn't want me playing basketball and getting a leg injury or breaking an ankle or something. I did the shot put and the discus in track, and JB and I were on the relay team. We ran the 440-yard relay together. Man, I was bringing it back then. I looked at guys in the next lane and would say, "This ain't no cakewalk, brother. I can run." Then we'd take and "bam" I'd leave him behind.

We beat some tough teams in track and field. I was always close to being an All-State track guy I didn't want it bad enough. I was so focused on football that track was just something to do to keep busy.

In football, we never finished higher than fifth in the state. We never failed to have fun, either. I was Jerome Bettis' guy on the offensive line. I was the right tackle and I was the left tackle. It just depended on which side we were going to run the ball. Other teams knew we were going to go that way and they still couldn't stop it. It was fun for me but it was bad for some of the other guys. They had to go play the other side because they couldn't block at the point of attack, or their guy was too powerful.

JB was a heck of a linebacker, too. His nickname in high school was "The Bear" because he was like a big old grizzly bear that would knock the hell out of you. He was a middle linebacker. I played defensive end, and behind me, all I could hear was crack, pow, bam and ouch when JB hit guys. He could run sideline-to-sideline like you wouldn't believe. I don't think he would have been a great linebacker in college or the pros. He was hell out there on the other team in high school, but he might've been too physical. He might've been so physical that his body wouldn't be able to take it.

He played running back with that mentality and it has taken a toll. I look at a man whose body is changing. JB doesn't walk the same anymore. You can tell he's taken a lot of hits. But you can tell he's still got that fire. You could shoot him and he'd still have that fire. He'd get across the goal line before he died.

I do his football camp every year. At the end of the camp, he tells the campers that I'm his boy, and all that, but that I never got a good hit on him. Not once. Not in high school and not in the National Football League. I tell the campers it isn't because JB is that elusive. It's because he never comes close enough for me to put on a lick.

When we graduated, JB went his way and I went mine.

He had all the Division I powerhouses after him and it looked like he was going to Oklahoma to be a Sooner. He was all set and then at the last minute there was talk about possible NCAA sanctions and he got scared off. He never told me where the story came from, and he wasn't sure there was anything to it, but he didn't want to take a chance.

That's how Jerome Bettis chose Notre Dame.

Of course, I ended up choosing Kansas. I played offensive line in high school, and I was pretty good at it, too. In fact, I was too good. I hated it because I had to sit back and take it from defensive linemen. I hated it. I had the attack mentality.

One of the reasons I went to Kansas, I'm sitting there and

Mrs. Ann Brown

discusses Gilbert's decision to attend Kansas rather than in-state schools Michigan and Michigan State, and how Gilbert found a way to stay connected long after the cord was cut:

"I think Gilbert really went to Kansas because he couldn't decide between Michigan and Michigan State. His high school coach, Bob Dozier, knew how it was around Detroit and he thought Gilbert would do better in Kansas. It was small just like where we're from originally, a little town called Beckley, West Virginia. When Gilbert was young we would go there on family vacations. It was quiet and he liked it. When coach Dozier got him connected with Kansas it was just what Gilbert needed. It was just what I needed, too, to get him out of the house. He was always under foot.

"Of course I missed him but it didn't bother me that much because he was constantly on the telephone. Shortly after Gilbert left for Kansas LeRoy moved there to attend Baker University. That made it a little easier on the phone bill.

"LeRoy would tease Gilbert and tell him he didn't have to call mama every time he had a hangnail. Gilbert still called a lot but half the time he didn't listen to me anyway. He even called when he was with Minnesota and they were playing an exhibition game in Germany. He called so often I thought they were going to take my telephone out."

listening to teams and I know they're going to put me on the offensive line. Michigan. Michigan State. Minnesota. They all wanted to me to be an offensive lineman.

Now, Minnesota was my team. The Minnesota Golden Gophers were my team since I was little. They had Darrell Thompson, who played with the Packers. I loved him. I really loved Ricky Foggie, the quarterback. They had the burgundy and gold. I loved those colors. Oh, my God I thought it was the coolest thing when they sent me a postcard with the number 77 on it and free shoes. I've still got the post-card. That's where I was going. It was Minnesota all the way. I got up and visited Minnesota, and I was disappointed right way. I got in the dorm rooms and they were touching each other. The rooms were so small it was nuts. I wasn't going to stay I that dorm room with another big football player. No way.

Let's see. I can go to Minnesota and be squeezed to death. I can go to Michigan, Michigan State or Notre Dame and be miserable on the offensive line. I can go to Kansas, play defensive tackle next to Dana Stubblefield and stay out of trouble because Lawrence is such a small town compared with Detroit.

KANSAS IT WAS.

CHAPTER THREE

Experiencing Growing Pains at Kansas

The University of Kansas was good to me in a lot of ways.

Getting an education helped prepare me for life after football. Playing nose tackle helped prepare me for the tremendous competition in the National Football League. Living in Lawrence prepared me for what it was going to be like in Green Bay.

It was small and it was quiet, especially compared with Detroit, and I liked that. My recruiting trip went well and I couldn't wait to start my college career. The summer after my senior year at MacKenzie High couldn't go by fast enough. I was bored, and I was tired of hanging out at the same places and living in the same house. I wanted a change, or so I thought. The fact is I was really nervous about leaving Detroit. It's all I had known my entire life, except for some family vacations to Beckley, West Virginia.

Lawrence reminded me of Beckley, which I liked, and it prepared me for Green Bay, which I also liked. The problem was I liked Detroit a whole lot, too. The fact is the day I left for Kansas I was homesick before I hit the highway. My mama and I were real close, and I spent a lot of time with her, so not seeing her was going to be different. So was not being able to hang out with my friends and family.

As much as I wanted to go to college and play football, I wasn't crazy about moving away from home. Now, I had no choice.

I caught two breaks when I went to Kansas.

One was having a chance to play defensive tackle next to Dana Stubblefield, who became a Pro Bowl player with the San Francisco 49ers. We didn't win a national title together at Kansas, but we definitely kicked a lot of butt. Dana was big, strong

Mrs. Ann Brown

discusses Gilbert's near-fatal accident in which he totaled his Chevy pickup truck en route from Detroit to Kansas for his senior year. His Detroit homeboy and Jayhawks' teammate, Kyle Moore, was a passenger when Gilbert fell asleep at the wheel. The accident occurred late at night due east of St. Louis:

"It was really bad. He fell asleep at the wheel and he had his baby, a little Chevy pickup truck, and he went down the embankment and ended up against a tree. He was situated upside-down and when he looked up the first thing he saw was a priest. He thought he had died and gone to heaven. The priest witnessed the accident, thought it looked pretty bad and decided to stop at the scene.

"The next day I talked to the man that pulled out the truck and towed it away. He said he didn't understand why those boys didn't get killed because there was nothing holding that motor in place but that very thin firewall."

and athletic. You know, just like me. Man, we tore people apart.

There are two types of competition and they're equally important.

There is the kind that Dana and I had when we were at Kansas. He wanted to out-do me and I wanted to let everyone know I could play pretty damn good, too. We were teammates, and we played the same position, but we also pushed each other.

Even when Dana was with the 49ers, we had that one-upmanship thing going on. He would tell me how San Francisco was going to beat our butts when we played. I'd just tell him that Adam Timmerman is telling everyone in Green Bay that he's going to kick Dana Stubblefield's butt. Dana would go, "Really? He said that? When I see that $#@$% I'm going to tear him a brand new you know what."

I still laugh because Dana would get so fired up about it. Part of it was that Dana wanted to beat the Packers, and part of it was that he wanted to prove he was the better player between us. The part I thought was funny was not telling Timmerman about it. There was one game where Timmerman comes up to me in the second quarter and says, "What's up with Stubblefield? He's acting like I disrespected him or something. What did I ever to do him?"

This is why I loved Adam Timmerman: He comes over and tells me that, and then he proceeds to give it right back to Dana. He blocks his tail off and makes Dana work hard for every inch of ground he'd get.

Dana and I have softened our views a bit over the years. We're not as ultra-competitive as we were in college and the pros.

The other type of competition is between teammates that have to face each other every day in practice. The offensive linemen compete with the defensive linemen. The quarterback competes with the safeties. The tight end and the strong-side linebacker get after it. And so on.

The best-case scenario is when a team has both.

They have players competing for roster spots, and they have players competing against each other in practice. That's what the Packers had in 1996, and what we lacked at Kansas for much of the time I was there. Glen Mason, the head coach, was OK but he didn't seem to warm up to me. I'm not sure why, but he acted like I was just this big thing taking up space and he never really made an effort to get to know me.

Our player-coach relationship took a turn for the worse going into my senior year. It was late in the summer – time for me and my good friend Kyle Moore – to report to Kansas for fall practice. We were supposed to leave at 6 o'clock at night. I had my pickup truck that my mom bought for me all packed and ready to roll by 5.

Of course, Kyle was nowhere to be found. Mr. Lance Romance had to visit his girlfriend one last time before he went off to school. You would've thought he was going to be gone for the whole year. Well, I wait around for Kyle to visit his gal and I'm thinking this isn't going to take long. Six o'clock becomes seven o'clock and then the hours start to go by. Now it's pushing midnight, I'm dead-dog tired and Kyle's got this dumb grin on his face and he's all set to hit the road.

I tell him to get some sleep while I handle the first shift. I was OK for the first couple of hours but then I started to get sleepy. I thought I was all right but I was nodding and I didn't know enough to pull over.

We were on the interstate about an hour east of St. Louis when I fell asleep. I don't remember falling asleep. I only remember waking up while my pickup truck was going down a steep embankment. It flipped over, skidded a few feet and slammed against a tree. I looked up and I was staring at my ceiling. I looked over at Kyle and he was all right, but he also was pretty shook up. He starts in about how I almost got us killed. Then I start in about how he had to take his sweet time getting on the road and that his you-know-what almost got us both killed. Then I look at my truck – my beautiful truck – and it's totaled. Gone. Wasted. Wrecked.

We were still buckled in and arguing when we noticed

the leaves on the branches of the tree we slammed into were moving. When they were parted I found myself staring at a priest. I thought, "This isn't good. An accident and the first thing you see is a priest? Maybe I'm dead. Maybe it's worse than I thought. Maybe he's here because he knows."

All that crazy stuff is going through my mind.

The fact is we were lucky to be alive, but you wouldn't know it by Coach Mason. At first, he acted like he didn't believe us and that we were making up an excuse for being late getting back. Then he acted like we must have been doing something wrong to get into an accident. Nice guy.

He made us run until we were sick. He worked us hard. He also demoted me from the starting lineup, which didn't make any sense at all.

All the while we're losing and my stock is dropping like a rock for the upcoming National Football League draft. I went into my senior season being rated by most of the scouts and the magazines and stuff as one of the top defensive linemen in the country. I was going to be a first-round pick. The only question was how high.

When I lost my starting spot it created a sense of suspicion among some scouts. They thought there must be some deep dark secret I was hiding. Why else would the coach put one of his top defensive linemen on the bench? Finally I got a chance to play again and eventually I won my starting job back. The trouble was the damage was done.

After the season, I wasn't being invited to the all-star games. That didn't make much sense, either. One day I got a telephone call from one of the organizers of the North-South Game down in Mobile, Alabama. He said that the committee wanted me to play in the game, and they wondered why I hadn't responded to their requests to set up a plane flight and accommodations and the whole deal. I told them the reason I didn't respond is because I never got the messages. Someone in the football office at KU said they thought Coach Mason was holding back the all-star invitations during the season so I would keep playing hard for him. Shoot. I would've played harder.

Well, I ended up playing in the North-South Game and I had a pretty good day. Some of the scouts told me they were really interested, and that included somebody with the Packers. All I could do was wait until the draft to see who was really interested and who was just trying to throw other scouts off the scent.

After the season ended, and I played in a couple of all-star games, I packed up and went back to Detroit. My father passed away the year before and I still wasn't over it. I still wasn't right, if you know what I mean, and I figured I would be better off in Detroit.

I played in Hawaii in the Aloha Bowl, one of the few bowls whose invitation I actually received, and then I stayed for another month at school before packing it up. Then one day I just left Lawrence. I guess it was losing my dad, and not having the senior year that I wanted to have, it all began piling up. Finally, it hit me like a ton of bricks were falling on my head. There was only one person that I wanted to be around and that was my mom. I was a notorious mama's boy, as you know, and she was the only person that was going to make me feel better. I had a lot of pressure on me. How do you learn to deal with it? I don't know. I guess you just do. It was an awful lot, though, so I left.

The days passed slowly after I left Kansas. It seemed like the draft would never get here. That '93 draft had some really good players in it. The Packers selected Wayne Simmons, the linebacker from Clemson, with the 15th overall pick in the draft. They took George Teague, the safety from Alabama, with the 29th pick. After that it was Earl Dotson, the right tackle from Texas A&I, in the third round. Ron Wolf also drafted Auburn linebacker James Willis in the fifth round, Louisiana Tech cornerback Doug Evans in the sixth round, Western Michigan left tackle Paul Hutchins in the sixth round and Navy defensive tackle Bob Kuberski in the seventh round.

Wolf hit it big on Simmons, Dotson, Evans and Kuberski. All four of those guys contributed to our Super Bowl XXXI team in a big way.

I'm proud to say that I did, too. It just took me a little longer, and a lot of heartache, to get to Green Bay.

When draft day finally arrived my mama threw a really nice party at the house. We had maybe 15, 20 people over to eat, drink and wait for my name to be called. Some of the guests were neighbors. Some were family. All of them were great. Everything was going just fine until the first round slipped by without a phone call.

Now I'm thinking that people might be wondering what round I would go in. If you slipped through the first round, would you slip through the second round, too? I knew it was possible but I didn't even want to think about it. I watched that whole first round, and then I watched that whole second round.

Nothing. The only phone call we got was a wrong number.

After the second round, ESPN switches its coverage of the draft to ESPN2, which was fine except for one problem. We

Mrs. Ann Brown

discusses Gilbert's disappointment at being bypassed in Rounds 1 and 2 of the 1993 NFL Draft. She also tells why the Packers didn't draft Gilbert in the first place:

"By the time the second round ended, Gilbert was upstairs in the bathroom crying because he felt like he'd let down the entire world. We didn't have ESPN2, which carries the NFL draft after ESPN wraps up the first two rounds, so it wasn't much of a party.

"That's when the telephone rang, but it didn't ring on the main phone because my daughter had another line into the house. Somebody finally picked up and the caller said it was Minnesota. Everyone froze until one of the men, a guy everybody called Gramps, stood up and said: Don't you know that's the Minnesota Vikings? Go get Gilbert!

"Gilbert got on that telephone and the Minnesota Vikings told him they were going to draft him. Finally, it was over, and he could relax and not feel embarrassed around his friends and family. I knew his appetite would return. He was happy in no time. He was very, very happy. He was so happy that he fixed two plates of food.

"What we didn't know was the way the Vikings were going to treat him. It wasn't very nice, and when he finally ended up in Green Bay, my whole thing was the Packers were the team that was supposed to draft him anyway.

"Before the draft in '93, the Packers sent one of their scouts or medical people or whatever to Detroit to weigh Gilbert. They wanted a current and accurate weight on him before they went ahead and drafted him. There was only one problem: The high school didn't have a scale big enough to weigh him. My sister was working at Henry Ford Hospital. I called and told her the situation and asked her if the hospital had a scale that big. She called back and said they couldn't find one, either.

"Now I wasn't sure what we were going to do. We started to call around to friends, and to businesses down on the loading docks. Maybe some of the big fishing boats had a scale. Then we decided to call some meat packing plants and so forth.

"Finally, we found a place called Meat Land. It was a meat store with lockers and a warehouse, and the man on the phone said, 'Bring him over. We'll weigh him.' Gilbert wouldn't do it. He wouldn't go. His thing was that he didn't want to be weighed like some type of cattle. He refused to do it.

"The Packers wanted an accurate weight on him, but Gilbert couldn't bring himself to provide it under the circumstances. That's why Green Bay didn't draft him."

didn't have ESPN2. We didn't have much of a party, either. As soon as the second round wrapped up, and ESPN turned it over to ESPN2, I said, 'God dang,' and then I went upstairs. I faked like I had to go to the bathroom, but the truth is I was in there crying my eyes out. Everybody came over, and so many nice people were rooting for me, and I felt like I let them down.

Now I'm in the bathroom crying when I hear my mama yelling something about having a phone call. I asked her to repeat it just to make sure. Then I got myself together, ran downstairs and took the call. It was Dennis Green, the coach of the Minnesota Vikings, on the line. He told me that the Vikings had selected me with the 79th pick overall, which was their second pick of the third round. He also told me that they thought I was a good player and they looked forward to getting me in there.

When I hung up I was numb.

I was in the NFL. I was making that next step. I did it. The Vikings did it, too. They took me in the third round. I was going to The Land of Purple. Well, I went up there for the post-draft mini-camp the next weekend and everyone treated me great. I met my position coach, John Teerlinck, and he was awesome. He gave me a bunch of drills to do and some workout routines he felt would help. He even came to Detroit a couple of times to meet with me and see how I was getting along. I thought we had a great relationship. I thought Minnesota was the perfect team to draft me.

I celebrated by buying a new truck with part of my signing bonus.

I thought, man, life is good. That was when life reminded me that there aren't any guarantees and everything can be taken away in the blink of an eye, or in my case, the pulling of a trigger.

I came home after the Vikings' second mini-camp with my new truck. Man, I was proud as a peacock, maybe too proud.

Myron, a buddy of mine, grew up next door. He was one of my homeboys and we were pretty close. He wanted to go for a ride in truck and I didn't make him ask twice. I had tunes and my rims were looking sweet, so I said let's roll.

My favorite food in the whole wide world is Church's Fried Chicken. I could eat Church's every day, three times a day. Everybody that knows me knows that's my favorite. Now, my mama hated for me to drive my truck at night. She knew about how the neighborhood was with all the car jacking stuff. I promised her that Myron and I would hurry up and get it quick. I figure I'm a grown man. I can handle myself. I wish my mama wouldn't worry so much.

We go get the chicken. Then Myron says he needs something to wash down the Church's and could we go to The Party Store. It was in a real bad part of town but I said all right. It's a corner store so I parked in front beneath the streetlights. The last thing I tell Myron is to hurry up. Of course, Myron doesn't listen at all.

He's messing around getting pop and chips and stuff. This dude walks into the store and looks at me and starts smiling like he's got something on me. I try not to pay him any attention and finally I drag Myron out of The Party Store. When we walk out the dude walks out right behind us. The guy comes up and smiles, and then he pulls a gun and sticks it in Myron's back.

Myron just about died right there. He had this look on his face like, "Please Lord, just give me one more chance."

Now I notice another dude walking across the street right at us. He's trying to act like he's got a gun, too. I take a look at the dude with the gun on Myron, and I'm thinking the gun looks like it's fake. It looked like a toy. I was just beginning to think I'd had enough of this bull when the dude shouts, "Give me the @#$#$# keys! Now! Give me the truck or I'm going to waste him!"

Myron was looking at me like, "Give him the keys, man." Now here I am, six-foot-three, 365 pounds, and I've got to give my keys to my brand new truck to this little @#$%^% who is about four-foot-two and weighs 125 pounds. Well, he's acting like the gun is real and I hated to do it, but I handed over the keys. I just gave them away to a guy that I could've choked with one hand.

I still didn't think the revolver was real. It had a funny shape and a skinny barrel, but I had heard that just because a gun didn't look real doesn't mean it can't kill you. It might've been one of those homemade numbers. Either way, I couldn't screw around. When I talked to Myron, he said that gun was real. I was like, "Myron, I just had my truck stolen. They took my keys, they took my truck with the rims and the new sound system, and worst of all they took my piping hot Church's Fried Chicken that was sitting in the back seat. I said, "Myron, I should have let him shoot you. Is there anything else you'd like from The Party Store as long as we can't go nowhere?" I knew he felt bad, and I was glad he was OK, so I added, "But you're my homeboy and I like you, man. Myron, if I didn't like you so much you'd be dead."

About this time a lady walks across the street and apologizes. She said she was so sorry that she didn't do anything to help us but her brother had just been killed by car-jackers a few weeks earlier in the same neighborhood.

She offered to drive us to the nearest police precinct and we accepted. It didn't do any good, though. The officer behind the desk wanted to know if we had registration for the truck. I told him the registration was in the glove compartment. Then he wanted to know if we could describe the vehicle, or the men that allegedly stole it.

I felt like telling him, "Yeah, I can describe the truck. It's the one with the piping hot Church's Fried Chicken in the back seat." As you can see we didn't get anywhere with Detroit's finest. I can't say that I blame them, though. There is so much crime and bad things going on to deal with, we were just one more carjacking.

Here's the worst part: Now I had to go home and tell my mama, who warned us not to go down to that neighborhood, and tell her that my new truck was stolen and we were almost shot in the process. That got me thinking about a lot of things.

That was my new truck that I paid for with my signing bonus. I could've been killed. I could've been shot. I may not have been able to play football again. It was a lot to consider after surviving a car accident in college, coming home, almost getting shot and then having to report to the Minnesota Vikings' training camp.

WHAT I DIDN'T KNOW WAS THE CARJACKING WAS THE FIRST IN A LONG LINE OF PROBLEMS THAT BEGAN THE DAY THE VIKINGS DRAFTED ME.

CHAPTER FOUR

A Purple Haze To Green Bay Reign

I reported to the Minnesota Vikings' training camp at Mankato full of confidence. The minicamps went smooth and I felt like I was going to challenge for playing time. All I heard throughout the mini-camps from my position coach and my teammates was, "You're the man. Nobody can block big Gil."

I was still really mad about my new truck being carjacked, but I figured that was behind me and I liked what was ahead of me. I also wanted to have my mind right so I could prove to the Vikings they made a great pick.

I'm feeling great. I get settled into my hotel room, check in at training camp headquarters and walk over to my first meeting with my position coach. We sit down for our first individual meeting – our first one – and I don't recognize the guy across from me. It looks like John Teerlinck, the defensive line coach, but it doesn't sound like him. This is not the guy I met during the off-season mini-camps.

He starts in on me without so much as a hello. He says, "You're a @#$^#$ rookie. You're #$%# horrible!"

I was blown away. I wondered where all this was coming from. Did they treat all the rookies this way? Did I do something wrong? How did I offend them?

I would have asked Teerlinck but I couldn't get a word in edgewise.

We get out to the practice field and it's worse. It's hot. It's humid. I'm mad because I just got cussed out by another grown man and there wasn't a thing I could do about it. At least, nothing I could do about it that wouldn't get me cut on the spot.

I thought I was one of the Vikings' homeboys. I thought we were all on the same team. It turns out all of that was bull. The Vikings treated their veteran players bad and they treated their rookies worse. It was like I got punished every day of practice because I was a rookie and I was fat. They made me feel expendable and I'd just gotten there. I felt like I wasn't a football player. I felt like I was a piece of dirt.

I roomed with No. 77, Brad Culpepper, before he went to Tampa Bay. Then I roomed with Esera Tuaolo, who had been with the Packers, for a little while. Then I roomed with some other big kid that I was battling with for the nose tackle job. I don't even remember his name any more. That's how bad I've tried to put this out of my mind.

It was a grind every day. I couldn't have number 93. I had to take 96. Then some of the guys on the defensive line were joking on me because they thought I looked fat in 96.

Some of the other guys chimed in, too. Cris Carter, the receiver, was one of the worst. I disliked Cris Carter with a passion. Every chance he got to stick it to me, he stuck it to me. Whenever it was his turn at the training table to decide which rookie had to sing for his supper, he would stand up and look all around the dining hall. He always ended up with his eyes on me, and I could hear some of the snickering in back.

Cris Carter would say, "Sing something for your supper. Sing your school fight song."

I said, "C'mon, man. I've had to sing every night this week."

Carter replied, "Get up on your chair and sing your song or you aren't going to eat. Get going."

I had to go through that just about every night. I thought I was playing professional football. There was nothing professional about the way the Vikings ran their operation. The practices were almost as demeaning as the evening meal.

Teerlinck would put two hoops on the ground and tell us to run around the hoops. It was like a figure eight. He would say, "OK, here's your challenge for the day. Gilbert Brown, you get up there, and John Randle, you catch him."

I had to start running around the figure eight and try to keep Randle from catching me. If he caught me, I had to run some more after practice. If I caught him, well, there was no way in hell I was going to catch John Randle. The guy was 100 pounds lighter, a Pro Bowl defensive lineman, and he could run.

I couldn't catch him. Every day I had to run extra after practice because of it. I never got a chance to show them what I could do because they always had me doing dumb stuff. They were always making me fight for this, fight for that, sing for this, sing for that. It was ridiculous. They never let me play. They were so busy worrying about the rookie hazing bull that they didn't bother to teach guys how to play.

After you sit there for a while, you start to think that you better find a way to get through it. You can't quit. You're in the NFL now. You've got to stick it out. It wasn't easy though. How could you make a team, learn your players, get to know your teammates and deal with all of that only to see these big veteran offensive linemen ripping bumpers off rookies' vehicles? That actually happened. They never got near my truck, and they're damn lucky they didn't. That's where I draw the line. You mess with my truck, and you mess with me, I will mess you up.

One of the linemen cut the tip of his finger off when he was tearing bumpers off cars. They taped him up and he went back out and played. I'm watching this and trying to comprehend how I'm going to learn this defense and make a place for myself on the team with all this bull going on.

It didn't help that I checked into training camp weighing 360, or somewhere in there anyway. I could have gotten down and given up but I stayed with it. I took Cris Carter's insults and pretended not to care. I sang for my supper but all the while I was thinking how I was going to tear up so-and-so in practice the next day. As much as I've got, I rallied, and I made it through the cuts, the running and the bull.

Sometimes I would dream that I was wearing a ski mask and I had a six-inch piece of pipe and I'd let these jokers have it. And these guys were supposed to be my teammates and coaches. I would wake up in a sweat and think, "This is crazy."

I went through all that stuff. I manned up. It was hard, but I did it and I didn't let my mama know anything about it. When I called I'd tell her everything was going great and that I was going to make the team no problem. I told her I had great coaches and teammates and we were going to be pretty good. It was all a lie. I didn't believe any of it.

I just didn't want my mama worrying over me because of someone that I didn't give a rip about. Finally, we have the final roster cut and I make it. I've got a spot on the Minnesota Vikings' 53-man roster. I was in the NFL.

We were getting ready for our first regular-season game when one of the administrative assistants comes and tells me that Dennis Green wants to see me in his office. He didn't say what Green wanted, only that the Vikings' head coach wanted me ASAP. I was in the facility at Winter Park, and I was sitting at my locker thinking about how I was going to make it work in Minnesota. I wanted to be a good teammate and I promised myself to do everything I could to make it happen.

I'm running up the stairs to Green's office wondering what he could want. I walk through the door, and I'm standing there, and he's sitting behind his desk. He says, "Sit down kid. Sit down." I sit down. Then he says, "You know what? You've got potential. You've got some things we really like. You've got some things that we don't like. I'm thinking while he's talking that he would've seen some things he liked if he'd have given me a chance to show it.

Finally, Green says, "We've got a situation here. We need a running back. I'm thinking of signing Barry Word and I'm thinking of letting you go. We'll pick up this guy, hide you for a little bit and then we'll bring you back on the practice squad."

I'm like, "What does that mean? I've got to leave? I'm done? I've got to go?"

I didn't say it like that. I'm more respectful.

Green told me to go back to my hotel room, hang out and wait and see what happens. I was stunned. I couldn't move. I froze. I was thinking what I could possibly tell my mama because she thought I was on the team. Hell, I thought I was on the team. The opening game was four days away.

Dennis Green had to tell me to get up. He said, "OK, I'm done. Go. Go on."

I got up and went to the hotel. I had no idea what I would tell my girlfriend or my mama or my boys back home. Actually, I didn't give a damn about anybody but my mama because she worried so much about me already, and I knew this might upset her.

I didn't know if what Green was telling me meant that I wouldn't get paid, or that I had to give back my signing bonus, which was spent my truck that was carjacked. I didn't know if I would have a chance to play somewhere else. I was in a daze. I was a young kid. I didn't know how all of this worked.

Practice squad? What does that mean?

I get back to the hotel and the people there are very nice. The women at the front desk stopped me and said, "You have a call from Gary Reynolds."

Gary Reynolds? I had no idea who that was until I checked out the message. It was Gary Reynolds from the Green Bay Packers. I must have cleared waivers. The Vikings cut me earlier that day, and they must have known I was gone. All that stuff Dennis Green was talking to me was a bunch of bull.

I was really mad. I was excited, too.

I was getting the hell out of Dodge, or in this case, Minneapolis.

I wanted to know more about Gary Reynolds and I wanted to know more about the Green Bay Packers. I called the number and he said, "Hey, man, how would you like to be a member of the Green Bay Packers?"

First thing I said was, "Can you do that? Minnesota drafted me."

Reynolds said that they could do that, and he wanted to know when I could be available to fly to Green Bay. He said the

Packers would purchase a plane ticket for first thing in the morning and he welcomed me to the franchise.

I thought about the plane ticket, and the Vikings, and all the bull I went through, and I said "Forget Minnesota! Forget this place!" I also told Reynolds that I didn't need a plane ticket. I told him I wanted directions to Green Bay because I was packing while we were talking and going to get the hell out of there – in Dennis Green's words – ASAP. I told myself to get out before someone changes his mind, or before I wake up because this had to be a dream. I told Reynolds, "I'll see ya'all tonight."

I threw my stuff in a bag, shot downstairs, threw the people at the front desk the peace sign and drove myself to Green Bay. Gone. I don't believe I stopped to get gas. I got on Highway 29 west and then Highway 41 south, according to Reynolds' directions, and I couldn't get there fast enough. Man, I was flying.

I didn't know a thing about Green Bay. I didn't know a thing about the Packers. I'm thinking, "Hmm. Wisconsin? That doesn't sound so bad. It had to be better than Minnesota."

I was thrilled that I didn't have to call mama and tell her I was a failure. I promised myself that whatever happened in Green Bay, no matter what, I was going to make it work. I called my mama and told her the news. She said, "You're going where? Green Bay?"

I said, "Yep. It's not too far, either. It's just right down the road. I'll be there tonight."

Then I hung up the phone and said, "Thank God."

The four-hour drive flew by. Still, I rolled in pretty late and I pissed off the dude that I was rooming with. He didn't know I was coming in and I'm stumbling and fumbling around and he got ticked off. I apologized, and then he did, too.

He fell asleep right away. I couldn't sleep at all. I was lying in bed thinking, "What in the world am I going to do? Whatever I do I'm going to do it at full throttle. I want these people in Green Bay to like me."

The next morning I come to the locker room and it's nothing like Minnesota. People are talking and laughing and joking and having a good time. The first two guys I saw were Earl Dotson and Paul Hutchins. They were rookie offensive linemen. They looked at me and I could tell they were thinking, "Who's this mother?"

Me? I'm thinking fat draws fat. We were the three fat guys standing around staring at each other. I just knew that we were going to end up being homeboys.

I made my way past Hutchins' locker and when I turned the corner he was there. It was number 92. It was Reggie White. I couldn't talk. I was speechless. When I was in Minnesota I could talk to Chris Doleman. Now he was a very good player, a strong pass rusher, but I didn't feel like I couldn't say hi. It was different with Reggie White. He was the Minister of Defense, the Big Dog, right here in front of me. I idolized him when he played for the Philadelphia Eagles and they were crushing people.

I was fired up. I had a great practice that day. I was out there killing people. I was battling James Campen, the center, and he was a very good player. Some of the other offensive linemen, especially the really young guys and the street free agents, wanted to dance with the defensive linemen. They were doing the brother-in-law thing. I won't make you look bad if you don't make me look bad.

I didn't like it. I told those boys to give me a little something to work on. I wanted to get better each and every practice. I was inspired because I had a new team and a fresh start and a teammate on the defensive line named Reggie White. We also had Bill Maas, Matt Brock, Tony Bennett, Bryce Paup and John Jurkovic. We had a pretty good defensive line even then.

Our defensive line coach, Greg Blache, certainly was no John Teerlinck. By that, I mean Blache knew how to coach, and he knew how to treat his players like men. Ray Rhodes was the defensive coordinator. I was shocked the first time I saw him playing dominoes in the locker room, and I was blown away the first time I heard him cussing and spitting tobacco in his cup and shouting, "This is how you do this! This is how you do that!" He was a mile a minute and he knew what he was talking about. He was great.

He didn't say too much to me, but what he did say was respectful. I felt 10 times better than I did at Minnesota in the first week. I got on my knees at midseason and thanked the Lord for getting me out of Minnesota and for putting me in Green Bay.

I still dislike Minnesota to this day. I hated going back there and playing them. I always worried that somehow I would end up having to stay. That was my nightmare. It was horrible and it messed up my mind. It might've cost me a career.

As bad as Minnesota was to play for, Green Bay was that good.

I played in a couple of games as a rookie. We were only so-so in '93. I thought we got better though. When you have guys like Reggie White around every day you're trying to learn what they know, and watching everything they do.

I was assigned jersey number 71. I wasn't crazy about it but it was better than 96. I worked my tail off that first season, and

Mrs. Ann Brown

discusses Gilbert's arrival in Green Bay and the positive influence head coach Mike Holmgren and defensive coordinator Fritz Shurmur had on him:

"I think he spent his first year in Green Bay just trying to get used to being in the NFL. But I also think his head coach, Mike Holmgren, and his defensive coach, Fritz Shurmur, played a big part in the player he became.

"I liked Mike Holmgren a lot. He said what needed to be said. He told Gilbert exactly the way it was and he didn't mind telling him that was the way it was going to be. I also like Fritz a great deal. He was really good for Gilbert. He stepped up and told Gilbert exactly what was expected. He treated him very good and extremely fair.

"Now, Gilbert had some lousy agents. He wanted to stay in Green Bay after the Super Bowl (in 1996) but his agents kept pushing him to do a deal with Jacksonville. One day this man called and we got talking about Gilbert. It was Fritz Shurmur. He told me how much Gilbert meant to him and to the Packers. He would call me back, talk some more, and finally he said: OK, we're going to do this deal. Fritz wasn't going to let Gilbert go to Jacksonville.

"When Mike Holmgren went to Seattle in 1999, Fritz wanted Gilbert to go with them, and I think he would have gone if Fritz hadn't become ill. Whatever Fritz told him to do, it was just like his Daddy telling him to do it. He loved that man just that much."

apparently the right people noticed. I was at my locker one day and Ron Wolf comes walking through. Ron hardly ever said anything to me. He just looked at me. It was like he was studying me, or maybe trying to guess my weight or something. So I'm sitting there and this time Ron stops and says, "Hey, Brown. What number would you like?"

I told him I always wore 93.

He said, "OK."

I didn't give it a lot of thought until I came in to work the next day. I walked into the locker room and the first thing I saw was a 93 jersey hanging in my locker. I couldn't believe it. I called everybody I knew. I told them that the GM, the main guy, gave me my old number. He gave me 93. That was one of the most memorable things that happened. The GM took the time to make sure I got the jersey number I wanted.

It made me feel wanted. It made me feel like I truly was a part of the Green Bay Packers. I called everybody I knew to tell them that Ron Wolf just did me proud. I also told them that I was going to make damn sure I helped Green Bay win a lot of games.

I was home at last.

CHAPTER FIVE

A Fantastic Front Four

Reggie White was the greatest player, and the greatest teammate, I have known.

There wasn't anything Big Dog couldn't do on the field, and there wasn't anything he wouldn't do for a teammate off it.

He taught me how to be a man. He taught me how to treat people with respect. He taught me how to take care of business, and how to realize the difference between taking care of your "true" friends, and your "so called" friends taking advantage of you.

When I came to Green Bay I had so much to learn about the league. Shoot, I had so much to learn about life.

The best way I knew how to learn about both was by watching Reggie.

I have always been one to sit back and take in everything that's going on around me. I guess you could say I'm an observer. I like to "people watch." I like to hear how they talk. I like to consider how they think. I like to see how they treat others. Best of all, I like to watch how they act when they don't think anybody is paying attention. It's easy to be nice and friendly when there's an audience.

I've been like that since I was a kid.

If I wasn't learning from Reggie, I was learning from Sean Jones. I liked the way Sean handled himself in any type of situation. He would yell at you when he was upset because of something you did, but he also got over it immediately. He didn't let it fester.

Sean was so smart that I felt intimidated around him.

I didn't talk to him for the longest time because I didn't know what to say.

It took awhile for that to change, and the biggest reason it did was Santana Dotson. When he came to Green Bay in March of '96 I didn't know what to expect. He was a big dude, about 6-foot-5 and 285 pounds, and he had a reputation as a good player with the Tampa Bay Buccaneers.

Santana was more of a pass rusher than a run stuffer, although he could and would do both. I trusted him on the field because he always did his homework. He left as little as possible to chance. His father, Alphonse, was drafted by the Packers in 1965 but instead decided to sign with Kansas City of the American Football League. Santana's dad played five seasons in the AFL, and he inherited his father's old-school style and appreciation for the players that came before him.

Santana was the missing ingredient in our defensive line. We were good before he signed with Green Bay, but when he came in we realized we had a chance to be great.

When Santana arrived I looked at our defensive line and thought, "This is perfect. There isn't a thing I would change. Why would you? We had Reggie who could it all at left end. We had Sean, one of the smartest and most experienced guys on the team, at right end. We had Santana and me taking care of business in the middle.

Santana was one of our speed demons. He had a move and a counter move for everything. He was so smart and so prepared it was crazy. I knew he would give us a push inside – a lot of tackles like to use power moves from that position – but Santana was a flashy type of player, too. He could mix it up. If they stopped his first move, he would just move on to the counter-move. He was one cool customer. I never saw Santana rattled in a game. He just rolled with it, and then he rolled over anything in his path.

We had size (me), speed (Santana), strength (Reggie) and smarts (Sean).

Reggie was special for a lot of reasons. Perhaps the biggest reason was that at any given point he could change the game. He was a game changer in every sense. When you sit up there and see the things that he does – like destroying an offensive tackle and making the game-clinching sack – he can change the momentum and the flow of the game in one play. When they say prime time players show up and make big pays in big games that was Reggie White. He was the best, bar none, at making an impact.

Everybody knows about the hump move, but to see him come off the ball with so much force and power, and to be next to him and hear it, it's crazy. It's like a car wreck. The right tackle's arms are flopping around and he's trying to get his feet set and I know he has no chance. It's like a locomotive. There was no stopping Reggie, and here's the thing that doesn't get talked about: What about all the plays that he wasn't involved in but he still beat the hell out of the guy opposite him?

We would sit in meetings and zero in on Reggie and whoever was trying to block him just for fun. We would watch the right tackle get his butt severely kicked, and we would feel pretty good about our chances in the upcoming game.

We had each other's back, too.

We also pushed each other so we wouldn't miss a day of work. The four of us were there for 75 of 76 possible starts in 1996. The only time one of us wasn't in the starting lineup was at Dallas when our defensive coordinator, Fritz Shurmur, decided to open with a 3-4 alignment. He started Ron Cox as the fourth linebacker in place of Santana. It was no big deal because Santana was on the field plenty.

In 1996 the defensive linemen had 21 ½ sacks, seven forced fumbles and an interception. A lot of it was because we had Fritz, and we had talent, but we also had each other and that meant everything.

It was one of those things where everybody knew his role and loved it.

Of course, Reggie was the man. He was the leader. Santana and I were younger players, and for Reggie and Sean to take us under their wings and to show us the things they showed us, and to tell us the things they told us – mostly about togetherness and being a close-knit unit – it is exactly like the picture on the back cover of this book.

It shows how close we were.

That was a Family Night scrimmage at Lambeau Field. Look how we're sitting. It's all four of us together. We always sat together like that for a couple of reasons.

First, every time we came off the field we wanted to be able to look at each other and make sure everyone was all right. That might sound dumb but it was true. We cared about each other as friends and teammates. It's a violent game, and we're OK with that, but that doesn't mean you shouldn't keep an eye out for your guys. That goes for high school football, college football and the pros. It is a good habit to get into.

The other reason we sat together was because it gave us a chance to talk. I wanted to know what Reggie was dealing with at left end. I needed to know how Santana was getting by – if everything was OK – because he was my partner in the middle. We needed to work in tandem to dominate. We needed to know what the other was thinking. We could talk about anything and never have to worry about hurting someone's feelings.

We were together all the time, yet the crazy thing is we never argued. We would fuss and crack jokes, but we never argued. Nobody argued with Reggie, of course, unless it was Wayne Simmons. We never did it. That's saying a lot when you're playing a game that's such high emotion and high intensity.

I looked at Sean Jones – the way he practiced – and I would see something that you hear coaches say all the time. Do not do what Sean Jones does in practice, but pay attention to how he turns it up on game day. Sean had the knack of chilling when he wanted to chill, but when it came time to get serious he turned it up to another level.

If Reggie didn't get the sack you knew Sean was going to get it. There was so much confidence looking down that line and knowing all that experience we had at left and right end. Reggie and Sean always knew what they were doing on the field. Sean was a student of the game and Reggie was damn near impossible to block.

Sean had this old flipper that he would bring out. It was a huge wrap on his left forearm and he put it to good use. It was funny if someone was trying to run a trap or a counter his way, it would be crazy to watch Sean come all the way from Macon, Georgia, and throw that thing and just block everything that was coming down his way. And you're looking to see some offensive lineman with his neck shortened because he almost got his head taken clean off. Sean had that pad on his arm for protection. You throw that flipper around for 16 games and it's going to take its toll.

It was amazing to see Sean be so durable. He was a professional and he played the game and the way he handled himself it was good to watch and learn.

Larry Brooks, our defensive line coach, was tremendous with us.

He played a long time in the NFL. He was a Pro Bowl defensive tackle for five straight seasons in the 1970s. He started for the Rams when they played Pittsburgh in the Super Bowl in 1980. He loved telling stories about the good old days and we loved listening to them. He was a great fisherman, and he and Fritz would talk fishing almost as much as they talked football. Larry was fun to be around, but he was like Sean because he knew when it was time to work and when it was time to play.

Gabriel Wilkins, that was Fritz's project. I have never seen anyone yell at someone as much as Fritz yelled at Gabe. He would yell at Gabe, and yell at Gabe, and I had to hear it. I knew where Fritz was coming from because he wanted Gabe to be the very best player he could be, and he wanted to be able to count on him in the clutch. That was a lot of pressure on Gabe, who was from a small college, and I could see it working on him. He was their draft pick and they needed him to shine. They wanted him to shine.

Gabe knew that if something happened to Reggie or Sean it was going to be Fritz or Larry saying, "Gabe, you're up!" The hard part there was that Mike Holmgren didn't believe in babysitting young players. If you were good enough to be on the 53-man roster, you damn sure better be smart enough to know your role and play it.

Gabe and I were tight, the best of friends, and we're still close.

Keith McKenzie was the other defensive end. There weren't many people that thought Keith was going to make the team. He was a late-round draft pick with really good explosiveness but not much size or strength. It would've been easy to dismiss him, but Fritz and his staff saw something they liked in Keith. I'm sure some of it was the fact that he kept fighting and scrapping throughout training camp. Then he put in extra time after practice, working on his craft, trying to get a position and keep a position on that defensive line. He wasn't the cutest guy, but he got the job done. He earned the position.

Bob Kuberski was another guy that played a key role. He kept us loose. He had a great sense of humor. He thought we were funny. Actually, Bob could play. He was good against the run, and he was athletic enough to get up field on passing downs. We never felt like it was going to be a problem whenever Bob came in to play.

We didn't have a catchy nickname or anything like that. We weren't the New York Sack Exchange, or the Purple People Eaters, or the Fearsome Foursome.

We were damn good, though.

We beat teams up.

We had a whole bunch of guys that played their roles behind us, too. They were unselfish. It was Santana's job and my job to make sure (George) Koonce made plays. When you've got two guys up front like that, it doesn't make your job easier, but it does make you more at ease. We told Koonce, "Don't worry about it. Just do your job."

Koonce did his job and more. It hurt me when he got hurt against San Francisco in the NFC Divisional Playoffs. He played so hard for so long that season and then he had to sit out the NFC Championship Game and Super Bowl XXXI.

I noticed the way he acted in the games after his injury. Koonce was still a team player all the way. He could have pouted about the injury or been angry and blamed it on a bunch of different things. He didn't. He studied and tried to lend whatever insight he could on Carolina and New England.

When we lost Koonce for the season, we plugged in Ron Cox and kept winning. Part of that is because he had big linemen in front of him to keep guys off his back. I didn't mind taking on two guys because that was my job. The word sack never entered my mind. When you've got guys like Reggie and Sean and Santana there was no need. My job was to crush the run, so that's what I did.

The thing that made the defensive line happiest was when Fritz would come to where we were doing our individual drills during practice and just watch. He'd just stand there, and he wouldn't say much, if anything. I think if he was having a bad day, or if the other drills weren't going so well, he came down and watched us to cheer himself up. If you're a defensive coordinator, and you're having a tough day, it's probably not a bad idea to remember what you do have: Reggie White and Co.

Fritz always told us, "It starts with the big boys up front." That was the greatest feeling just knowing he had our back.

We didn't have to bring up a guy to the line and blitz to get to the quarterback. We did it to create problems for the opposing offense, or to change it up, but the four of us allowed the linebackers and defensive backs to roam, freelance and make plays.

LeRoy was perfect in that playmaker role.

We used to toy with offenses and tell them it was coming.

LeRoy hated Santana for this. Santana would get down there, and we knew LeRoy would be shooting the gap, and Santana would say, "LeRoy, are you coming through this hole right here?" LeRoy wouldn't respond but right after the play he'd tell Santana, "Man, don't do that anymore. I'm trying to sneak up on these clowns."

But Santana did it anyway, and it still worked. LeRoy would complain, and I can see his point, and then he would make the play anyway. It was a beautiful thing.

So was that defensive front four. The Fantastic Front Four: Reggie White. Gilbert Brown. Santana Dotson. Sean Jones.

THERE WAS NO PLACE FOR BALL CARRIERS TO RUN, AND THERE WAS NO PLACE FOR QUARTERBACKS TO HIDE. THAT WAS THE REAL DEAL. THE BOMB! I CAN'T HELP GETTING EXCITED THINKING ABOUT MY BOYS UP FRONT.

Sean Jones Comments

on Gilbert Brown's ability to play nose tackle at a Hall of Fame level:

"Gilbert is a guy that took me a while to get to know. Gilbert became a different person when he and Santana (Dotson) lined up next to each other. I swear for two years I didn't hear a word out of Gilbert. He didn't talk. He didn't joke. He didn't say anything.

He went "Hmm." That was it. That was the extent.

The old joke used to be whenever anybody asked what Gilbert thought about anything, the stock answer was, "Hmm." I am proud to say Gilbert outgrew his shell. He was as good as any of the defensive tackles I played with. Ray Childress. Doug Smith. Bill Pickel. Reggie Kinlaw. Those are pretty special guys. Gilbert and Doug Smith are the two most talented defensive linemen I ever played with. The things Gilbert could do at 300-whatever pounds were amazing."

George Koonce comments

on life as a middle linebacker behind Reggie White, Gilbert Brown, Santana Dotson and Sean Jones:

"When you're in the midst of that storm it's easy to forget everything around you. But that front four made my job a lot easier. I think it made it easier for the other seven players."

Thursday's Practice…

…Sunday's Victory!

CHAPTER SIX

For Starters "Goods vs. Goods" As Good As It Gets

They say practice makes perfect.

I can't say we were perfect in 1996, but we tried to practice that way.

If you ask any of the players off that Super Bowl XXXI championship team they will tell you that Thursday was the day they looked forward to the most. Of course, Sunday was everyone's favorite day, or Monday if we played on Monday Night Football.

The reason we looked forward to Thursday was because that's the day the No. 1 offense and the No. 1 defense got to get after each other. We called it "Goods versus Goods" and it was all of that. Most National Football League teams, from what I am told, do the same thing that coach Mike did on Thursdays.

We worked on the 2-minute drill, the red zone and short yardage situations.

Obviously those are three key areas in each game.

The 2-minute drill was Brett Favre's time to shine. If we needed a last-minute touchdown or field goal to win that was when the offense had to go to work. There was no room for error and coach Mike was a real stickler during the 2-minute drill. He would be moving around and not missing anything and making sure that Brett and the offense got the play, called it at the line and kept moving the chains. He also used it to discuss strategy. He talked about when to spike, or clock the

Mike Holmgren,

head coach

"It was very competitive. I just kept my fingers crossed that no one would get nicked up and hurt, but they learned how to practice fast. What helped that team that year was a healthy respect between offense and defense. We had good players on offense. We had great players on defense. It takes both to win. There was a good respect there."

football by snapping it and throwing it into the ground to stop the clock. He talked about using timeouts. He talked about what yard line the offense had to reach for Chris Jacke to be in field-goal range.

On defense, Fritz used the 2-minute drill to first of all make sure we had the right personnel on the field. He would go absolutely crazy if we had 10 men, or 12 men, on the field or if guys were running on or off while trying to pull their helmet on and get the call. It's a recipe for disaster and Fritz knew it. So he wouldn't tolerate it.

Fritz also liked to use the 2-minute drill to knock other teams out. He didn't want to drop back in that dam prevent defense, or as Fritz called it, "Prevent? The only thing it does is prevent us from winning." That's why he would like to have specific blitzes in his bag of tricks all ready to go. He might pull one out for the right moment when a sack, and maybe a fumble, can end the game on the spot.

The red zone – when the offense is inside the defense's 20-yard line – is critical for obvious reasons, too. Red zone offense and defense usually decides which teams are going to go to the playoffs and which teams are staying home.

When our offense got inside the red zone it was deadly. Sherman Lewis, our offensive coordinator, was really good in there. He could draw up things you couldn't even dream of or imagine. The tough part of the red zone offense is that everything is shrunk down to a small area. Offenses can't run their usual plays because they won't work in such a confined area. Trust me, the defenses know it and plan for it. That's why Sherman and the offense had to be creative.

On defense, we really focused on reacting to the football and we tried to be super alert in that phase. I mean we concentrated on every snap. Our deal was to try to knock offenses out 1-2-3. We wanted them gone in three plays and punting so we could get back to the sideline, watch Desmond Howard try to return it for a touchdown, and then settle in and see Brett and those boys go to work.

The short yardage work was intense but we tried to not make it crazy. The last thing coach Mike wanted was to get somebody nicked up or hurt in Thursday's practice because it means you've got one less weapon and you've got to get someone else ready. One of the things that coach Mike did – and it made a lot of sense – was demand that the backups be ready to go the same as the starters. That was his insurance policy in case something went wrong late in the week. It's pretty foolish to build a large part of a game plan around a couple of guys and then have an injury mess up what you've practiced. I've seen it happen and it usually isn't pretty come Sunday. That's when mistakes occur.

Between the 2-minute drill, the red zone and the short yardage plays, we probably spent a good deal of that 90-minute practice or whatever on Thursday.

The competition was intense, as you might imagine, even though we weren't working on things we were going to see from the other team on Sunday. It was still football. Can you cover me? Can I block you? It was that sort of thing and it was fun.

We had guidelines during the "Goods versus Goods" and coach Mike would go ballistic if we didn't follow them. The biggest one was keeping guys off the ground. When guys were lying down around a pile, which meant they were lying down around other players' legs, the chances of injury went way up. It's common sense.

The other thing that was so important was the ability to know the difference between practicing really fast, I mean as

Brett Favre, quarterback

"To this day, the thing I look forward to most in practice is the actual competitive part. You hate to go against your defense all the time because that's not the defense you're going to see, style or pressure, but there's no substitution for goods against goods and bringing out the best. In those days, it was like, 'We'll see how good you are and you'll see how good we are.' "Can you beat the cornerback across from you? Can you block these guys?' LeRoy Butler would always be running his mouth. He'd be talking smack. It brought out the best in me. I still look forward to those drills, but it's not the same."

close to game speed as possible, and practicing out of control. Fans might laugh but it's almost an art. Coach Mike preached on that all the time because he knew the faster and smarter we practiced the more likely it was that we would play that way on game day.

Thursday's practice featured some battles that were epic. I mean this was the best game in town on a lot of weeks. They didn't sell tickets to it but they damn sure could have, and they would have made a lot of money doing it.

For starters, we had Brett Favre – Mr. MVP quarterback – going up against our safeties in the 2-minute drill and the red zone. LeRoy and Eugene loved trying to fool Brett into thinking he'd read them off one receiver so he could throw to another. That battle was ongoing and nobody knew who would win. It was a week-to-week thing.

Brett loved to look off the safety, especially LeRoy, and make a big completion. But if LeRoy ever got an interception it was crazy. He would sprint toward the other end zone and if Brett got near him like he was going to pretend to make the tackle, LeRoy would hoot and holler and put the football right in his face mask. Brett hated that, but I think he loved it, too.

There were some other interesting battles out there.

My favorite was Wayne Simmons, our strong-side linebacker, going against Mark Chmura, our big tight end. Simmons wasn't quite as vocal as he would be in the game, but still let Chmura know that he thought he could shove him around. Wayne was naturally strong and he had long, powerful arms that were perfect for getting leverage. When Wayne got his hands on you it was lights out. Game over. Done.

He did things to the 49ers' Brent Jones that shouldn't be allowed. He tried to do the same stuff with Chmura, but you've got to remember Chewy was no lightweight. He also had a reputation to uphold. He was regarded as one of the best blocking tight ends in the entire NFL, and he was all of that and then some. So you'd have Wayne trying to throw Chmura around, and Chewy trying to manhandle Wayne, and it was awesome.

Brian Williams, our weak-side linebacker, often had to chase either Dorsey Levens or Edgar Bennett out in the flat. Most of the time it was Dorsey because he was our single back and coach Mike liked to go with four wide receivers in the 2-minute drill. Can you imagine B-Dub – who could really run – getting after Dorsey? Edgar had great hands, too, and when he got busy inside the red zone it was the same thing. Could B-Dub get there in time before Edgar could catch the pass, give a shimmy shake and get to the sideline or the end zone? That was always the question. It's been 10 years and I'm still not sure what the answer was but I'd have to put my money on the defense.

People ask what I think would happen if the offense and the defense scrimmaged for four quarters. Who would win? I guess I tend to agree with Ron Wolf's opinion. Wolf said he thought the offense's playmakers and firepower eventually would win out. He felt that given enough time, Antonio Freeman, Robert

Brooks, Andre Rison, Keith Jackson, Mark Chmura, Dorsey Levens and Edgar Bennett would find a way to beat the defense. He just wasn't sure if cornerbacks Craig Newsome and Doug Evans could hold up.

I see what he is saying because Free and Brooks and K-Jack and the boys were really, really good. That's why we liked getting off the field in three plays. We could sit down, kick back and watch them tear defenses apart.

I also know that Wolf added this: "The offense's playmakers would probably win out, but that's if the offensive line could hold up against that defensive front. And that's a big if."

MIKE HOLMGREN PRE-GAME SPEECH

"Men, this is what we've worked for since that first meeting in training camp. We're here for one reason, and that's to win the Super Bowl. It was a long, hard road. It's why we went through all the ups and downs, just to be here in this position we're in right now. So don't let it slip away. Enjoy yourself and remember this moment forever. Now let's get out there and ***GET AFTER IT!"***

CHAPTER SEVEN

Super Memories From Super Bowl XXXI

The night before the Super Bowl was supposed to be like any other night.

That's what the coaches wanted us to believe.

The truth was we were playing at the pinnacle of our entire profession, and it was like no other night in my life.

Oh, it began routine enough.

We got something to eat on our own, just like always, and then we went to our first meeting at seven-thirty. Back in those days, I liked to eat and then come back to the hotel room and lie down and relax before the meeting, which is what I did.

I had my usual pre-game meal at a restaurant in New Orleans.

I got a nice big porterhouse steak. Medium rare. I want something that is going to fill me up. I also had mashed potatoes, sweet corn, crab legs and mussels. I skipped the salad. I'm a meat-and-potatoes man, as if you couldn't tell.

Some guys eat like it's their last meal the night before a game. I just eat the same usual, which I suppose is like some players' last meal. After my nap, which was about the only sleep I had between our seven-thirty meeting Saturday night and Sunday's kickoff, we went to the meeting room. The walk there was one of those surreal deals.

It was Santana Dotson, Gabe Wilkins, Reggie White and myself. We were joking and messing around all the way on the walk to the meeting room.

Looking back, I think we were jacked up and we also were trying to get rid of the nervous energy. If it wasn't the Super Bowl, we probably would have played cards and shot the breeze in someone's room – usually the room closest to the elevator for convenience – or we might've just sat in the hallway and killed time. We tried to keep it the same so people wouldn't choke each other.

I didn't do much drinking of alcohol during the week. It was New Orleans, and Bourbon Street, and it was tempting but I decided to wait until after the game. When I drink I like to switch it up. A little Crown, Tequila, beer or whatever is at hand. A lot of guys can't do that. When they try to drink what I drink they usually hit the floor.

That would come later. I had serious business to attend to.

Our first meeting was the defensive team meeting. It goes about 30 minutes. Most times our meeting would get over before the offensive team meeting and we'd have to wait for them to wrap it up. There wasn't an official seating chart but guys ended up sitting in the same places all season. Most of the time the older players would stay in the back of the room and the younger players would scoot up front. We also sat with our position group because that made it easier for Fritz Shurmur, our defensive coordinator, to address a specific group at once.

Fritz opened by talking about what we needed to do to defeat New England's offense. How to attack their strengths? How to take advantage of their weaknesses? It was a lot of what we covered all week. It was the last refresher before the final exam.

If something popped into Fritz's head he would say it.

We watched film of certain plays. We started with the run and then the pass. Fritz loved to use the overhead projector. That was his favorite thing. I used to hate that thing. During the week that thing is sitting right in front of me. Fritz is sitting up there talking and spitting, and stuff is running off the overhead projector, and he keeps rolling along. He is old school all the way. Now they have the computers and the special markers and all that stuff. Fritz had the overhead and a marker. He didn't dress like it was prom, either. He always wore a golf shirt, slacks and comfortable shoes.

The way Fritz opened the meeting depended on the mood. Not our mood. His. He didn't want anyone to be overtired. He didn't change much. He kept it real.

We met for thirty minutes. He didn't believe in meeting to death. He thought it was better to hit the high points, emphasize the key elements and get out of there.

With New England we talked about their blocking scheme on the offensive line, and we talked about their running back, Curtis Martin. He was the featured back, but we also had to watch out for Keith Byars because he was a crafty veteran. Reggie knew him real well from their time together in Philadelphia, and he knew how bad Keith wanted to win the game because he'd never been on a championship team in the pros.

The Patriots didn't have a powerful offensive line. We viewed them as a unit that was going to show up and play and probably not make many mistakes along the way. Their offense had a lot of weapons, but Curtis Martin was a guy we couldn't forget.

Max Lane, a young offensive lineman, drew the awful assignment of having to try to block Reggie. During that season, even though Reggie was 36, it didn't matter who was across from him. You could see the change in Big Dog as the season unfolded. He was so focused on getting to the Super Bowl he began slowly fazing out everything else. It sounds corny but that's what made other guys begin to tune in and focus. We followed his lead, and his moods, and we knew we had to be heading the right direction.

There is a difference playing in the Super Bowl as opposed to playing in any other game. Most people don't see that jump. The players feel it. The competition takes a jump from the regular season to the playoffs to the Super Bowl.

We didn't have one or two guys that were the emotional leaders. Everybody knew Brett Favre and Reggie White were the leaders, and everybody rallied behind them, but we had different guys take over that emotional deal on different weeks.

We never really knew who it would be, but someone always seemed to step up. For example, Wayne Simmons was not the leader, but his play, intensity and attitude for what he was doing would rub off on the rest of us. When a guy is out there doing his thing and pumping his fist in the air, everybody wants to ride that wave. Everybody wants to go out there and help.

I couldn't relax the night before Super Bowl XXXI.

We had the same format in meetings but the attitude felt different. Everybody was focused. Too focused. We needed something to break the ice. Fritz did that with his talk.

The speech was about a relative that was dying of cancer, his brother of all things, and looking back it is eerie because that was how Fritz died. He talked about it a bit and then he somehow tied it all into the game. By the time that meeting was over just about everybody was to the point of crying. Guys were turning their heads away from each other, or looking down at their shoes, so they didn't have to face each other or Fritz.

It was so quiet, and so touching, it put everybody in the mood to focus on what we had to do. It relaxed us and it got us fired up, too. I know that doesn't make sense, but if you were keyed up about a game, and then Fritz told you that story, you would just naturally slow down, and come down, and then he brought it all back to the job at hand.

He was amazing that way.

If anyone tells you that the coach's talks in meetings and their pre-game speeches aren't important they're full of it. Fritz was the master. We were like, 'Let's go kill!'

I was looking at Craig Newsome, and the defensive backs were always laid back because they don't have to hit anybody, but to see Craig and Doug Evans and those boys tearing up was a sight to behold. I could see that this game meant more to them than any game they ever played in, and Fritz meant more to them than any coach. When that meeting was over we gave him a couple of pats on the back. We loved him, but we didn't want to get too mushy the night before the Super Bowl.

Fritz wrapped up his deal and everyone was talking about how we were going to do this and do that to New England. Then it got quiet. We needed an icebreaker.

Wayne Simmons, of all people, delivered it. He shouted, "Let's go mess 'em up! Let's go!" We were ready for the team meeting now.

Coach Mike (Holmgren) always opened the team meeting with a highlight film. They put something together for each game of the playoffs and it really got us going. We saw each other kickin' butt and the music was blasting and we were revved up.

This time, when we walked into the team meeting, the offense was sitting down. The highlight film hadn't started and we looked like our eyes were glazed. The offense was like, "What's wrong with these dudes?"

We were looking at the offense wondering the same thing. Are they ready to play? Are they ready to kick butt? That offensive line was hard to read that year. We couldn't tell if they just got chewed out by Mike or pampered.

Mike's thing was to keep everyone calm, but to make sure you knew that you had a very important job to do. Certain guys had certain things. Mike had a way of looking right at you while he was talking. When he wanted to get his point across, I mean really hammer it home, he would look at somebody and let them know he was talking about them – to them – without pointing a finger or saying a name.

Mike opened with a general comment that covered all three phases: offense, defense and special teams. It was never in-depth. He was just hitting all the points we went through during the week. That night he didn't need to motivate us. He just wanted to get us in, go over the material and get a good night's sleep.

We wrapped up with a film showing highlights of the offense and the defense. It was a good mix of certain plays and certain guys. It went about 20 minutes.

After the meeting we went to a cafeteria area in the hotel and got a snack. I always sat with William Henderson at the evening snack. It just started one night and we kept with it ever since. I usually sit and eat with Will but this was one of those nights where if I eat I'm just being fat. I didn't want to feel like I was weighed down.

I believe George Koonce and LeRoy Butler and a couple of the wide receivers were at our table for the late-night snack. The guys tended to gravitate to the same table all season long. Will and I made a strange combination – he was a fullback and I was a nose tackle – but we clicked. I think the thing with that was I respected his game and he's told me that he respected mine. That was one of the other things that made that team special. It wasn't just guys hanging out with their own position group, or just the offense if they played on offense. Guys mingled and it wasn't something that was forced. It just sort of happened over time, and especially in the years leading up to 1996.

That's how Will and I started hanging out.

It's funny because William will tell you that he isn't superstitious but that's not true. He and I had been sitting together all year and we decided it wouldn't make sense to change. Now, I will admit it. I am superstitious. I have one where I will do things seven times on game day. If I shower I will rub the shampoo through my hair seven times. If I brush my teeth, I will brush back and forth seven times. If I comb my hair, it's seven times. It's stupid, I know, but I do did it all the time. I don't tell anyone. Are you crazy? They'd think I was obsessive-compulsive. I don't know what that is but it can't be good. That habit started in college and I've been doing it ever since.

While we were at the table guys were talking about what they were going to do when they were introduced before the game. We were trying to figure out what other guys should do, and then we got into guys' personalities, and I started telling everyone what I thought they should be doing. The one thing we didn't do was get Reggie involved in the conversation. We didn't bring Reggie in because he was already focused beyond belief. It's like Fritz during the game. You don't mess with him.

When we got tired of joking and messing around it was time to head to room for a good night's sleep. Yeah, right. I wanted to focus all week, which is why I didn't get tickets for anybody but my high school football coach, Bob Dozier. I didn't get tickets for my family, not my mama, not my brothers and sisters or friends or anyone.

I wanted it to be special for coach Dozier. I also didn't want to be distracted. I knew that he wouldn't impose on me. I put him and a friend up in a nice hotel. I took care of everything. I wanted him to have a great time because I wanted to thank him for being my coach and for driving my dumb butt to school each morning my senior year.

My family is so cool to understand. Not a single one of them gave me grief about it. They just said they understood and that was that. I bet there aren't many pro athletes – NFL players especially – that would be so lucky. Well, I've got to be honest. I did catch it from a few people, and I understand that, too.

Now, the next year it was a whole different deal in San Diego. When we went to Super Bowl XXXII to play Denver, I got tickets for everybody and my brothers. It was nuts. It was like that for a lot of the guys. I don't believe that's the reason we lost to Denver. I'll save that for the next book. But it certainly couldn't have helped.

Well, Gabe and I went back to our room. It was time to get some sleep. Try as I did I couldn't catch a wink. I sat in bed all night long with the lights on. I was just sitting there thinking about everything that had happened during the season leading up to that point, and I was thinking about what might happen in the game.

I kept thinking about what Fritz said during the film. I thought about all the people I left at home. I was thinking that we damn sure better win this game. I was thinking about Dan Marino and Bart Starr and all the greats that came before me.

Now how are you going to sleep with all that going on inside your head?

Funny thing was I didn't feel tired the next day. Not one bit. I slept about 20 minutes in the locker room once we got to the Superdome. That was about two hours before kickoff. Otherwise, I was awake and ready to roll.

My roommate, Gabe, was altogether different.

He was snoring the second his head hit the pillow. He was gone. I was alone.

I tried to call my girlfriend and she said, "You better try to get some sleep because it's a big game. You're not going to play well if you don't sleep."

This was at midnight.

Then I talked to my mom, my brother LeRoy, my homeboy Kyle Moore, and just about anybody whose phone number I had so I could call. This went on for about two hours. Now it's almost three o'clock in the morning. Gabe is sleeping like a baby. I'm pacing like a cat – a really big cat. The reason I'm pacing is because there was nobody left to call, and nobody left to talk to.

I didn't want to bother Gabe so I left the light on in the bathroom. I just stared at myself in the mirror for what seemed like forever. I was shadow boxing and thinking about how I was going to play and what moves I was going to use.

Then I got my Sony Walkman out of my bag and went back into the bathroom. I was listening to all kinds of music, mostly stuff with a good beat to it. I was moving and bopping so much I started to break out in a sweat. Finally, I went back to the bedroom, turned up the air conditioning and laid down. I knew I needed to do that, even if I didn't sleep, because I wanted to have my legs.

The trouble was I couldn't do it.

I just couldn't sleep.

There are only two nights in my life that even come close. There was the night my son was born, and there was the night my daddy died. Those two nights had really different emotions, and neither one was anything like the night before Super Bowl XXXI.

When Gabe woke up in the morning I was just sitting there. He asked me what was going on. I told him I couldn't sleep. The other thing about me was that I didn't eat before games. I might have some Gatorade or water, but I don't eat. I won't do it. For some reason my body feels sluggish if I eat and try to play. Now, after the game I'm hungry enough to kill. I'm starving like you wouldn't believe.

Once Gabe got up and we started the pre-game routine I

was edgy. I tried to mess around with guys in their rooms, joking and teasing, but it didn't work. I was too wired. Guys would ask each other how they slept. I said I didn't catch a wink. Guys thought I was nuts and they acted real cool, like they all slept like babies.

I think they were lying.

George Koonce said he was light's out the second he went to bed. I said, yeah, you're full of it, too.

I was ready to get to the Superdome by the time the first bus pulled up in front of the team hotel. I didn't get on though. The first was a little more uptight. Mike was on the first bus. Most of the coaches were on the first bus, too. So were most of the young guys. All the older, cooler guys took the second bus. It's a little louder and we're all acting like The Thing on The Fantastic Four going around saying, "It's clobberin' time."

Brett and Reggie always took the second bus. It got to be a tradition so that's what I stayed with. It was the same in the locker room once we got to the dome.

I never got my ankles taped. I just show up and get dressed. That's what I do. Sometimes I hate putting my pants on because they're so tight, and I use the big pads for my shoulder pads, and I've got to have my knee pads and my thigh pads.

I didn't need anything taped though. I was a youngster then.

The only thing I had was a superstition about marking my pads. I know I have to put that one in first, that one in second, that one in third, that one in fourth, and then my belt. Then I lay my pants and my shoulder pads down and I let them sit there. I don't put my stuff on until I have to. I have shorts and a T-shirt on. Some guys like to whirlpool, but I don't do that stuff.

I like to come in and look at the guys.

I listened to music then. I tried to calm down. If somebody's cracking jokes I tried to scoot over there and listen in. Wayne Simmons always joked that I was going to have a snow cone machine during training camp, and I'd have a flavor called "gravy" and I'd be turning it on all the time. The guys thought it was funny. I didn't but I rolled with it.

The game is still a blur to me. I've watched it on ESPN replays and I remember everything then, but if you ask me to take you through it I can't. That's because I was so focused on what I was doing down there in the trenches on every play.

When I look back I do think of the Patriots.

Curtis Martin, their running back, is a future Pro Football Hall of Fame back. He was a real good player, very consistent, and we knew we couldn't go to sleep on him. I remember one drive when Santana Dotson had to come out for a breather. We brought Darius Holland in and I thought, "Oh, boy." I told Darius that New England probably would try to run a screen or a counter play or a trap, and that he should be head's up.

I told him, "Darius, we might need you on this one." As soon as Santana came out, sure enough, they went right to Curtis Martin and right where S.D. had been. Darius didn't listen and the Patriots ended up getting a pretty decent gain. We hated to give up a first down, let alone a gain of 10 yards or more, so we weren't happy.

Sometimes you could just tell that something bad was going to happen when one of the big guys up front went out.

Martin finished with something like 42 yards rushing so it wasn't like he went crazy. We controlled him. The problem was they had other weapons. Ben Coates was a great tight end. Their receivers were pretty good, too. Keith Byars was all-purpose and Reggie kept telling us that he still could hurt us if we didn't pay attention.

The guy we were most concerned about was the Patriots' quarterback. We always wanted to take away first down and second down, and then pin our ears back on third down and get after the quarterback. That was the pretty much the plan going into every game, and that was the plan going into Super Bowl XXXI.

Stopping Drew Bledsoe was the main thing. We had to be aware of the whole field, but Bledsoe made it happen for them. He made them go. He was big and strong. You couldn't arm tackle him. You had to wrap him up. You had to put a body on him.

It took a while, but we finally did put a body on him: Reggie's body.

My best memory of that game was Reggie getting the three sacks, especially the two sacks late that shut down the Patriots. It goes back to what I always said about Reggie. He was a prime-time player that could change the whole game in one play. He was 36 years old when he played in Super Bowl XXXI. It didn't matter. He didn't play like an old man. He played like a grown man. Now matter how old he was he always gave it everything he had, and he really wanted that ring. He wasn't going to be denied. He wasn't one of these guys that was hanging around and biding his time.

He went out and made it happen.

When I saw Reggie come off the field after the first sack he went straight to the oxygen tank. Guys were trying to high-five him and jump on him but he didn't want any part of it. He was too busy trying to catch his breath and calm himself down.

Fritz was like that, too. When the game was going on you didn't bother him. Nobody went over and messed with Fritz during the game. He was so focused and into calling plays and getting a feel for the game that he didn't have time for anything else.

There's no time for playing around when Fritz had the headsets on. A lot of defensive coordinators sit up in the coaches' box. They're all comfortable up there with their coffee and their lemonade or whatever. Not Fritz. He was down in the trenches right where he belonged. He was like a general down there with his troops. He wanted to deal with the heat and the cold just like we had to. He was with us all the way.

When we took control of the game in the fourth quarter, I remember sitting next to Santana and thinking that clock would never get to zeroes.

It gave me time to think about things.

I looked at our cornerbacks – C-New and Doug Evans – and I always thought they were really good and really underrated.

I thought about where our victory in Super Bowl XXXI began. That was the win in San Francisco in '95 in the NFC Divisional Playoffs. Craig Newsome made the big play that day when he scooped up that fumble and took it in for a touchdown.

That was where it all began.

That game brought us closer together as a team. Usually we watched film and went home, but for that specific game – that 49ers game – we were all in the film room as a unit after practice every day. We said we were going to win that game no matter what. We knew what was riding on it.

I also thought about the Dallas Cowboys, as crazy as that sounds, but it's true.

The last game we lost in 1996 was the game at Dallas on Monday Night Football. We ran the table after that to win the world's championship. That game motivated us. All those doggone field goals drove us insane. We lost but we didn't let the Cowboys get into the end zone. We were determined not to let them and we still lost.

We put so much into that San Francisco game to get to that point it might have taken something from us. We had no choice though. The ball was rolling and we wanted to get to that NFC Championship so we had to take care of business with the 49ers first.

When we went to Dallas and lost that day to end the 1995 season, I hate to say it but the Cowboys were probably the better team. That was the only time I saw Reggie get really frustrated. The Cowboys' Erik Williams, their right tackle, had a way of being able to get under Reggie's skin. That was the only guy that could it. When we saw that it was like, "Oh, no." Somebody just threw Kryptonite on Superman's cape. When your leader is going through the ropes with this cat, Erik Williams, it didn't do much for our confidence or our chances to beat them. Every time Reggie tried to assert himself against Williams, he'd almost get the edge or use the "hump move" to bowl him over. Almost. It never quite happened.

Plus, we always had to play them in Dallas. That got old, too.

I give Dallas credit. That offensive line was pretty damn good. They had Williams and

Mark Stepnoski at center and Nate Newton and Larry Allen. That was a great offensive line, to be honest. I think we lost to them all the time because our defensive line was our strength, and their offensive line was their strength, and we couldn't seem to get the better of it.

I thought about Brett Favre and Reggie White. You don't just go to the Five & Dime and buy something like that. It was a blessing for me. I love all my teammates from those days, but I thank God I played with Reggie White and Brett Favre.

I was proud of Brett, and happy for him, too.

That had been a really rough season. It was shocking when I heard about the addiction to painkillers and that he was going to a treatment facility. I know he's not perfect. I'm not. Nobody is. But for him to come back and play at the level he did, and to win the Super Bowl, that guy just amazes me.

What you see is what you get with that guy. Brett walks it. He talks it. He does it.

That's why you could take an offensive lineman, and he may not be that good, but he'll block his butt off because he's got Brett Favre behind him. Offensive linemen know that guy will play his ass off to win. You know that guy behind you is going to tear his nuts off to win. You knew Brett didn't always make the best decision with the football, and that he took some chances, but you also knew he always had your back.

Mike Holmgren was the same way. I have to say that besides my high school coach, Mike was the best coach I ever played for. He had a knack of being hard, fair and smart all at the same time. It's rare that a coach has that type of combination, and he could motivate guys, too.

He could do things to where you didn't think you could do. When you have a head coach that everybody loves and respects you want to go out and play your heart out for them. We knew he was an offensive coach, and I know the offensive boys had a little edge over us with the head coach. That was OK. We had Fritz, and it was good to see Mike get mad at us on Thursdays when we had those practices.

Mike always told us, "You show respect to your teammates, but you've also got to have your teammates' back."

Santana and me, that's my boy, we talked all the time. We were tight. The Super Bowl was winding down and we just looked at each other and grinned. We were looking at the clock, we were looking at the score, and we were smiling. It was coming close now. We were going to be the champions of the world.

That game was like a movie. The ups and the downs and up again. It's so amazing to see that clock and know that it doesn't tick down fast enough. I wanted it to hurry up.

I looked up and down the sideline and saw Eugene Robinson just standing there. He had this look on his face of deep satisfaction. He seemed to be soaking it all in. I think Eugene loved being a part of it. He knew what he was doing. If he told Craig something, he did it because he wanted Craig to be better. It wasn't criticism. It was being helpful. It was the same thing with Santana and myself. We were there to work together, and that meant sharing information and caring about each other.

Nowadays, if you tell a young player something it seems like they don't listen. They're too busy saying, "Who are you? Why do I have to listen to you?" They fight each other right down the line. If you're messing up, and you don't try to listen and do it better, you're not going to win.

It can't happen. It won't happen.

I was so glad I didn't have to deal with it in Green Bay. In fact, the hard part was trying to move on after doing something like winning the Super Bowl. It's very hard to deal with the reality of having to let go of that high.

We could have gone three times in a row. We should've won that 1997 debacle. You think about all that stuff. The opportunity was there. Pay attention to what's going on around you. If you don't pay attention, you're not going to get where you want to go. That's what happened to us. We should've, could've and would've but we didn't.

That's another reason 1996 was extra-special right down to the victory parade in Green Bay. The thing about that damn parade, everybody had their coats and their bags still on the airplane. We were told it would be OK because we were going to get a ride on a bus through town. We were told how cool it was going to be. Well, it was cool all right. We got on the bus and the windows were down. It was nice to be cheered like that, but the people that had gloves on – I hate to say it – we were snatching their gloves off them and their hats off them. That route took forever to get back to the stadium.

Everybody had a party that night. Everybody had something going on. I went home. It was late. I wanted to go home and watch TV. I wanted to hear them talk about us. I wanted to hear about how we dominated. I wanted to hear all of that.

It was everything we thought it would be and a little more.

It was wonderful. So was that damn parade. It was cold as hell, but I had fun. When I saw Mike Holmgren borrowing a police officer's jacket to stay warm I laughed. If I could do it all again, parade included, I would do it. I swear to God I would.

CHAPTER EIGHT

Life After Football And Beyond

Some people play it down. Some don't. I think it's big.

Winning Super Bowl XXXI was a tremendous team accomplishment in the most terrific team game there is in all of sports. It's an individual award to go to the Pro Football Hall of Fame or to be a Pro Bowl player, but it's a team award to go to the Super Bowl and to win makes it extra-special.

You did something together. You share it with 52 other guys. You did something for a cause, your team and its fans, and there aren't too many people that can say that they are world champions. People treat you differently, that's for sure. After you win a Super Bowl, you walk into a place at a league-connected function or what not and there might be 15 former NFL players in there, but there's probably only one Super Bowl winner. Everybody recognizes it because everybody wants that hunk of ice. They want that ring on their finger. There's something almost magical about it.

The important thing is never to gloat. Nobody wins a Super Bowl by himself. I'm appreciative of it. I respect it. Super Bowl championships don't come easy. You've got to work hard at it. You've got to be the best guy on the best team that year.

That's saying something.

People ask what I want for myself in 10 years.

I would like to be healthy. I have three wonderful kids. I want to see them grown and loving what they do. I believe my connection with auto racing and the Milwaukee Mile will be something

Mrs. Ann Brown

discusses Gilbert's decision to play the 2003 season despite a torn biceps muscle, and why she suspects her son is popular among Packers fans:

"I never really understood the decision to play. I drove to Green Bay and I was waiting on him to go to the hospital, and waiting on him to make a decision on his career. To me, he should have had the (torn triceps) taken care of. I left it up to him and he decided not to do it. He gets stubborn. He thinks he's doing the right thing but he isn't. He shouldn't have played that season, but I think (Packers) fans respect him for it.

"He's a likeable kid. He's also generous. He'll buy shoes for kids whose families have lost everything in a fire. He'll pay his friends' light bill if they're struggling. He does a lot of nice things for people but he will never tell you that he did them. I think that has a lot to do with the way people feel about him.

"I also think a lot of it – as my mother once told me – was that he didn't get to Green Bay on his own. He got to Green Bay because of the people that were behind him, and by The Man Upstairs. I think God put him where he wanted him to be, and I think God touched him even though a lot of things Gilbert does he shouldn't do.

"I tell him where you live and what you have is because God mapped it out. He needs to start thanking God more often. Let's hope he sees that pretty soon."

exciting for me. My charitable foundation is helping in the Milwaukee and Detroit areas and it's growing. That means a lot to me.

I plan to continue pursuing my love of cars. Being in Detroit, the Motor City, and growing up around all types of cars – my uncle and father and their friends always had cars – it rubbed off. Just to see my dad working on cars was fun growing up. He was very good at it, too. There wasn't anything he couldn't fix. And he was always customizing them, too.

Sometimes he got carried away, and he would get a spray can and spray-paint gold or whatever. The good Lord upstairs blessed me with the opportunity to get to know about cars and work on them and enjoy them. My dad was a Chrysler-Mopar man. He had a love of cars. I share that with him.

Some days I'll walk through the garage and look at my little car collection and think about my dad and my uncle and their friends. I'm so appreciative of what I have. Every now and then I'll pull one out and let my daughter, Jada, go for a ride with me. She loves the cars and her favorite is the orange Dodge Super Bee 440. That movie, Cars, she calls my car Lightning McQueen after the car in that movie. That's what she calls my car. She loves to go fast.

I've got one car that he really loved, a 1971 Roadrunner. Mine is the 440 six-pack pistol grip and he had the same car. Every time I sit in that car and grab that pistol grip, I can see myself sitting on the passenger seat or the backseat and remembering his hand go through the gears. It's like I was 8 years old again watching him do those things.

I'm part owner plus the deal closer at the Milwaukee Mile. My title is director of new business development. I can watch how things are going. Make sure my investment is doing great. Make sure we get more people in there. Commercials. Appearances. It'll bring in more sponsors. To help out the track be even better and to put fans in the seats.

It's funny. In football they say offense puts fans in seats but defense puts team in the Super Bowl. I'm glad to say that I've had the chance to do both.

There's so much stuff you think about. The main thing is to be healthy. My father passed away at 48, if I can get past that and be there for my kids I'll be very happy. I'm feeling great. I'm really great. I'm blessed. I wish I could get a couple more years of football, because I look at myself and know what I can do. I played 10 years, and I'd to play 12, but I feel like I'm punished for playing with a torn biceps.

You look at loyalty. I was always loyal to my friends, my family and my Packers. Loyalty is when I took less money, I always came back and I put it on the line. I felt like when it was my turn to finally get some loyalty for myself it didn't happen the way I hoped it would have happened.

You start second guessing yourself.

I should have had my arm fixed by the doctors, or I should have gone to the Washington Redskins when I had the opportunity. It was a lot more money than Green Bay was offering, but I'm a loyal guy. I bleed green and gold.

I talk about what I might've done but I wouldn't do it. I didn't do it.

I'm a Green Bay Packer and I always will be.

IT'S AN HONOR JUST TO KNOW THAT OF ALL THE GUYS THAT PLAYED IN THAT PACKERS UNIFORM THAT YEAR, THE ORGANIZATION CHOSE ME TO BE THE REPRESENTATIVE OF THE SUPER BOWL XXXI GAME AGAINST NEW ENGLAND, TO BE THE HONORARY CAPTAIN FOR THAT GAME, IT TRULY IS THAT.

"WE GOT IT BACK!"

WE WON'T COME HOME
SUPERBOWL EXPRESS
1967 1968 1997
PACKERS
WITHOUT IT!

The Fans

Rison to Victory
the Superbowl
Is not Favre away!
PACKER
BACKER

OUR FUTURE
GO PACK
IS
#84
A. RISON
GREEN BAY PACKERS

LUTHERAN
CHURCH
POLARIS
GREEN BAY
PACKERS

LAMBEAU
LEAP
10.0
LAMBEAU
LEAP
9.7
LAMBEAU
LEAP
9.9
LAMBEAU
LEAP
9.8

PANTHERS

Sprint
OFFICIAL CARD OF THE NFL
DRINK Coca-Cola
CIGNA
TIMEOUT
PATS 21
PACKERS 35
6:43
Bud

NFL 1996 Final Standings

AMERICAN CONFERENCE

EASTERN DIVISION

New England	11-5
Buffalo*	10-6
Indianapolis *	9-7
Miami	8-8
N.Y. Jets	1-15

CENTRAL DIVISION

Pittsburgh	10-6
Jacksonville *	9-7
Cincinnati	8-8
Houston	8-8
Baltimore	4-12

WESTERN DIVISION

Denver	13-3
Kansas City	9-7
San Diego	8-8
Oakland	7-9
Seattle	7-9

NATIONAL CONFERENCE

EASTERN DIVISION

Dallas	10-6
Philadelphia *	10-6
Washington	9-7
Arizona	7-9
N.Y. Giants	6-10

CENTRAL DIVISION

Green Bay	13-3
Minnesota *	9-7
Chicago	7-9
Tampa Bay	6-10
Detroit	5-11

WESTERN DIVISION

Carolina	12-4
San Francisco *	12-4
St. Louis	6-10
Atlanta	3-13
New Orleans	3-13

Note I: * Wild-card qualifier for playoffs

Note II: Home team is upper case

THE POST-SEASON

AMERICAN CONFERENCE

Wild-Card playoffs: Jacksonville 30, BUFFALO 27; PITTSBURGH 42, Indianapolis 14

Divisional playoffs: Jacksonville 30, DENVER 27; NEW ENGLAND 28, Pittsburgh 3

AFC Championship: NEW ENGLAND 20, Jacksonville 6

NATIONAL CONFERENCE

Wild-Card playoffs: DALLAS 40, Minnesota 15; SAN FRANCISCO 14, Philadelphia 0

Divisional playoffs: GREEN BAY 35, San Francisco 14; CAROLINA 26, Dallas 17

NFC Championship: GREEN BAY 30, Carolina 13

SUPER BOWL XXXI: GREEN BAY (NFC) 35, New England (AFC) 21 at Louisiana Superdome, New Orleans, Louisiana

A Statistical Analysis Of The 1996 Packers

		NFC RANK	NFL RANK
Points scored	456	1st	1st
Points allowed	210	1st	1st
Net Yards Gained	5,535	2nd	5th
New Yards Allowed	4,156	1st	1st
Sacks Made	37	9th	15th
Sacks Allowed	40	10th	18th
Punt Returns	15.1 net	1st	1st
Punt Coverage	8.2 net	6th	10th
Kickoff Returns	22.1 net	8th	14th
Kickoff Coverage	21.7 net	8th	15th

1996 Packers Individual Awards

Pro Bowl selection

Safety LeRoy Butler; Quarterback Brett Favre; Tight end Keith Jackson; Defensive end Reggie White; Center Frank Winters

All-Pro selection

Safety LeRoy Butler; Quarterback Brett Favre; Punt return specialist Desmond Howard; Safety Eugene Robinson; Defensive end Reggie White

Acknowledgements

GILBERT BROWN

THANK YOU'S …

I would like to thank my Dad for all he has done for me and my brothers and sisters. I miss you so much and I love you.

To my Mom, without her in my life would not be the person I am today. I love you more than anything. …

To LeRoy, Carla, Carlos and Joann Brown – my brothers and sisters – I want for them the very best that life has to offer.

To Coach Dozier – my second Dad – you mean the world to me, I love you.

To Fred Roll – my son Jesse's god father – without you my football career would not be whole. Love you.

To Ma Bee, Ma Hill, Uncle Chip, Aunt Sparkie, Uncle George, Reen, Jessica, Uncle Gilbert – who I am named after – all of my Dad's sisters, my Grandma and Pa Brown, I love all of you and thank you.

To my boys, Whitt, Jermaine, Troy, Joe, Lehier, Walt, Brian, Nard, Boz, Phil, Jerome Bettis, Pepper, Matt, all my MacKenzie High boys to name a few. Thank you.

Kansas crew Kyle Moore (Jamal's god father), Dana Stubblefield, Chris, Guy, Brian, Larry, Boss, Tony Sands, Ron Page, so, so many thanks and I miss you guys.

Thank you to the Minnesota Vikings for getting me into the National Football League and also thank you for cutting me.

Thanks to all my coaches, friends and teammates at the Green Bay Packers – it was a good ride, I loved it all. Thank you.

To my line mates, Reggie you are and always will be the man. I miss you and you are always on my mind. Sean, to learn from you and Reggie as a young player was priceless. Thank you. Santana – Jada's god father – you are my friend and one of the best guys I ever played with my boy S.D.

To LeRoy Butler, you mean the world to me.

To Jermaine Smith, thanks for being real and being one of my best friends. …

To Jerry Iverson for making sure I'm riding in style.

To Gabe Wilkins, a great friend and roomy.

To Chuck and Indry Haun, Mr. AC, Mr. Gil, Sheryl's mom Doris and who ever knows me on a family or personal level, and if I missed somebody I'm sorry.

To my kid Jamal, Jada and Jesse, I love you with all I got.

To Carla, I love you more than I love myself.

To Sheryl (I'm sorry for whatever happened and I love you).

To Linda Rogers, thank you for everything.

To Carrie, you are the best.

To the fans of Green Bay you are my family. I miss and love you guys.

Monday nights and Sunday nights – for 10 years – I was your "Hall Guard" and no one ever got through even if they said they had a hall pass, so says The Gravedigger. Most of all to Isabella, I love you baby. … RIP

Chris Havel

THANK YOU'S …

To Dad, Mom and Sis for keeping the project alive. I love you!

My parents, John and Carole, for blessing me with the best childhood possible. To my sister, Teresa, for making that whole experience and beyond a shared adventure. To my daughter, Josie Rae, you're always on my mind. I love you honey.

To my aunts and uncles on both sides of the family. You are the best people and relatives in the world.

A heartfelt thanks to Gilbert Brown, the Gravedigger, whose wit, wisdom and generosity are legendary. He is truly one of the most caring, unselfish and sincere professional athletes I have ever met.

A special thanks to Elizabeth Krogwold, a Hall of Fame graphic artist whose excellence while setting a book-publishing speed record is nothing short of amazing.

To Pete Petasek, whose friendship and perseverence was priceless along the way.

To Paul Kennedy, my friend and fellow publisher, for sending the best gift (Elizabeth Krogwold) ever.

To the Green Bay Packers and Bob Harlan for their support in reliving the great 1996 Super Bowl XXXI championship team.

To Worzalla Publishing, Stevens Point, for being helpful and providing a reason to visit my alma mater.

To William Henderson, Sean Jones, Brett Favre, George Koonce, Edgar Bennett, Kyle Moore, Fred Roll, LeRoy Brown and Carlos Brown for tremendous contributions.

To Mrs. Ann Brown, a sweet, classy lady.

To my co-workers who understand, accept and acknowledge.

To the men I've shared many an afternoon with: Johnny Gray, Harry Sydney, Brian Noble, Mike Counter, Kevin Garthwaite, Mike, Matt, Jimmy C. and all the rest.

To my pals B.J., Norm, David, Fidel, Arnold, Mark and the gang. Thanks for being good (and bad) company.

To my girls Marie, Mugsy, Linda and my friends Leslie, Jane and Sue Burke. … Thanks for keeping me down the straight and narrow. … I love you guys!